The Essential Guide to

Fly
Fishing

IN BRITISH COLUMBIA

Neil Cameron
Jim Crawford
Rory E. Glennie
Robert H. Jones
Martin Lamont
Ralph Shaw
George Will

Edited by Robert H. Jones

Blue Ribbon Books

JOHNSON GORMAN PUBLISHERS

Johnson Gorman Publishers
2003 – 35 Avenue SW
Calgary Alberta Canada T2T 2E2
www.flyfishingsource.com

Credits
Cover design by Duncan Campbell
Text design by Dennis Johnson
Cover photo courtesy of Keith Douglas
Printed and bound in Canada by Friesens for Johnson Gorman Publishers

Acknowledgments
Financial support provided by the Alberta Foundation for the Arts, a beneficiary of the Lottery Fund of the Government of Alberta.

COMMITTED TO THE DEVELOPMENT OF CULTURE AND THE ARTS

National Library of Canada Cataloguing in Publication Data
Main entry under title:
The essential guide to fly fishing in British Columbia
Includes index.
ISBN 0-921835-60-4
1.Fly fishing—British Columbia. 1. Cameron, Neil, 1958–
SH572.B8E87 2001 799.1'24'09711 C2001-911606-3

5 4 3 2 1

Contents

Introduction

ROBERT H. JONES

A FEW YEARS AGO, publisher Dennis Johnson suggested that I consider writing a book about fly fishing in British Columbia. The more I thought about the suggestion, the more I realized how much such a book was needed. But the publisher wanted me to cover the entire province. All of it. I pointed out that the sheer size of British Columbia was only one of several major stumbling blocks. There was also its geography, which ranges from flat prairies to rugged mountains, arid cattle country to ocean shores. Then there was the diversity of fish species, which range from warm-water critters like largemouth bass and walleye to arctic grayling, pike and lake trout, to sea-run steelhead and five species of Pacific salmon, to native rainbow, coastal and westslope cutthroat trout, and to dozens of species of saltwater bottom fish. To name just a few.

To be honest, I couldn't think of any one person who could write such a book and do it justice, but I knew a few who could come close. So being a staunch proponent of the old adage about many hands making light work, I jotted down the names of a potential "dream team," then contacted each with a proposal to write about the specific region with which they were most familiar. To say I was surprised and happy that each one agreed would be an understatement. After some discussion among ourselves, we set about to get the job done, and here it is.

I hope that you will find it as interesting, exciting and helpful to read as

I did to edit. And if it makes you do some serious daydreaming about visiting a few of the many lakes, rivers and saltwater destinations we have mentioned, our project has succeeded.

Chapter 1

Welcome to British Columbia

ROBERT H. JONES

ONSIDERING THE VARIETY and sheer abundance of game fish in British Columbia, it is little wonder that legions of resident anglers are joined by hundreds of thousands of visitors every year, a great many of whom are fly fishers. Some are making their initial visit, but many return annually or even more often, knowing they will find limitless opportunities to cast their lines in spectacular settings that range from tiny, crystal-clear tarns nestled high in the Rocky Mountains, to the wave-tossed waters of the Pacific Ocean. Within British Columbia's borders are over 30,000 lakes, and no fewer than 11,000 pristine rivers and streams flow into the Pacific and Arctic oceans. Most are surrounded by some of the most beautiful wilderness scenery imaginable, but there are excellent freshwater fishing opportunities within the city limits of large metropolitan areas like Vancouver and Victoria, both of which provide memorable saltwater fishing within sight of their skylines. This happy situation is repeated in smaller coastal cities like Nanaimo, Port Alberni, Powell River, Campbell River, Port Hardy, Kitimat and Prince Rupert. Inland, nearly 50 of the best-known rainbow trout lakes in the world-famous Thompson–Nicola region are within a 25-mi (40-km) radius of Kamloops; in the Cariboo, Williams Lake's namesake offers rainbow and kokanee; and in the Okanagan, residents of Penticton and Kelowna share Okanagan Lake's bounties. All are also excellent destinations for family vacations. While it may be hard to believe, there are many interesting activities other than fly fishing to occupy one's time. Or so I'm told.

The two key words concerning fishing in British Columbia are *road accessible*. A road map of the province reveals seven main highways: the Trans-Canada Highway 1, Yellowhead Trans-Canada Highway 16, Yellowhead Highway 5, Crowsnest Highway 3, Cariboo Highway 97, Highway 93/95 from the Montana border northward to Golden and Island Highway 19/19A on Vancouver Island. Although the southern portion constitutes barely one-fifth of the province's land mass, the area from Vancouver northwest to 100 Mile House (no, we don't call it 160 Kilometer House), then due east to the Alberta border is covered by a maze of roads. Northward, however, the remainder of the province—roughly 300,000 sq mi (777,000 sq km)—is relatively free of roads. Highway 97 wanders northward to Dawson Creek, where it becomes the Alaska Highway and swings northwest to Watson Lake, Yukon, just over the British Columbia–Yukon border. Highway 16 cuts in a westerly direction from Jasper, Alberta, to New Hazelton, British Columbia, then turns south toward Terrace and Prince Rupert. A few miles beyond New Hazelton at Kitwanga, Highway 37 branches off almost due north toward Cassiar, crossing the British Columbia–Yukon border at Upper Liard, a bit west of Watson Lake.

These are the main thoroughfares from which branch thousands of secondary roads, private logging and mining roads, and other routes, some which are little more than twin tire tracks. The amazing thing is that it is nearly impossible to drive, ride or hike on any of them without passing beside or over water containing fish.

Now, revisit that map and see how much territory remains roadless. There remain countless lakes and streams, but getting to them requires other means of travel—aircraft, boat, horseback or hiking. Usually, the farther off the beaten track one travels, the better the fishing—but not always. Many fishing lodges and resorts are situated at locations with outstanding freshwater and saltwater fishing, so anglers have a wide range of choices to consider when planning a trip.

British Columbia is divided into six tourism regions, each of which has distinct characteristics. Let's start up in the northeast corner, then work our way through them to see what they have to offer.

The Northern British Columbia region covers four topographical zones—the flat prairies of the Peace district, rolling foothills, five rugged mountain ranges and the Queen Charlotte Islands. The number of lakes and rivers is staggering, and most are remote and roadless.

The British Columbia Rockies region is known locally as the East and West Kootenays. The East Kootenay has about 70 remote, high-elevation lakes that are stocked with westslope cutthroat trout. These hike-in lakes offer excellent fishing in true wilderness settings. Lowland lakes and rivers yield rainbow, cutthroat, bull and brook trout, kokanee, plus lake and mountain whitefish. Several lakes and sloughs at the south end of Kootenay Lake contain largemouth bass, some reaching double-digit weights.

The West Kootenay is home of the gigantic Gerrard strain of rainbow trout found in Kootenay Lake. Behemoths weighing 20–30 lb (9–13.6 kg) are caught each year, but mostly by trolling with salmon-weight tackle and downriggers. However, there are also outstanding fly fishing opportunities for rainbow, westslope cutthroat, bull and brook trout, kokanee, largemouth and smallmouth bass, walleye, and lake and mountain whitefish.

The Thompson–Okanagan region consists of the arid Thompson–Nicola cattle country and the lush Okanagan Valley with its fruit orchards and vineyards. The Okanagan has westslope cutthroat trout in high mountain lakes, trophy-sized rainbow and bull trout in lowland waters, plus lake trout, Dolly Varden, brook trout, kokanee, and lake and mountain whitefish. In addition, some lakes offer excellent largemouth and smallmouth bass fishing. The Thompson–Nicola is where ardent fly fishers from around the world make annual pilgrimages to challenge the famous Kamloops strain of rainbow trout. Also available are trophy-sized brook, lake and bull trout, and large kokanee. The Thompson River and its tributaries are world-renowned for summer-run steelhead that are well above average in size and strength and noted for taking dry flies.

The Cariboo–Chilcotin region offers some of the highest catch rates, yet has the least crowded fishing in the province. Inland lakes contain trophy-sized rainbow, lake, bull and brook trout, kokanee, and lake and mountain whitefish, while coastal lakes produce some of the finest cutthroat trout and Dolly Varden fishing imaginable. In addition, there are 13 steelhead systems, including the Chilcotin, Chilko, Dean, Atnarko and Bella Coola rivers.

The Vancouver, Coast and Mountains region encompasses the Fraser Valley, Lower Mainland, Whistler and Sunshine Coast. Of 60 streams in this region, the Vedder River receives the best returns of winter-run steelhead and coho salmon. The Fraser River yields steelhead, coastal cutthroat, Dolly Varden, plus migratory coho, chinook, pink, sockeye and chum salmon. The most popular river for rainbow trout is the Skagit near Hope, but other rivers in the area also offer good fishing in similar wilderness surroundings. Coastal cutthroat and rainbow trout are available in virtually all lakes throughout the Sunshine Coast, Whistler and Fraser Valley, kokanee are found in many lakes, and several small lakes and sloughs in the Lower Mainland area offer huge black crappie.

The Islands region also includes a sizable chunk of remote real estate on the lower Central Coast. Vancouver Island alone has over 100 steelhead-bearing rivers and creeks, and there are several more on the mainland portion. The most productive systems are the Stamp–Somass and Gold on the west coast and the Cowichan, Salmon and Quatse on the east coast. The Cowichan has a good population of trophy-sized brown trout, which are also available in the Little Qualicum and Adam rivers. Hundreds of lakes contain native rainbow and coastal cutthroat trout, Dolly Varden and kokanee, and some southern Vancouver Island lakes offer introduced brown trout and truly trophy-sized smallmouth bass. The latter are also present on Saltspring Island.

Operating in conjunction with the six tourism regions, BC Tourism provides an excellent information package for anglers interested in fishing coastal fresh and salt waters. All you have to do to start planning a trip is contact 1-800-663-6000 or 1-800-HELLO BC (435-5622), or visit the tourism website at www.hellobc.com/index3.jsp. For specific information on freshwater fishing visit the British Columbia Fishing Resort Owners Association website at www.bcfroa.bc.ca, and for saltwater fishing, the Sport Fishing Institute website at www.sportfishing.bc.ca.

Be warned that such diverse fishing opportunities throughout the province come with a wide range of fishing regulations. Nontidal waters are managed by the provincial government. The province is divided into eight management regions, each with a section in the *Freshwater Fishing Regulations Synopsis.* While general restrictions and regulations apply throughout the province, each region has site-specific restrictions on such topics as access, tackle, use of bait, possession limits and the use of motors on boats. Considering the large area and wide range of fish species involved, these regulations are easy to use, and you need only read the section covering the region where you intend to fish.

The *British Columbia Tidal Waters Sport Fishing Guide* is produced by the federal Ministry of Fisheries and Oceans Canada. It details everything you can and cannot do while fishing in saltwater. The coastal region is divided into 29 inshore and nine offshore management areas. General regulations and restrictions apply coast wide, but some management areas may have site-specific restrictions or closures, spot closures during certain periods or adjusted size and possession limits.

Whether fishing fresh or salt water, be sure to familiarize yourself with the regulations concerning size and possession limits, and the wrapping and transportation of fish. It can save you a lot of grief should you happen to be stopped at a road check.

Chapter 2

Planning Your Fly-Fishing Vacation

ROBERT H. JONES

THE BOTTOM LINE when planning a fishing vacation depends on three things: what you want to catch, how much time you have and how much you can afford. Accommodations vary enough to suit everyone's bank account. You can choose from rustic campgrounds lacking running water or electricity, fully serviced RV parks, bed and breakfast operations, hotels and motels (some of which offer fishing packages), and fishing lodges and resorts that range from meeting basic requirements to those catering to your every whim as you lounge in pampered luxury.

There are numerous road-accessible resorts on the Sunshine Coast and Vancouver Island, plus several remote fishing lodges located on the central and northern mainland coast, the west and northeast coast of Vancouver Island and the Queen Charlotte Islands. While most cater to saltwater anglers, many also offer freshwater opportunities. Most operations throughout southern and central British Columbia are road accessible, but a few require the use of 4-wheel-drive vehicles, horses, boats or aircraft to reach. In northern British Columbia, the majority of lodges and resorts are in remote, fly-in locations.

When selecting a destination give each a five-star rating: excellent, good, fair, adequate and poor. Get rid of the chaff by making your minimum standard good. It's your time and money, so why settle for less? The paramount point should be the fishing potential based on the numbers caught or, if you are seeking trophy fish, the average and largest sizes of your target species.

Rate the accommodations, facilities and amenities available, plus the type and size of boats and motors used. In the case of saltwater and large lakes, bigger boats are usually better. If a package deal is available, determine precisely what is included. Check the following basic points:

1. What are the travel arrangements? If location is remote, are connecting services provided?
2. If air travel is involved, what is the maximum allowable luggage weight?
3. Do meals include early and late breakfasts, boxed lunches and snacks? If required, can hosts cater to special dietary needs? Are alcoholic beverages supplied or available for purchase?
4. Are fishing tackle and rain clothing, including footwear, provided? Are local fly patterns available?
5. Are cleaning, freezing, packaging and shipping of fish included?

Some lodges offer guided and unguided packages. First-time visitors generally use guides, but repeat customers often learn the areas and techniques well enough to fish unguided. Ask the following questions:

1. Is guided fishing provided as part of the package or does it cost extra?
2. Are the boats suitable for fly fishing?
3. Are the boats equipped with such equipment as a marine chart, compass, VHF radio, depth sounder and Global Positioning System?

Information packages from reputable operations usually include recent catch statistics, pictures of guests with fish and a list of personal references. The latter can be an excellent source of information. Nothing beats personal points of view and advice from people who have experienced one or more stays at a particular resort. The best indication of an operation's overall quality is the number of repeat visits guests make each year.

Most avid anglers would rather stay at a rustic camp with limited services and good fishing than at a luxury resort with only modest or poor fishing; however, it is possible to get the best of both worlds. In most cases, all it takes is a bit of homework on your part.

TIPS FOR INTERNATIONAL TRAVELERS

When crossing the border into Canada, visitors from the United States may be asked to provide a birth, baptism or voter's certificate as proof of citizenship. Naturalized American citizens should carry their naturalization certificate, and permanent residents who are not residents, their Alien Registration Receipt Card.

Citizens of all other countries must be in possession of a valid passport and, in some cases, a visa. Each child accompanying an adult must have a birth certificate. Visitors under the age of 18 who are not accompanied by an adult must have a letter signed by a parent or guardian permitting them to travel in Canada. Pets must have a current rabies certificate.

All vehicles should carry a motor vehicle registration form and proof of insurance. Vehicles not registered to the driver require a letter of authorization. A rented vehicle must carry a copy of the rental contract, and it must be endorsed for entry into Canada.

Currency can be exchanged at prevailing rates at Vancouver International Airport or at any bank, trust company or credit union. Problems exchanging currency can be avoided by using Canadian funds or major credit cards like Visa, Master Card, American Express, Diners Club and Carte Blanche. Using your credit card to withdraw Canadian funds from bank machines yields the best daily exchange rates.

You can bring alcohol and tobacco for personal consumption, but check the current regulations concerning quantity.

DON'T EVEN THINK ABOUT TAKING A HANDGUN

Carrying handguns in Canada is illegal, and attempts to smuggle them across the border will result in their confiscation. Period. Then it gets nasty. Visitors entering Canada are warned twice that any weapons they intend to take into the country must be declared. Properly documented rifles and shotguns for use in hunting activities or competitions are permitted, but as handguns are strictly prohibited, arrangements will be made to store those which are declared. They will be returned when the owner leaves Canada.

If you attempt to bluff your way through and get caught, you will find that no one is exempt. Over the years, thousands of people have tried, including U.S. law enforcement officers, and all have received the same treatment. Confiscated weapons become the property of the Canadian government, and all violators have their vehicles seized. The call then goes to the Royal Canadian Mounted Police to investigate and determine whether charges should be laid—and they usually are. Friends, this is not a great way to start your fly-fishing vacation in British Columbia.

Northern British Columbia

Chapter 3

Welcome to Northern British Columbia

ROBERT H. JONES

NORTHERN BRITISH COLUMBIA is a land of dramatically changing geography between the Alberta border and Pacific Ocean. The 19,900 sq-mi (51,537 sq-km) Peace region alone covers three distinct topographic zones: flat prairies, rolling plateaus and the Rocky Mountains. Beyond are the Muskwa and Swannell ranges, the Omineca and Cassiar mountains, the Stikine Ranges, and the Skeena and Coast mountains. Just below the Alaska Panhandle, this region continues 37 miles (60 km) offshore to encompass the Queen Charlotte Islands, also known as Haida Gwaii. This vast northern region offers the most diverse range of freshwater fishes found within the entire province.

Native species in the northeast Peace district include rainbow, bull and lake trout, arctic grayling, mountain and lake whitefish, pike, walleye, yellow perch, goldeye, burbot and, farther north, inconnu in the Liard system. In addition, depending upon location, there are introduced brook trout, kokanee, limited numbers of westslope cutthroat trout, and rainbow that have been stocked well beyond their original range in the Peace River drainage.

From the western slopes of the Rockies, stretching across the top of the province to the Alaska Panhandle, you will find lake trout, arctic grayling, lake whitefish and pike. Fly-ins from Atlin, British Columbia, will also put you on coastal rivers with steelhead, coastal cutthroat, rainbow and bull trout, Dolly Varden, chinook, coho, chum and sockeye salmon.

Farther south, Skeena system tributaries like the Babine, Bulkley and Kispiox rivers are legendary among fly fishers seeking summer-run steelhead, plus trophy-sized chinook and coho salmon. Lakes in these southern climes contain coastal cutthroat, rainbow, lake trout, introduced brook trout, plus lake and mountain whitefish. Several rivers on the Queen Charlottes have winter-run steelhead, coastal cutthroat trout and excellent runs of coho and chum salmon.

Much of northern British Columbia was uninhabited until 1942, when the 1,500-mi (2,414-km) Alaska Highway was constructed during the Second World War. A map of British Columbia illustrates that while there has been growth since the war years, most of this region is still very much a new frontier. With the exception of small, scattered communities, the largest area of development is about two-thirds of the way up the British Columbia–Alberta border, where Dawson Creek, Fort St. John, Hudson's Hope and Chetwynd form a rough square about 35 x 60 mi (56 x 97 km) The only other communities of any size are Tumbler Ridge and Mackenzie to the south and Fort Nelson over 185 mi (298 km) to the northwest.

A map also reveals why even the smallest of communities have a charter air service, for there are few alternatives. Highway 97 stretches north from Prince George, curves northeast toward Dawson Creek, then bends sharply northwest to Fort St. John, Fort Nelson and the Yukon border (where it becomes Highway 1). Along the way, you won't find many branch-offs and secondary roads.

Southern approaches in the west are similar. Highway 16—the Yellowhead Trans-Canada—heads northwest from Prince George to Prince Rupert, and Highway 37 branches north near Kitwanga. Highway 37A from Stewart, at the head of the Portland Canal, joins at Meziadin Junction and that's it until the Highway 1 connection in Yukon at Upper Liard. The only other roads of note are Highway 7 running due south from Jake's Corner in Yukon to Atlin, British Columbia, the Whitepass Trail that cuts through the northwest corner of British Columbia from Skagway, Alaska, to Carcross, Yukon, and Highway 7 from Haines, Alaska, to Haines Junction, Yukon.

From fly-in trips to remote resorts to wilderness camping trips to float trips on the larger rivers, the possibilities for exciting and memorable fishing adventures are endless. However, this frontier country can be very unforgiving to the inexperienced or unprepared, so visitors are well advised to use the services of the various available lodges, guiding operations or packers.

Chapter 4

Fly Fishing Northern British Columbia

MARTIN LAMONT

THERE WAS A TIME, not so long ago, when northern British Columbia was a truly remote, inaccessible wilderness containing mystical places and mountains unnamed, rivers and lakes untouched by anglers. Map makers seeking boundaries for the new province of British Columbia arbitrarily drew straight lines along the 120° west meridian of longitude for its eastern border with Alberta, and the 60° parallel of latitude for its northern border with the Northwest Territory and Yukon. A diverse topography, indeed.

For eons this land supported native inhabitants. Then came the explorations of European trappers and prospectors. None had much impact, and this area still remains sparsely populated. The urgency of the Second World War saw construction of the Alaska Highway (Alcan), after which mining and oil patch enterprises opened up the northeast and Cassiar, after which came the inevitable secondary logging roads. Finally, in the late 1970s, the Dempster Highway created a link to Inuvik and the Arctic Ocean.

This northern area encompasses more than half the land mass of British Columbia, so visiting fly fishers venturing north need a focus. Decisions must be made beforehand regarding destination, timing, targeted fish species tackle requirements and length of stay. All are essential elements of a successful trip. Join me as we work our way northeast from Prince George to the Peace Region, then westward along the British Columbia–Yukon border—

with even a few stops in Yukon locations, for we now have a joint license for transboundary waters. Then we will work our way southward to the Skeena Region with its multitudes of lakes and rivers. It's a vast area, so I will use mileage points throughout to help you locate various places on a map.

NORTH CENTRAL BRITISH COLUMBIA

Let's use Prince George as a starting point. To the west and northwest are three groups of large lake systems with interconnecting rivers that eventually converge to form the Fraser River. The largest have lake trout and kokanee, while smaller lakes and rivers provide rainbow and whitefish.

The first group of lakes to the west was formed by the Alcan Project and the Kenny Dam, 60 mi (97 km) southwest of Vanderhoof. The Nechako Reservoir group includes Ootsa, Whitesail, Eutsuk, Tetachuk, Natalkuz and the Knewstubb chain of impounded lakes. This system is joined by Cheslatta Lake and the Nechako River, joining the Fraser at Fort Fraser near Vanderhoof. The Nechako has resident rainbow, Dolly Varden and whitefish, and there is fairly good access via a logging road.

The second group consists of Burns Lake and the Endako River, and, 19 mi (31 km) south of the town of Burns Lake, Francois Lake and the Stellako River. Crossed by Highway 16, the easily accessed Endako is a good rainbow fishery offering quality and size. Nearby Francois Lake is 75 mi (121 km) long. Except for smaller trout taken during the early mornings or evenings, it rarely provides surface-feeding rainbow for fly fishers. Better options are found in smaller lakes like Takysie and others via Southbank and Ootsa roads. The Stellako, a Classified Water (meaning an additional license is manda-tory) is accessible via Francois Lake Road west of the town of Fraser Lake. This fair-ly short freestone river—7 mi (11 km) long—flows north, but only 2 ½ mi (4 km) is open. The water is so clear that trout and whitefish can be easily sight-ed. Access by hiking is limited to a bank-side trail, but drifting the river in a pontoon boat is a good option that takes most of a day to complete. Get local information before attempting this float for the first time. The lake's outflow section is flat water with moderate wadeable depths and even flows, but the river descends and narrows in the middle area to pools and white water, and there is a portage around a lower dam. The take-out is at the Highway 16 bridge.

The Stellako's fly hatches pick up through June and peak around mid-

July with mayflies like blue-wing olives and western green drakes. When mayfly spinners are on the water, try the ever useful gray-brown Adams. There are good hatches of brown, green and yellow-bodied caddis, plus large golden stoneflies. Small green stones like the Lime Sally continue throughout the season, so match the hatch during this classic dry-fly fishery with artificials like the Lime Sally. Fall fishing peaks in September, when trout plunder the redds of Fraser River sockeye, gorging on their eggs. Try single or double egg patterns like Roe Bugs, Double Egg Sperm Flies and Babine Specials in red or orange.

The nutrient-rich Stellako system produces plentiful numbers of trout averaging 15" (38 cm). My tackle preference is a 5- or 6-weight, 9' rod with a floating line and a long leader with a fine tippet. Cover the water with dead-drifted dry flies or a twitched dry when caddis or stones are on the water. Downstream wet-fly techniques with an emerging nymph will also work.

The third group of lakes is in the remote northern Skeena and Omineca mountain ranges. It starts with the Driftwood River, a feeder stream to Takla and Trembleur lakes, which eventually empty into the 40-mi (66-km) -long Stuart Lake. Stuart, which also receives water from Pinchi and Tezzeron lakes to the north, drains through the Stuart River to connect with the Fraser east of Vanderhoof. Not far west of Prince George, the Chilako River drains Tatuk and Finger lakes. Access is via Highway 16 and local logging roads, which follow the Chilako for most of its length. Smaller rainbow are present in fair numbers, and there are occasional Dolly Varden. A few words here on Dollies *(Salvelinus malma)* and bull trout *(Salvelinus confluentus).* These closely related members of the char family overlap, so there is often some confusion over which is which. Generally, bull trout are the larger with longer and flatter heads, and larger mouths. Rather than muddy the water further, I will use whichever name is commonly accepted in the area being covered.

High-elevation mountain lakes are subject to sudden afternoon thermal storms. Anglers are forewarned to use only seaworthy boats and to have experience handling them in rough waters. However, topographical maps of the Fort St. James and Vanderhoof areas reveal multitudes of small lakes that are worthy of consideration and not as subject to such conditions. To check these out, try the BC Fisheries website (http://www.bcfisheries.gov.bc.ca/fishinfo-bc.html) and use the Fish Wizard, which gives detailed maps at 1:50,000 scale of lakes and rivers, and the information on fish distribution, ranges, stocking locations and history, lake topography, depths and elevations is very useful.

After several exploratory trips to these smaller lakes, the summer development of warmer surface water forced my partner and I to adopt new tactics. We were sure the rainbow were feeding on emerging chironomids, but they were too deep for normal sinking line techniques. Afternoon thermals created stronger winds, making fly fishing an even greater challenge. After studying the lake's hydrographic chart, we chose lines of drift running downwind that would parallel underwater ridges, drop-offs and the edges of shoals. To slow down the drift of our 14' (4.3 m) aluminum boat, a drogue of nylon mesh was fastened midship. After fine-tuning its position, the boat slowed to a crawl and drifted broad-beam to the wind. Working from bow and stern, we easily cast ultrafast sinking lines very long distances downwind, well ahead of the boat.

We tested the depths by counting down and eventually found the trout feeding at 15–20' (4.5–6 m). By retrieving our lines almost vertically—just as chironomids emerge—we hooked several deep-bodied rainbow that frequently jumped 3' (1 m) into the air. If faced with windy conditions anywhere else, give this technique a try—it works.

Kokanee are present in most large lakes in the Skeena and Omineca ranges. They feed predominantly on photosensitive zooplankton, which experience phenomenal growth spurts during the long daylight hours of summer. This peaks in June and July, providing a bonanza for kokanee. They follow the feed, which responds to light levels by moving up and down vertically in the water column. Therefore, on dull, overcast days, or in early morning or late evening, kokanee are closer to the surface and can be taken on flies.

Find creek mouths and locate the drop-offs with a depth sounder. If a kokanee school appears, approach quietly to avoid disturbing them. Fish light and gentle, with long, fine leader tippets, casting to the side or ahead of the fish. Dry flies like a No. 16–12 Royal Wulff or Adams will work, as do wets like a Gold-Ribbed Hare's Ear. When kokanee are deeper, I prefer peach pink or fluorescent green Baby Dolls, using a deeply sunk line and determining their depth by counting down.

Two distinct subspecies of rainbow have developed in this region: a predominantly smaller strain that feeds primarily on insects, and a larger, deeper-swimming strain that feeds on fish. Both strains coexist quite well, occupying different niches in the food chain. The *Freshwater Fishing Regulations Synopsis* offers clues about which is which. Where there are numerous insectivorous rainbow, the catch limit is generous, but if trophy-sized trout are present, it drops to zero or possibly only one fish of over a specific length. These large lakes present challenges when casting flies, but if you don't have a problem about deep trolling with large streamers, you might well net and release a trophy 20-lb (9-kg) rainbow.

The river systems interconnecting the lakes in this region are all freestone gems containing prime wild rainbow trout. There are also many fly-in lakes with larger-sized fish, with Fort St. James the center for arranging fly-ins.

PRINCE GEORGE & EAST FRASER RIVER

Close to Prince George, many small- to medium-sized lakes contain rainbow and stocked brook trout. Some are nutrient rich and productive; others are variable or poor depending on overwintering conditions. The best advice is to get current information at local tackle shops or the provincial fisheries office. Lakes like Crystal, Emerald, Firth, Junker and Ness have large rainbow trout. Also popular is Carp Lake north of Prince George, in Carp Lake Provincial Park, accessible via Highway 97.

East of Prince George, the Fraser River originates in the Rocky Mountains. Its heavily silted meltwaters offer little for fly fishers, but there are numerous tributaries like the Castle, Doré, Giscome, Goat, Holliday, Holmes, Horsey, Moose, Robson and Slim, and the larger Salmon River to the north. All of them fish best after spring runoff subsides. Try the clearer waters at confluences with the Fraser, or, better yet, hike upstream where average anglers hesitate to go.

While I was fishing a Fraser tributary many years ago, a large bull trout frequently emerged from the pool's depth to follow my fly right to my feet, then turned and slowly swam back to deep water. One cast accidentally hooked a small salmon fry, which the big char—fully 10 lb (4.5 kg)—immediately inhaled. After the ensuing battle, the bull trout simply opened its tooth-studded maw and the dead, badly mauled fry came free. Obviously, to attract these big bruisers, your fly should resemble a baitfish and have lots of flash. Incorporating metal barbell-shaped eyes and cone heads with Woolly Buggers or Matukas in combinations of black, red, purple and silver—for flash—can be quite productive. Use a fast sink-tip line, and present your fly by casting across or slightly upstream, followed by rapid upstream line mending to create a dead drift during the deep swing downstream through the pool. Simulate an injured fish with rapid, intermittent twitches, and hang on—bull trout hit hard.

Larger Fraser River tributaries like the Willow have access off highways 16 and 97, and 50 mi (80 km) northeast of Prince George the McGregor offers small rainbow.

WILLISTON LAKE & PEACE RIVER WATERSHED

I have driven along the John Hart Highway 97 and completed the 1,250-mi (2,012-km) drive on the Alcan to Yukon many times, but there is always a sense of adventure. It is now paved throughout its entirety, in stark contrast to those early days of bone-shaking potholes, washboard surfaces and shattered windshields. Fish populations change dramatically in this Arctic watershed, with grayling, whitefish and lake trout predominating. All Peace River waters flow to Slave Lake, where they are joined by the Athabasca system.

These eventually form the Mackenzie River, which empties into the Beaufort Sea far to the north. Highway 99 ascends north from Prince George, then at the junction with Highway 39, north to McKenzie, it swings northeast toward Chetwynd. North of the junction, in the great Rocky Mountain Trench, Williston Lake is hemmed in to the north by the Muskwa and Misinchinka ranges and to the west by the Omineca and Finlay ranges. This long trench was dammed by the W.A.C. Bennett Dam east of Hudson Hope, creating a huge reservoir consisting of three arms. The south arm is fed by Tchentlo Lake and the Nation River, and the Parsnip, Arctic, Crooked and Summit systems. The Nation River, accessed via Fort St. James, has good rainbow trout and grayling fishing.

The Parsnip is a large river originating from Arctic Lake. It flows 150 mi (241 km), and while often slow and silted closer to Williston Lake, upstream it has pools and stretches of rapids with fair fly fishing in the fall for smaller grayling and bull trout. The Crooked, an even smaller river about 60 mi (95 km) long, is nice to fish for small rainbow and bull trout.

The north arm of Williston is fed by the Finlay River, while the Mesilinka and Omineca rivers flow from the west. The Finley is often silted, so look for better bull trout fishing in the clear mouths of tributaries. The

Mesilinka is renowned for large grayling, rainbow and bull trout. This area requires a long drive via Takla Lake and Germansen Landing on the Omineca River to the west, or from Mackenzie–Windy Point Road on the west side of Williston Lake. An alternative is to hire a guide in Mackenzie and go in by jet boat or floatplane for a wilderness camp-out.

Williston Lake's east arm, the Peace Reach, offers rainbow, whitefish, grayling, kokanee and bull trout. There is fairly good road access to camping and boat-launch sites, but be warned that this large lake is subject to violent storms that blow up suddenly, making it very dangerous. Williston has special quotas to protect bull trout and grayling populations, so check the regulations.

Southwest of Mackenzie is road access to Tchentlo and Chuchi lakes and the Nation River. Back on Highway 97, once over Pine Pass, the road descends to follow closely beside the Pine River. This pretty freestone stream heads east toward Chetwynd, then north to Hudson Hope to join the Peace River. The Pine is currently closed to fishing pending environmental rehabilitation efforts after an oil pipeline spill in 1999.

The Sukunka and Murray rivers join the Pine east of Chetwynd. Access is near East Pine on Highway 97 and from the Tumbler Ridge highway. Both rivers contain grayling, bull trout and whitefish. Also worth trying is the nearby Wapiti River, east of Monkman Park. The upper Murray is accessed by a gravel road from Tumbler Ridge to the provincial park's entrance. From there you must hike in, ride on horseback or launch a boat at a downstream bridge and then head upstream. The Murray is joined at Tumbler Ridge by Flatbed Creek and the Wolverine River, both accessible by hike-ins. Farther downstream, 5-mi (8-km) -long Gwillim Lake fishes well for bull trout, lake trout, burbot, pike, whitefish and grayling. Its outflow feeds into the Murray River, which joins the Pine River at East Pine Park, where there is a boat ramp for shallow-draft river boats.

Other lakes in this area are Monkman, source of the Murray River, and Moberly, 12 mi (19 km) north of Chetwynd off Highway 29. Both contain lake trout and pike. Southeast of Tumbler Ridge, try Hook and Stony lakes for pike. In the Chetwynd area, Heart and Sundance lakes have rainbow and some lake trout.

Farther north at Fort St. John, the region's largest city, nearby Charlie Lake produces pike, walleye and yellow perch, and northwest on Highway 97, Inga Lake offers good rainbow fishing and introduced brook trout.

North and west of Fort St. John, Peace River tributaries and rivers worth fishing include the Graham and swift-flowing Halfway. The latter can be accessed 19 mi (30.5 km) east of Hudson Hope, again from the Alcan at 95 mi (153 km), close to the hamlet of Wonowon, and at 140 mi (225 km) at Pink Mountain Road. Along the Alcan, at 75 mi (121 km) access is available to the Blueberry, Beatton and Doig rivers. All offer grayling, whitefish, rainbow trout to 2 lb (.9 kg) and larger bull trout. Fly fishing is best July to September; however, stretches close to the road are subject to heavy fishing pressure, so it's necessary to explore farther afield for better results.

One concern for hike-in anglers without a Global Positioning System (GPS) is becoming lost. After a good day's hike through the bush on these rivers paralleling the highway, disorientation sets in easily. If you don't use a GPS, then carry a topographical map and compass, and take note of features like taller than average trees, unusual land formations and the river's shape to assist with your bearings.

LIARD & YUKON RIVER SYSTEMS

The next destination on the Alcan is Fort Nelson at 300 mi (480 km). All waters from here north to the Yukon flow into the Liard and Yukon drainage, which finally reaches the Bering Sea and Pacific Ocean in northwestern Alaska. Here, vast areas of inaccessible muskeg, freshwater marshes and sub-arctic willow and pine forests extend to the horizon in all directions. Lakes like Maxhamish (fly-in), Tuchodi (pack-horse trip) and Muncho (road access) all have lake trout and grayling, some walleye and large pike. Within relatively short flying distances from Fort Nelson are Muncho and Watson lakes, and the isolated Netson, Pike, Moose, Redfern and Trimble lakes, which are rarely visited but well worth a trip. Renowned for grayling of exceptional size, they receive only light fishing pressure. Netson Lake and the Netson River wind through mountain valleys, and the Kechika and Gataga rivers join the Rabbit River and ultimately the Liard River. This trip can be done by canoe or inflatable over a period of two weeks, offering excellent fishing for grayling, bull trout and lakers. Fly-ins to Fern, Chesterfield and Haworth lakes in Kwadacha Provincial Park offer similar high-quality fishing.

South of Fort Nelson is the Prophet River at 223 mi (359 km), Bucking Horse at 175 mi (282 km), and Sikanni Chief at 159 mi (256 km), all of which have limited access along the Alcan.

Within a day's drive north of Fort Nelson, the Muskwa is a short hike from the highway. A pleasant river to fish, its main stem and braided side channels are full of grayling. I like to match the hatch with dry flies, then sight-cast to rising fish. The most useful dry flies are the Royal Wulff, Adams, Blue-Winged Olive (BWO), Humpy, Tom Thumb and Elk Hair Caddis. Grayling often lie in swift water, hugging the bottom in the shelter behind boulders. From these slack pockets, they watch the surface for insects, rise rapidly, then drift back with the current to intercept the insect, often with a deliberate, splashy take. Feeding is most active during midday, when the warming temperature triggers a hatch.

On days when the fish don't show on the surface, I fish the deeper pools, channels and pocket water with a weighted hellgrammite pattern. The dobsonfly nymph is a large, fearsome predator of lesser aquatic life forms on the river bed. Its black body is long with distinct segmentation, and multiple legs protrude laterally along the body. I fashion mine on a No. 8–6 hook with an extra long shank, which might seem much too large for grayling. However, hellgrammite patterns work well if fished along the bottom, and my largest grayling have all been taken this way.

While attending a World Fly Fishing Championship in Europe several years ago, we Canadian team members were introduced to the Polish Nymph, an ultra-fast sinking fly, which, when used with the high-stick method of fishing, can be used effectively in short drifts. It was exactly the hellgrammite presentation we had used with great results years earlier on Muskwa grayling. Using a longish rod, say 9–10', cast a short line upstream and allow the fly to swim deeply, virtually right at your feet. If the grayling are in deeper water, follow through with a dead drift, but always maintain contact with the fly by keeping your line and leader taut. With no slack, you can feel their rapid takes.

North of Muskwa is Lake Tuchodi. About 119 mi (191.5 km) southwest of Fort Nelson, its outflow is accessed by fly-in or pack-horse trail, and it is well worth a camping trip. The Tuchodi River is relatively fast, dropping 1,000' (305 m) in the first 40 mi (64 km). It joins the Muskwa and makes for a fabulous wilderness float trip all the way down to Fort Nelson.

The nearby Tetsa River is named after the Slave Indian word for boulders, and after many trips there, I know why: The river bed is covered with round rocks, each the size of a bowling ball, which makes it tough to wade without soft metal-cleated wading boots. Access it almost anywhere from 363 mi (584 km) to 392 mi (631 km) along the highway.

At 419 mi (674 km), Racing and Toad rivers are worth exploring. When they run clear, grayling, bull trout and whitefish are available. There is a hiking trail at this point, where the Alcan bridge crosses the Racing River. From here, there is downstream fishing on the west side for 7 ½ mi (12 km), and an overnight camp at its confluence with the Toad River completes the first leg. On the following day or two, return southwest along the southern bank of the Toad River, heading upstream for 9 mi (14.5 km). This brings you back to the highway at 425 mi (684 km), close to your starting point. The nearby community of Toad River has good eating facilities, cabins, RV parking and other services. The Toad River is also suitable for exploration with a flat-bottomed jet boat.

Surprisingly, during mild years when the river ice breaks slightly early in April, fly fishers can get access to open water for a shot at mountain whitefish and grayling that are migrating toward the headwaters from their over-wintering grounds in the main-stem lower reaches. Be warned, however, that this can be dangerous. One year, while spring fishing on the Tetsa, I ventured out onto a thick ice pan to fish for whitefish schooled in the deeper central flow. I was using Wire Nymphs, which are simply hook shanks wrapped with colored wire—copper, green, red, yellow—with two turns of sparse, similar-colored hackle at the head. They are presented deeply using a fast sink-tip line, with repeated upstream mends to rapidly sink the fly. I took a few fish to 2 lb (.9 kg) by striking at the least feeling of hesitation during the fly's drift. Whitefish take a fly very gently, just sucking it into their soft mouth only once before rapidly rejecting it. This demands fine tactile perception and a rapid strike response from the fly fisher.

While out on the ice I had a growing feeling of unease because of the day's warmth and constant dripping of water off of the icicles. I had no sooner retreated to the riverbank when the entire ice pan separated and quickly broke up, before being washed downstream. Weak-kneed from the experience, I vowed never again to walk on river ice. Which, come to think of it, you shouldn't, either.

At 457 mi (735.5 km), Muncho Lake is an oasis on the highway, a place to relax for a night's stopover with good food and lodging. In cooperation with Liard Air, local lodges operate many fine fly-in trips for daily fishing and river float trips in the spectacular back country. About 8 mi (13 km) long, Muncho Lake sits atop a limestone formation, but it is still nutrient poor. Surprisingly, it produces some large lake trout to 20 lb (9 kg) every year, but years of angling pressure reflects the fragility of northern waters affected by overfishing. Muncho is at its best from late May to July, and local streams remain silted with meltwater until after July. At ice-out, grayling schools often cruise in the lake's shallows and along the ice-pan edges, but, they soon disperse into its northern outlet, the Trout River, which parallels the highway for almost 25 mi (40 km). The trout fishes well for adventurous day hikers in early and late summer, and it also contains rainbow trout, which seems an anomaly so far north.

The next section is north of the community of Liard River and the hot springs at 498 mi (797 km). Liard Hot Springs offers an interesting side trip, so take your swim suit for a welcome dip. Accessed by a boardwalk through lush wetlands warmed by the thermal springs, the springs remains ice-free and green with vegetation for extended parts of the year. This area is frequented by browsing moose that are well equipped to walk on the soft, damp ground. While fly fishing there, I have often been startled by close encounters with moose because, despite their size, their approach is silent.

The Liard River is the system's main stem. Although known to contain substantial fish stocks, the river receives little pressure as it is colored by run-off for most of the open-water season. The Alcan follows the Liard closely for the next 90 mi (145 km), but unless it is running clear during the early spring or fall months, only the tributary streams and their confluences are worth exploring.

Next stop is the Smith River at 515 mi (829 km), where a road north leads to the community of Smith River. The road parallels the river, which is worth testing for a day's exploration. Coal River at 537 mi (864 km) offers a short, interesting hike along a tumultuous river of rapids and falls with good pocket water for fly fishing.

Nearby, the Rabbit, Kechika and Red rivers need a more ambitious hike or fly-in that requires planning and time, as does the wilderness farther southwest for the Turnagain and Gataga rivers. Fly to South Gataga Lake, then float the Gataga River 25 mi (40 km) downstream to a take-out at Fireside on the Alcan. Another fly-in is to Dail Lake for a float down Dail River to the Turnagain River, which joins the Kechika River 50 mi (80 km) upstream from Fireside. An alternative to flying is an organized pack-horse trip down established wilderness trails with a guide, which requires several days of camping out.

At the small community of Lower Post, the drainage is from the south-western Cassiar and Kechika ranges. This is close to the lengthy Blue, Rapid and Dease river system that enters the Liard at Lower Post, which is accessed from Highway 37. The Blue River bridge is 34 mi (55 km) from Watson Lake, Yukon.

About 14 mi (22.5 km) north of Watson Lake, 635 mi (1,022 km) on the Alcan, the road divides. Highway 97 branches off to Cassiar, Dease Lake and Stewart, which are about 403 mi (649 km) away. The Alcan continues by the Rancheria and Swift rivers for 750 mi (1,207 km) into the British Columbia–Yukon transboundary area. This is the great river divide where the Rancheria flows to the Mackenzie River and Beaufort Sea, and the Swift flows to Yukon and the Bering Sea. All have grayling, bull trout and whitefish, and can be fished all summer and fall.

During the spring, clouds of recently hatched, blood-sucking mosquitoes can drive you crazy. Be prepared by taking ample insect repellant, and invest in a bug-proof jacket and head net. This far north the midsummer sun barely kiss-es the horizon, which is almost due north, then quickly rises low in the sky again. If you camp out, whenever possible set your tent in shaded areas out of the rising sun's path. It's no joy to have a brief sleep disturbed by late evening sunshine, then early in the morning have your tent overheated by the rising sun.

The whole of the northeast region is beautiful during late fall. The yel-low of aspen trees clashes delightfully with intense blue skies, and distant mountains are dusted with fresh snow. More important, the air is devoid of insects—no mosquitoes, blackflies or horseflies to torment fly fishers.

Fall flights of sandhill cranes signal the end of the fishing season. This great migration from Arctic tundra to southern wintering grounds starts with the first frosts of fall. Great waves of birds pass overhead in V formations, their melodious calls filling the air. This is also time for fly fishers to return south, for snow will soon be falling.

BRITISH COLUMBIA & YUKON TRANSBOUNDARY LAKE DISTRICT

In the old days, the Alcan was slippery, treacherous driving whenever recent-ly graded sections were wet and muddy. Other hazards included flying rocks from passing trucks, deep potholes from ice-heaves and the blinding dust of summer. Now almost completely paved, it is a pleasure to drive. One of the greatest hazards these days is avoiding the ever-present threat of driving fatigue or rounding a bend to suddenly encounter several Stone sheep on the road. Expect to encounter them anywhere near the mountains in this region, and bear in mind that they are quite common on roadways where they are looking for salt licks.

You have finally arrived in Yukon, North of 60, and your next destination is the outstanding Lake District. This group of very large lakes is part of the Yukon watershed, ultimately draining a major portion of Yukon, plus central and western Alaska, northwest into the Bering Sea.

The first lake encountered as you journey north is 94-mi (151-km) -long Teslin at approximately 812 mi (1,307 km) on the Alcan. Its upper third lies south of the British Columbia border. The community of Teslin, Yukon, is on the north shore, and there are boat launching facilities at Dawson Peaks Resort 7 mi (11 km) south of Teslin and at Johnson's Crossing on the Teslin River.

Apart from typical northern fish species, this area also has a hardy race of chinook salmon that make an amazingly long journey from the Bering Sea, migrating up the Yukon River to spawning beds in rivers and creeks feeding Teslin Lake. These fish can be spotted on their redds in August. They are dark, battered and unsuitable for consumption and so deserve to remain unmolested after their incredible 1,875-mi (3,017-km) ordeal.

Right off Teslin community is a group of rocky islands and reefs that fish well for lake trout averaging 8–10 lb (3.6–4.5 kg), with occasional monsters to 35 lb (15.9 kg) turning up. In the spring, the southern part of the lake is colored with meltwater flowing from the Nisutlin River. For some reason, during this period lake trout and inconnu actively cruise and feed along the boundary of clear and colored water. As red and white Dardevles are the most popular lure, try large saltwater streamers like a red and white Sea-Ducer, Sea Bunny, Lefty's Deceiver or Clouser Minnow. During the fall, inconnu— occasionally to 20 lb (9 kg)—stack up at cliffs near the Teslin bridge. You can take them using ultra-fast sinking lines with vertical retrieves up through the schools.

Teslin Lake's primary feeder streams are the Teslin and Jennings rivers. The Teslin's clear, shallow oxbows have fairly large pike, from 12–15 lb (5.4–6.8 kg), that can be targeted with big streamers. Smaller pike are found off any creek mouth, river deltas and big bays in Teslin Lake. The river also has inconnu to 20 lb (9 kg). Big, silver-scaled and tarponlike, these fish-eating predators also are found in large rivers like the Yukon and Kluane in Yukon, and the Liard in British Columbia. However, being in remote areas where rivers are often silted and difficult to fly fish, inconnu are seldom targeted. The Teslin and Jennings rivers at the south end of Teslin Lake are accessible by jet boat, and here fly fishers can make exploratory trips seeking these large, hard-fighting, elusive members of the whitefish family.

Not long after ice-out, inconnu move upstream from their over-wintering grounds, which are probably in the lake itself. They follow schools of whitefish, suckers and grayling on their upstream migration, feeding voraciously. By midseason—July and August—water levels recede and clear up, which is the prime time for flies that represent these baitfish. Many patterns that work for lake trout and pike do fine for inconnu: Mickey Finn, Deceiver, Thunder Creek, Matuka and Zonker. However, make them big—No. 2–3/0 hooks—with additional weight and a little Flashabou. Fish them on short, strong leaders.

Because of the inconnu's migratory nature—here today and gone tomorrow—keep moving so you are constantly covering new water. One general principle is that inconnu avoid fast water, preferring a river's slower-moving inside bends, the openings to sloughs, drop-offs, obstructions, holes and bars, so never pass up fishing a back-eddy. Present your fly deeply, close to the bottom on a full-sink or fast sink-tip line and retrieve slowly to imitate the intermittent swimming action of a baitfish. If a surface disturbance gives away an inconnu's position, try a floating line and unweighted fly presentation down and across the current. Stripping the fly back quickly on the surface will often trigger an attack, and be warned that inconnu hit hard. I find a stout 8-weight outfit is the minimum for casting large, heavy flies.

The Laidlaw and Morley systems connect with the Teslin system, adding more flow to the Yukon River. Farther west, the Bennett and Tagish system—both of which extend into British Columbia—is located on the Carcross loop created by Highways 5 and 6. This area is serviced by the Village of Carcross, Yukon.

During spring snow melt, usually in May, occasional floods may wash rocks and debris down onto the roads or take out bridges, so take care while driving. This, too, is a time awaited by fly fishers, when lake ice is thinning and cracks form, allowing blue-green water to seep on top of the ice. A sense of anticipation grows as anglers wait for a series of warm days after which an overnight wind will result in ice-off. Frequently, the shadowy gray forms of grayling schools may be seen out in a lake, cruising the edges of drifting ice pans. Diligent casts onto an ice pan with a dry fly, followed by gently pulling it forward to drop softly onto the water, will be rewarded by the rapid rise of a grayling. This is easily repeated until you become bored.

If seeking larger targets, think lake trout. They are available at ice-out for a brief period before the surface water warms. Averaging 5–30 lb (2.3–13.6 kg) and more, lake trout require cold, unpolluted water and prefer temperatures less than 50°F (10°C). Being slow-growing, they are susceptible to climatic changes and over-fishing. Fly fishers should follow a no-kill policy on these big char.

Spring water temperatures are still cold enough that lake trout are free-ranging, and in the early mornings they can be seen cruising into the shallows. A fly fisher slowly walking the lake shore, eyes attentive to moving underwater shadows, can target individual fish rather than casting blindly. Sight cast with the sun behind you, and if the surface is riffled, look for windows of increased visibility between the crest and trough of the wavelets. There is no greater thrill than spotting a fish and casting close to it. Your retrieve often stimulates a laker to take immediately, but more often than not it will follow your fly hesitantly, then take by rolling over it before turning away toward deeper water. These takes frequently happen almost right at your feet.

Look for surface disturbances when lakers are rounding up schools of fry. Large ones even eat their own, often targeting smaller lake trout. Try slow-sink or sink-tip lines and baitfish-style patterns in No. 6–4. Those incorporating rabbit strips or marabou with Flashabou are effective. A few well worth trying are the Muddler Minnow in silver or gold, Zonker, Matuka, Woolly Bugger and Egg-Sucking Leech.

At times there are large overnight hatches of caddis, and lakers cruise the surface scooping up the fluttering Tricoptera. Anticipate the cruising path of a fish and cast a big Goddard Caddis or Elk Hair Caddis in front of it. On the hook-up they are strong fighters, tending to head to the drop-off and bottom out in deeper water. This initial run is often the most thrilling part of the event, as big ones feel like logs when bottomed out, and they take time to work back to the surface. I much prefer smaller fish up to 10 lb (4.5 kg) for sport.

As summer warms the surface waters, lake trout descend deeper, seeking colder temperatures. Now available only to trollers with downriggers or wire line, it's time for fly fishers to seek grayling in the rivers until fall. Then, as the cool weather arrives, lakers are again available as they move onto their shallow spawning grounds. Although they are not leader shy, I prefer longer leaders for fishing the shallows, a minimum of 9' (2.7 m). Rods generally need be on the heavy side: 8-weight for deep fishing and a 7-weight for shallow water.

Don't overlook trolling. I believe big white bucktails like those used on the coast for Pacific salmon will out-fish most trolled hardware. Use a 10-weight outfit with a fast-sink line and a large fly on a long line. When a fish hits, kill the motor and play it hard.

The spectacular scenery of Atlin, British Columbia, attracts many visitors annually. A thriving gold-rush town of 5,000 at the turn of the century, its permanent population now hovers around 500. It is reached via Highway 7, a 61-mi (98-km) -long gravel road that cuts south from Jake's Corner, Yukon, at 870 mi (1,400 km) on the Alcan. This junction can also be reached from Skagway, Alaska, via White Pass and Carcross. Atlin Lake is the largest natural body of water in British Columbia, and its northern tip is barely in Yukon. Nearby Surprise Lake (B.C.) and Little Atlin Lake (Yukon) are also in this system.

The Atlin River has some dangerous rapids, but with good boating skills, it can be run upstream to Tagish Lake for an exceptional wilderness camping trip. Surprise Lake, 12 mi (19 km) east of Atlin, has a good gravel access road. The outlet area and Pine River easily provide a good day's sport for feisty grayling and lake fish, some of which are up to 21" (53 cm). This entire area in British Columbia and Yukon has multitudes of seldom fished fly-in locations worthy of exploration, so check at local communities for air charters.

New licensing regulations allow these border-crossing waters to be fished with either a British Columbia or Yukon angling license. All lakes yield lake trout to 20-plus lb (9 kg), grayling in feeder streams and rivers, and some lakes have pike in some lakes to 30-plus lb (13.6 kg).

Look for pike in big bays with a sandy bottom, but if feeder streams and creeks are warmer than the lake water, shift your attention there. You can often spot pike off weed beds, appearing as stationary gray shadows. Shortly after ice-off it is possible to exploit these spring spawners' territorial behavior. They aggressively protect their area from intruders and are likely to attack flies with incredible ferocity. They are omnivorous, eating fish, of course, but also creatures like shrews, muskrats and ducklings with equal gusto, so think big, surface-disturbing flies or poppers. I favor a No. 2–2/0 Dahlberg Diver attached to strong wire leader to avoid cut-offs from their sharp teeth. Remember a hemostat or long-nosed pliers to retrieve your tattered flies.

To the southwest, not far from Juneau, Alaska, and the open Pacific, is the Taku River and its tributaries, the Nakina and Inklin. This Pacific drainage river is being managed by the Taku–Atlin community fisheries group and Tlingit First Nation in an effort to restore declining numbers of chum salmon. It has a few road accesses and can be approached via boat in the lower reaches or by fly-ins about 56 mi (90 km) south of Atlin for Dolly Varden, steelhead and salmon.

THE STIKINE & NASS SYSTEMS

From the north, this area is accessed via the Highway 37 (Alcan) junction a few miles north of the community of Watson Lake, Yukon. The road climbs southward toward the Cassiar Mountains and Blue River, 125 mi (201 km) north of Dease Lake, which has spring and fall fishing for bull trout (occasionally large ones) and grayling. Its source, Blue Lake, offers pike and grayling. The road continues south, close to Boya Lake Provincial Park near Cassiar, then crosses over the continental divide at Dease Lake. Boya is a nice location for camping. Its beautiful aquamarine color is created by light reflecting off the white marl bottom. From Boya Lake, the Dease River flows north out of the mountains through rolling plateaus to Lower Post. A week-long river trip through this wild country requires an experienced guide who is familiar with the river. It ends at Lower Post on the Liard River near the British Columbia–Yukon border. The small town of Dease Lake has accommodation for travelers, an airstrip and charter air services for local fly-ins. The lake is 29 mi (47 km) long with a fishing season from June ice-out to October. It produces lake trout to 20 lb (9 kg), grayling and pike. There is a floatplane base on the lake, where boat launching also is permitted.

The road follows Dease River in a southwesterly direction for almost 22 mi (35 km), and hiking access is good all summer for grayling and bull trout.

The Dease River, a gentle, shallow flow with only minimal rapids, lends itself to fishing by canoe, inflatable or shallow-draft river boat. There are numerous locations for launching and take-out, which allows for varying trip lengths. Midway on the river is McDame, an old gold rush trading post. It has lots of riverside camping spots but is heavily used by moose hunters in late August and September.

The surrounding region has many lakes with lake trout, pike and grayling. Nearby Joe Irwin Lake is small but has cartop boat launching that provides access to good grayling and lake whitefish fishing. For even more information on accessible lakes in this area, refer to topographical maps, ask for advice from the locals or consider a fly-in.

Dease Lake is 312 mi (502 km) from southerly Kitwanga Junction and 212 mi (341 km) from Meziadin. It is a long, straight, boringly somniferous drive south, but it takes you into a new watershed hemmed in by the western Coast Mountains, which make the Swiss Alps look like they were executed in miniature. There, drainage to the Pacific flows west and south. The road crosses tributaries of the Stikine, Tuya, Klappan and Tanzilla rivers, then heads to Telegraph Creek 282 mi (454 km) north of Kitwanga. The mighty Stikine has many other tributaries—the Klastline, Pitman, Spatsizi and Chukachida—but they are remote and require assistance to access. The Stikine's lower reaches and main stem are always heavily glaciated in summer, but tributaries can be fished in spring and fall for rainbow, Dolly Varden and whitefish. Although a Pacific watershed, the Stikine system also is an anomaly in that arctic grayling have colonized it. In fact, the Tanzilla River is good for grayling in June and July. Accessed by flying from Wrangell, Alaska, lower reaches of the Stikine offer cutthroat trout, Dolly Varden, chinook, coho and steelhead.

To the east, the headwaters of three large river systems originate in Spatsizi Plateau and Wilderness Park, which is often enveloped by storms dumping rain that creates the watersheds of the Stikine, Nass and Skeena rivers. Farther south, the Iskut River has road access via Iskut Village, but only to its upper reaches and drainage from Kinaskan and Natadesleen lakes. This is close to Mt. Edziza to the west and about 185 mi (298 km) from Stewart. There is a chain of five lakes located there in a magnificent wilderness setting, and while all offer reasonably good rainbow trout fishing, they receive little angling pressure. Kinaskan Lake also has lake trout.

Farther along Highway 37 are Bell Irving River and Bowser Lake. The river is close by Highway 37 for 25 mi (40 km) north of Meziadin Junction (Highway 37A to Stewart). Because it colors up from glacial melt in summer, it is best fished in spring and fall for rainbow trout, Dollies and grayling.

The Meziadin River, 102 mi (164 km) north of Kitwanga, flows a short distance from Meziadin Lake into the Nass River. The lake has rainbow and Dollies, and some shoals and weed beds occasionally produce larger fish. Being orientated to the salmon stocks, both can be taken on fry patterns and, in season, egg patterns. The Meziadin River has rainbow, coho and a fall run of steelhead. Downstream a short distance is the main stem Nass River, where the water level was so low one year that my fishing partner and I had the river to ourselves. The Meziadin Lake outflow was stacked with coho waiting to ascend into the lake and its upper tributaries. While I fished the outlet for numerous feisty rainbow, my friend was hooking coho by drifting a Woolly Bugger deeply below the bridge a short distance away. Many threw the hook shortly after striking his fly, but each coho that was well hooked ran downstream hard and fast, more out of the water than in, using the turbulent flow to power their descent downstream to the Nass.

There is currently no fishing for salmon in the Meziadin, and the Nass is limited to pink salmon retention only. The Nass can be fishable in the late fall when the water is clear, but it is heavily glaciated for most of the spring and summer.

On the south side of the Nass, the Ksi Shi Aks River (formerly the Tseax) is 72 mi (116 km) north of Terrace. It has cutthroat trout, Dolly Varden, coho, chinook and steelhead.

Continuing southwest, Highway 37 parallels the Nass River to New Aiyansh and Greenville, then continues down to the Portland Canal, which leads out to the Alaska Panhandle and open Pacific.

THE SKEENA, KITIMAT & KITLOPE

Geographically bound by the Alaska Panhandle on the Pacific Coast and the northern Cassiars and vast Tweedsmuir Park to the south, this premier river-fishing area has the greatest density of government-regulated Classified Waters in British Columbia. Many fly fishing devotees from around the world arrive annually to fish for summer-run steelhead and resident rainbow trout. This whole area has been an angler's dream destination for over 50 years, during which time many dedicated people have established lodges and guiding services. Whether you are an experienced old pro fly fisher or an inexperienced, downy-cheeked neophyte, you will find the services of the people in this region invaluable. For information, check with the Guide Outfitters Association of British Columbia at PO Box 94675, Richmond, B.C., v6y 4a4 or visit their website at www.goabc.org. The e-mail is goabc@dowco.com.

Praise must also be given to the numerous fly fishing shops found in most of the communities you may visit. The staff are usually dedicated fly fishers themselves and always forthcoming regarding current fishing conditions and current productive patterns.

The Skeena is the second largest river system in British Columbia, with numerous tributaries and headwaters of considerable size, like 112-mi (180-km) -long Babine Lake. The general timing of migratory stocks in the Skeena system depends on the species. An early run of chinook enters in May, but the larger run is in July. Coho arrive in September and October, but during the mid- to late 1990s, the returns were alarmingly poor, so serious fishing constraints were rightfully imposed to protect these weakened stocks. Indications at the time of writing are that Skeena stocks are rebuilding.

Summer-run steelhead migrations occur from August to late fall, and winter steelhead from December to April. The former travel throughout the system into the headwaters, while the latter usually frequent tributaries closer to the ocean. With no hatcheries on this system, all the fish are wild. For summer-runs, the prime time is from the third week of September until the second week of October. This is the time when every steelhead fanatic and his dog wants to fish the system. Typically there are few fish earlier in the month. On the other hand, there are no crowds. The other alternative is to visit in late October, but wet weather and high water levels can contribute to poor conditions.

At Kitwanga Junction, Highway 37 joins Highway 16. The nearby Kitwanga River drains from Kitwanga Lake and runs south beside Highway 37, draining into the Skeena. It has steelhead and coho in September and October.

Highway 16 follows the Skeena down to Terrace, then continues on to Prince Rupert. The Gitnadoix River, 44 mi (70 km) east of Prince Rupert, flows north and enters on the south side of the Skeena. It has Dollies, cutthroat trout and salmon in its lower reaches, but with no road access, it is necessary to take a river boat across from the Exchamsiks River on Highway

16 to fish it. A southern road leaves Highway 16 at Thornhill, near Terrace, ending at Kitimat at the end of Douglas Channel.

The scenic and productive Kitimat River is 20 mi (32 km) south of Terrace, where Highway 25 parallels it for almost 19 mi (31 km). It offers winter steelhead from late November through to March. December's high water brings in a run of fresh winter steelhead, which move up into the smaller headwaters and tributaries to hold there for spring spawning. They often stack up in groups, and several can be hooked from the same pool before being spooked.

April rains increase water levels in the main stem Skeena, and steelhead holding there are stimulated to move into smaller systems like the Kitimat and Kitsumkalum (known locally as the Kalum). By May the steelhead are spawning, but some new fish still arrive on each incoming tide. These late-comers quickly spawn and return to the ocean. The Kitimat gets a run of summer steelhead in August, which can be fished if the river is clear. This is the same time the Kitsumkalum gets a big run of sockeye and pinks. Cutthroat trout and Dollies are available all year round due to the abundance of fry, eggs and salmon carcasses—virtually a never-ending supply of food.

The Pacific salmon cycle on lower Skeena tributaries starts early in June with returns of big chinook salmon and continues through to July. As the Skeena drops and clears, it is possible to hook chinook on the fly. These silver powerhouses, often fresh from the ocean for only a few days, are a formidable challenge to land and the ultimate test of your stamina and tackle.

Chinook, which commonly attain 30 lb (13.6 kg) and more, require equipment to match, preferably 10-weight rods with fast-sink or sink-tip lines to present big, weighted flies. You want a deep, slow presentation that delivers your fly right on the schooling chinook's nose. Cast far upstream and across, and mend continuously to achieve a deep dead-drift, always mending as necessary to control and slow your line. Good patterns are the Teeny Nymph, Woolly Bugger and Egg-Sucking Leech. Under normal daylight conditions, use dark color combinations of black, green and purple, but in dull light combine black with bright fluorescent orange or chartreuse. When hooked, the chinook will put up a long, stubborn fight that will disturb the other fish. Further fishing usually requires a change of location until the school settles down.

By late July and August, the Kitimat has a chum salmon run, and early coho show up through to September. All small tributaries of the lower Skeena—including the Zymagotitz, Zymoetz, Lakelse, Ishkeenickh, Gitnadoix, Exstew, Exchamsiks and Ecstall rivers—are good in September for coho.

A few miles from Thornhill on Highway 16, the Lakelse River enters the Skeena on the south side, as does the Zymoetz (Copper) River 5 mi (8 km) from Terrace. Both have Dollies that turn up during the salmon runs from August to October, and some are of good size. There are cutthroat trout and spring steelhead in April, chinook in July through August, coho in August through September and fall steelhead in September. Lakelse Lake is worth exploring for good-sized resident cutthroat to 6 lb (2.7 kg).

Downstream from Kitnayakwa to the Skeena, the Zymoetz River receives heavy fishing pressure yet still produces steelhead to 20-plus lb (9 kg) during the September to April season. The river is subject to high turbid water levels, and as flash flooding can permanently alter pools and fish-holding areas, they must be rediscovered each season.

Back on the main-stem Skeena and farther upstream, the Kitsumkalum River enters on the north side about 3 mi (5 km) west of Terrace. Winter steelhead are present from mid-December to late May, and cutthroat and Dolly Varden for a good part of the season. The river is about 13 mi (21 km) long, and the upper 5 mi (8 km) must be accessed by drift boat due to an impassable canyon in the middle section. During the winter and early spring, water levels are usually low, and the river can be drifted, but from June to November, high water makes this infeasible. As Terrace enjoys fairly moderate winter temperatures, unlike rivers farther inland, the Kitsumkalum is fishable. Typical of other "canyon-type" coastal rivers that are filtered and buffered by headwaters lakes, winter rains seldom cause flooding.

The Cranberry River is at the junction of Highway 37 and Aiyansh Road, 52 mi (84 km) north from Kitwanga. It is glaciated in the summer, so fishes best in spring and fall for rainbow, Dolly Varden, whitefish and steelhead.

Leaving Kitwanga on Highway 16/37 and heading toward Smithers, you cross the world-famous Kispiox River near Hazelton. The Kispiox has chinook in June through July, coho in September through October and steelhead in September through November. A small river by northern standards, the Kispiox has an easily wadeable flow, and its steelhead average 12 lb (5.4 kg). Its claim to fame is a 35-plus-lb (15.9-kg) steelhead caught on a fly in

1962, which is unlikely to ever be bettered. The best section of river has good road access and is found in the lower reaches above Hazelton.

At this lower end, the main-stem Skeena is often colored for much of the season, so fly fishing is infeasible. However, it is joined by eastern headwater tributaries like the Suskwa, Babine and Sustut, which are fishable. The remote Sustut was once world renowned for late summer and fall dry-fly fishing for steelhead. Unfortunately, this stock is now a shadow of its former glory, but the river is still worthy of a trip. For glimpses of those nostalgic times of dry-fly steelhead, read *Steelhead Paradise* by John Fennelly (Mitchell Press, 1963).

Babine Lake is 47 mi (76 km) northeast of Smithers via Smithers Landing Road, and can also be accessed by a southerly route from Topley to Topley Landing and Granisle, and from the town of Burns Lake. This big lake is famous for large resident rainbow to 10 lb (4.5 kg), and fishing is best in June to August. At its northern extreme, right beside Fort Babine, 7-mi (11-km) -long Nilkitkwa Lake is known as "Rainbow Alley." Technically still part of the Babine River—merely a widening and slowing of its flow—it is Class I Water and fly fishing only. Nilkitkwa's unique habitat and high density of large rainbow attract many of fly fishers annually. Usually in May, a mass exodus of sockeye smolts migrating out to the ocean provides a feast for the trout. Fairly large Deceivers, Clouser Minnows, Muddler Minnows and similar streamers are always effective. In May–June there are prolific golden stonefly hatches in Rainbow Alley, plus mayflies and caddis in slower-flowing sections. The favored fishing technique is sight-casting to individual fish, either while anchored or drifting in the slow current. From mid-August to the end of September, salmon stocks—sockeye in particular—return in vast numbers to spawn. Their eggs and the flesh from dead carcasses add even more biomass to the food chain and growth of the trout.

Almost 112 mi (180 km) long, Babine is the second largest natural lake in British Columbia. It is drained by the Babine River, which joins the Kispiox near Hazelton. Babine River steelhead average 8–13 lb (3.6–5.9 kg) and are usually taken on deeply sunk flies like the aptly named Babine Special. This river is often unfishable in the late fall because heavy rains bring high water. The upper reaches are accessed via Smithers Landing and the lower reaches from Hazelton.

Ice-out in Babine Lake is some time in early May, after which anglers may fish through until November for wild stocks of rainbow, cutthroat, lake trout, lake whitefish and steelhead, plus sockeye, pink, coho and chinook salmon. A main attraction for fly fishers is the rainbow fishery based on the emergence of sockeye fry from small creeks and rivers, plus artificial spawning channels located in the Fulton River near Topley Landing and Pinkut Creek near Donald Landing. Millions of fry descend into the lake, which will be their nursery for the following two years. Rainbow and Dolly Varden concentrate at the creek mouths, feeding voraciously on dense schools of fry as they ball up tightly for group protection. As the fry schools disperse into the lake so, too, do the trout and char.

South of Hazelton are the Suskwa and Bulkley rivers accessed via Moricetown, where the canyon falls are impassable by boat. Here you can watch First Nations people fishing by traditional methods. Perched precariously on slippery, mist-drenched board walks and rocks, they gaff or dip-net salmon and steelhead that are leaping upward through the raging rapids. New Hazelton to Smithers is 42 mi (68 km) on Highway 16. The Suskwa River, just northeast of Moricetown, is accessed by local logging roads. This fairly fast-flowing river has some steelhead available to fly fishers.

Upstream from Smithers, the eastward-flowing Telkwa River joins the Bulkley. The steelhead tend to average slightly smaller in these rivers. The confluence is a good place to launch for a day's downstream drift to a take-out just below Smithers, close to the falls at Moricetown. The river is wide in parts, with a nice, even flow, where summer-run steelhead hold in long, shallow runs. In early September, this section can be effectively fished with floating lines. Make long casts with large, high-floating patterns like No. 8–4 Bombers, Air BC and the Bulkley Moose, and skate them on the surface. Steelhead in this section seldom move to a dead-drifted fly. Later in the season, wet-fly techniques succeed with small, dark patterns like the Skunk, Purple Peril or Undertaker.

The Bulkley is a very beautiful river that originates in Bulkley Lake near Houston and flows to Hazelton. From Houston to Hazelton is 84 mi (135 km) via Highway 16, but the meandering river is almost 94 mi (151 km) long. Like the Morice, it is less likely to blow out with fall wet weather. This water is effectively fished by Spey casting, an Old World fly-fishing technique pioneered in this area by Mike and Denise Maxwell of Gold-N-West Flyfishers in Vancouver.

The Telkwa River, 10 mi (16 km) upstream from Smithers, silts up during storms, but steelhead and salmon timing is similar to other Skeena tributaries: September to late November. In addition it yields occasional resident rainbow, cutthroat, Dolly Varden and whitefish.

Just southwest of Houston, the Morice River is the final western tributary of the Skeena system via the Bulkley River. Morice Lake is approximately 53 mi (85 km) southwest of Houston via the road that closely parallels the Morice River. There is a campsite at the lake, where anglers can stay while fishing for rainbow to 6 lb (2.7 kg), occasional cutthroat to 3 lb (1.4 kg) and more elusive lake trout to 15 lb (6.8 kg).

Many of the best holding sections of the Morice and Bulkley rivers are just upstream and downstream of their confluence. Some coho arrive in the Morice from August to September, and steelhead are best from September to October. Almost 50 mi (80 km) long and fairly fast flowing, the Morice is a wonderful river to hike along and fly fish, with the added attraction of steelhead and resident rainbow that come nicely to dry flies.

The Skeena River and most of its tributaries can be fished from drift boats and jet boats. However, unless you have the proper equipment plus the knowledge and experience to use it safely, you are advised to hire a local guide. During the early season, high runoff or heavy rains may cause quick spates, so caution must always be exercised.

Fly fishing for Skeena summer-run steelhead involves a few basic principles. As water temperature approaches the 50–60°F (10–15°C) range, steelhead become active and will chase a fly. Use 7-weight rods and floating lines with long leaders to make surface presentations with dry or waked flies like a No. 10–6 Western Steelhead Bee, Riffle Dancer or Bomber. For wet-fly presentations, try stonefly nymph imitations like a No. 8–4 Golden Stone, Black Stone, Montana Stone or Teeny Nymph. These techniques are most effective in the smaller tributary rivers. The fish hold in specific lies, but if you are new to a river, concentrate on the slick water at the head and tail-out of a run or pool.

Clear water conditions seldom exist in big rivers. Glacial melt and silty conditions require sunken-line techniques and big flies. In the Skeena and its larger tributaries, it is standard to use No. 2–4/0 flies to improve their visibility. Black General Practitioners and Woolly Worms are popular standards and are regularly used on short, strong leaders. In analyzing the fly box contents of many anglers, I have concluded that everything will work at some time or another. While some flies occasionally hint at imitations of insects, prawns, ghost shrimp, worms and fish eggs, other are often fanciful creations, some bordering on psychedelic.

A general observation is that closer to saltwater you fish, the more you should use larger, colorful patterns incorporating some flash. For upstream locations, smaller, darker flies get the nod. For summer-run fish in the upper tributaries of any watershed, the dry fly is the best choice. Its success is related, I think, to the warmer water temperatures of summer and early fall, which make steelhead more metabolically active and reawaken their juvenile habit of rising to natural insects. Skating or waking a dry fly or using the greased line technique is, in a way, matching the hatch. Never mind that you are presenting a "natural" about 10 times life size. You are triggering an innate response, which is really all that matters.

The technique for landing big steelhead is now a well-practiced routine that has proved to work efficiently. With about two rod-lengths of line and leader from your rod tip to the fish, hold your rod tip up or tilted sideways and slowly back out of the river. As the fish enters shallow water, its tail has little thrust and swimming becomes ineffective. It may flop or roll about, but there is still enough water that it won't damage itself. After a quick release, simply point the fish's head into a good flow of water until it is ready to swim off under its own power.

While I will be the first to admit that I have enjoyed excellent fishing throughout British Columbia, I think it is fair to state that my most exciting and memorable experiences have always occurred in this marvelous north country. May it ever be so.

Near the historic gold rush town of Atlin, Chuck Cronmiller probes the picturesque Pine River for grayling.

Located near Atlin, Surprise Lake yields trophy-sized arctic grayling amid alpine splendor.

Arctic grayling, one of British Columbia's most beautiful freshwater fish, are common throughout the northern region.

Stuart Richter with a prime Babine River steelhead.

Chuck Cronmiller lands a grayling at Suprise Lake near Atlin.

Southern British Columbia

Chapter 5

Welcome to Southern British Columbia

JIM CRAWFORD

IT CAN TRULY BE SAID that almost anywhere in British Columbia where there's water—fresh or salt—there are fish to be caught. In particular, four regions in the southern half of the province include some of the most productive fly fishing waters in the world. From east to west they are the Kootenays and the Cariboo–Chilcotin, the Thompson–Okanagan, and the Lower Mainland.

A provincial map shows two main highways traversing the province. Highway 1, the Trans-Canada, goes for more than 500 mi (800 km) in British Columbia, crossing the three southernmost regions. Beginning at Horseshoe Bay near Vancouver, it passes through the heart of the Fraser Valley, turns due north at Hope, then at Cache Creek cuts east past Kamloops and continues across the province through the Rockies into Alberta. To the south, along the U.S. border, Highway 3 winds 600 mi (960 km) from Hope eastward through the south Okanagan, then across the West and East Kootenays to end at Crowsnest Pass on the Alberta border. Great road access affords out-standing fly fishing opportunities everywhere within this region.

Accommodations throughout these regions range from sparse camping to regular motels to exclusive fishing lodges. Food and other services are available along any main road. Vancouver has an international airport with virtually every major airline represented. Other airports with scheduled flights are located near Vancouver in the Lower Mainland; Kamloops and

Kelowna in the Thompson–Okanagan region; Williams Lake, Quesnel, Prince George, Bella Bella and Bella Coola in the Cariboo–Chilcotin; and Castlegar and Cranbrook in the Kootenays. With the exception of remote destinations, vehicle rentals, including motor homes, are available at most airports.

As part of the provincial highway system, there are ferry services across Lower Arrow Lake from Needles to Fauquier on Highway 6, Upper Arrow Lake from Shelter Bay to Galena Bay on Highway 23 and Kootenay Lake from Balfour to Crawford Bay. These services are free, and like many free things in life, sometimes there is a waiting period. If that happens, don't hesitate to walk down to the shoreline and cast a fly. You never know. . . .

There are 15 Customs and Immigration border crossings into southern British Columbia from Washington, Idaho and Montana, making it easy to pick your fishing destination and then checking a map to determine the most convenient crossing point. Double-check times, though, because many border crossings are open only during the day.

Chapter 6

Welcome to the Kootenays

JIM CRAWFORD

OUTHEASTERN BRITISH COLUMBIA is chunked into a geographical region known simply as the Kootenays. The region is bounded by the Rocky Mountains and Alberta to the east, Washington, Idaho and Montana to the south, the Monashee Mountains along the west flank, and, to make it easy, the Trans-Canada Highway on the north. Within this section is some of the most rugged and stunningly beautiful mountain scenery in Canada, and the fishing is to die for.

Continuing east along Highway 3 from Osoyoos, in the mountains just beyond Grand Forks, you enter the West Kootenays. At Castlegar and Trail, roads seem to head off in every direction and, indeed, no matter which way you travel, there will be fishing along the way. Past Trail, Highway 3 rises over Kootenay Pass and rolls down across the Kootenay River at Creston. From here, Highway 3A winds north along the eastern shore of Kootenay Lake to Crawford Bay, where a ferry crosses the lake and puts you back on the west side about 20 mi (32 km) above Nelson. After leaving Creston, Highway 3 eventually connects with Highway 95 at Yahk, which marks the beginning of the East Kootenays. Another 40 mi (64 km) brings you to Cranbrook, where Highway 3/95 meets Highway 93 from Montana. This confusing maze of roads untangles as Highway 3 splits off and heads east through Fernie and Sparwood to the Alberta border, while Highways 93/95 continues northward through the Columbia River Valley.

About halfway up Highway 93/95 near the town of Canal Flats is a barely perceptible land-rise. This innocuous high spot at the south end of Columbia Lake, at an elevation of 2,651' (808 m) above sea level, separates the Columbia River headwaters from those of the Kootenay River watershed by mere feet. Cradled by the Canadian Rockies on the east and the Purcell Range on the west, the Columbia River flows due north from here, cutting through the glacier-gouged Precambrian sediment of the Columbia Trench, far up into British Columbia before making a U-turn at Mica Dam and heading back south.

The Kootenay River flows south into Lake Koocanusa (created from the names Kootenay, Canada and USA), down into northern Montana (where the spelling changes to Kootenai), then back north into British Columbia between the west flank of the Purcell Mountains and the eastern Selkirks to create Kootenay Lake. After rambling hundreds of circuitous miles and picking up many dozens of tributaries along the way, these two great rivers eventually merge at Castlegar, right in the heart of the West Kootenays, to form the main stem of the Columbia, about 100 crow-fly mi (161 km) from their beginnings.

At certain locations along their courses both offer excellent opportunities for fly fishing, but these are big, imposing rivers that are unforgiving. What gets the attention of fly fishers are feeder streams like the Elk, St. Mary, Skookumchuck, Spillimacheen, Incompappleux and Duncan, and smaller flows like Bobby Burns Creek and Howser Creek. All offer bounties of westslope cutthroat, rainbow, brook and bull trout, plus mountain and lake whitefish.

There are lakes to fish in the Kootenays, too. The Purcell Mountains stretch from Libby, Montana, north to near Golden, British Columbia, where they meet the Rockies. The northern terminus of the region ends at the Bugaboos, world famous for vertical peaks, glaciers and helicopter extreme skiing. Lakes along the east slope of the Purcells generally lie in a shallow channel formed by a ridge that seems to have just leaned away from the main mountains. Most are deep, long on the north–south axis and narrow east to west. Some—like Whitetail, Jade and Mitten—are full of Pennask strain rainbow, legendary for performing numerous high jumps and strong runs when hooked, along with a few lakes containing hard-pulling Gerrard strain rainbow.

High on the east side of the Rocky Mountain Trench are uncountable numbers of alpine lakes, small rocky tarns located in natural crevices and at the bottoms of slides, which are usually stocked with native westslope cutthroat. Lower down in recesses of the foothills are larger lakes like Premier, Whiteswan and Loon. These are planted with rainbow, but others have westslope cutts and brook trout. Fortunately, these low-elevation valley lakes reach ice-off by late April or early May, which extends the season here for fly fishers by up to two months.

Across the Purcells to the west lies 80-mi (129-km) -long Kootenay Lake, ancestral home of giant Gerrard strain rainbow that can exceed 30 lb (13.6 kg). Obviously, taking a trout that size on a fly is a fantasy, but not too many years ago, Gerrards to 12 lb (5.4 kg) and some very large kokanee were common on the fly from boats drifting the West Arm outlet above the Balfour ferry dock. This fishery declined in the mid-1980s, and while trout that size are still available in the spring and fall, they are fewer and fly fishers must work at it.

Northward up Highway 31, Duncan Dam holds back Duncan Lake. The Duncan and Lardeau rivers and Howser Creek feed into the lake and are also the Gerrards' spawning grounds. The dam put a severe crimp in their free migration, and, despite all efforts, the population of these largest of all lakebound native rainbow trout continues to be vulnerable. In an effort to protect the last remaining spawning areas used by these truly unique fish, the Duncan River is closed to all fishing between the dam and Kootenay Lake, as is the Lardeau River below the Trout Lake outlet. There is fairly good fly fishing in Duncan Lake at times, especially the far end, where the Duncan River enters. There are no clean roads into this area, which, no doubt, accounts for better than average fishing. Trout Lake itself has excellent fly fishing for trout and kokanee right in front of the campground near the old ghost town of the same name.

Back at the south end of Kootenay Lake, where the Kootenay River flows in alongside Highway 3A, is an immense slough area of backwater channels and ponds containing largemouth bass that provide excellent fishing during the summer. One caution: Regulations for the entire Kootenay Lake region, all tributaries and its outlet are many and varied, so be sure to read the *Freshwater Fishing Regulations Synopsis* before making your first cast. Once that's done, welcome to the most fabulous fly fishing in the Pacific Northwest!

Chapter 7

Fly Fishing the Kootenays

JIM CRAWFORD

BECAUSE OF HIGH, MOUNTAINOUS TERRAIN in the Kootenay region of southeastern British Columbia, lake and stream fishing success is always determined by the amount of winter snow and the spring temperatures controlling its melt. And, because trout are really the only fish in which we are interested, determining when to be there becomes a pretty simple procedure. Lower elevation lakes are almost always ice-free by late April. Fishing will be good to excellent from ice-out until July and throughout the summer if the weather stays cool. By the end of September, storms start affecting the fishing, but it can be good until mid-November. Higher elevation lakes are totally at the whim of weather, and ice-off will be at least two to four weeks behind lakes at lower elevations.

Rivers are normally fishable any time from mid-June to early July, but some years a week can be subtracted or added on either end, depending on snow pack and spring storms. The timing for fly fishing in rivers is perfect because they begin picking up just as lake fishing starts declining. Once the water has dropped to normal summer levels, fishing will be excellent right into fall. Then, again depending on storms, it can be good right through until freeze-up.

As a fly tier, I pride myself in creating patterns that take fish in lakes and rivers wherever I go, but after intense days on the water that might stretch from six or seven in the morning until after eleven at night, I never have the energy to tie flies for the next day. I usually recommend buying flies locally, but, unbelievably, most stores in the entire region sell only generic patterns that hardly match anything that trout eat. In fact, 9 of 12 tackle shops and stores I visited during this trip carried the same brand of offshore-tied flies! Only one, the St. Mary Angler Fly Shop in Kimberley, had a complete selection of flies custom-tied to local specifications. Therefore, as I cover the various aquatic critters that trout consume and the flies to match them, keep in mind that unless things change during the interim, most patterns may not be readily available locally. To avoid disappointment, plan on taking along the flies described or tie your own after you arrive.

Check on motel accommodations, campgrounds and restaurants before your trip. Guides usually have excellent contacts, especially if they offer a package program. If you decide to fish this country on your own (and the Kootenays are very amenable to that), contact Tourism British Columbia (www.tourism.bc.ca) at 1-800-663-6000 for a brochure to guide you. Most towns of any size also have a website with links to various services available in their area.

LAKES

On this specific trip, I chose five lakes to fish in five days. I picked early June because chironomids (midges) would still be emerging, and if I hit a few warm, sunny days the region's renowned damsel emergence would occur. Later on, any time after mid-June, large lake caddis (locally called traveler sedges) will also emerge, and while these don't quite equal the fabulous sedge hatches in Kamloops-area lakes, they certainly hold their own.

Although the specific lakes mentioned are located in the East Kootenays, I wanted them to be typical of lakes throughout southeastern British Columbia, so all are popular, heavily fished waters. I felt that if I could be successful, then anyone else could as well. For careful readers, the strategies and techniques described will work in still waters everywhere across the southern region (including Vancouver Island), and there are also clues on specific aquatic structure to look for that will give you an edge when fishing lakes.

Echo Lake

Echo Lake is an hour and a bit north of Kimberley on the Purcell Mountain Range side of the valley. A few years back it was poisoned to remove trash fish and stocked with Pennask strain rainbow. The lake is about a half mile (805 m) long and maybe 600' (183-m) -wide with wonderful marl shoals, a steep drop-off, and deep undercuts at both ends and several places along both sides. For those who don't know about marl, it's the whitish residue covering the shallows of many lake bottoms. It forms when aquatic weeds and algae decompose, and is predominant in lakes that lean toward being more alkaline than acidic on the pH scale. Marl is home and nursery to a wide variety of aquatic insect larvae and pupae, leeches, scuds and other critters that live inside the residue and surrounding weed beds.

I started out in nice, clear weather, but after leaving the highway and enduring a fairly grueling 12-mi (19-km) trek (the final quarter mile in 4-wheel drive through mud), the weather turned ugly. Frequent rain squalls moved through with thunder, lightening and brisk winds. There were periodic sunny breaks, but it was generally cold—not a great day to fish over hatches. This weather pattern was to occur every afternoon until the last day of the trip.

I headed for a marl shoal at the far end in my 8' (2.4-m) pontoon boat. The fair-sized shoal starts in a reed bed at shore and gradually slopes down into about 16' (4.9 m) of water before dropping off into a deep center channel. A few damsel nymphs were climbing the reed stalks, and the odd sedge scampered across the surface, but I didn't see fish taking anything on top. There also were some Callibaetis mayflies coming out, but what caught my interest was a strong emergence of black chironomids.

I rigged my usual 18' (5.5-m) leader and 5x tippet on a floating line, and tied on a No. 14 black Bead Head Chironomid to match the rising pupae. A nice 15" (38 cm) fish hit within a minute, followed by a scrappy 14-incher (36 cm) a short time later. The secret to this technique is to cast downwind, throw a bit of slack to let the weight of the bead take your fly down, then put the rod tip underwater and slowly hand-twist in just enough to keep a fairly straight line. By keeping the rod tip down, the wind and wave action won't lift your line. As soon as anything out of the ordinary happens, lift. It may only be a twitch in your line where it enters the water or a sensation that "something" is there (and often nothing is), but sometimes you'll be surprised. This technique of fishing lakes with weighted nymphs using a floating line and long leaders was the natural spin-off from sinking-line methods developed by fly fishers around Kamloops in the late 1950s. The technique has resulted in some of the largest trout I have ever seen taken.

Wanting to see more of the lake and take some bottom readings with my portable sounder, I cruised the perimeter while staying out over deep water. There I could look in along the shallows and see shoals clearly. In several places spawning fish had cleared the marl down to gravel to create redds. Trout require clean, flowing streams in which to spawn, but they often perform their age-old rite in still water. Young are not produced, but it allows mature trout to avoid becoming spawn-bound by releasing their eggs and sperm. Most redds had beautiful, full-colored fish in residence—several of 24" (60 cm) or more—but I shied away from them. Spawners take just about any fly presented to them, which I don't consider much of a challenge.

Farther along I watched several trout nosing right down into the marl bottom, obviously picking up something. Several casts with my chironomid elicited looks but no takes. I changed to a little Bead Head Leech fashioned from brown cat fur, and a 16-incher (41 cm) grabbed it immediately and almost got into the backing on its first run. I spooned its gullet (the area at the back of its throat) rather than down in the stomach, which can injure a fish. I found a couple of adult gammarus shrimp and some tiny seed shrimp—pale green masses of jelly with two clearly distinguished eyes and a dark vein along the back. With nothing to match these little seedlings, I continued using conventional nymph patterns and picked up a few more fish, all about 14–16" (36–41 cm). Generally, I took one fish on a pattern, then had to change.

About 7:00 P.M. three guys arrived on pontoon boats and surrounded the big shoal along the west side, where they started casting over the spawners I had observed. When I left at 9:30 they were still whooping and hollering and having a grand time. I have no doubts they were taking some clean fish along with the no-brainers, but fishing over redds—even nonproducing ones—is not my idea of fair play.

There is a little mystery attached to Echo Lake. At the far end is a swampy passage that leads to a smaller lake with the same general shape as the main lake (hence, I assume, the name Echo). It is purported to have fewer but much larger fish, but I didn't take time to test it.

On the way out, just before dark, I watched a herd of eight elk feeding in an open meadow next to a shallow, reed-filled pond. I also surprised a beautiful black bear eating greens along the road, causing it to stand at full height to identify what I was before dropping down and heading into the brush. Then, back on the highway, I spotted five more elk and two whitetail bucks with velvet antlers. Normal stuff for British Columbia.

Premier Lake

The next morning I headed to Premier Lake on the Rockies side of the valley. Premier was named, so the story goes, when British Columbia Premier W.A.C. Bennett and a group of moneyed oil people from Alberta tried purchasing all of the land at the lake's north end to make it their exclusive playground. No one got too excited about it until the road into the lake was paved by the provincial Department of Highways and declared "private." At that point an opposition Member of the Legislative Assembly determined that the action to privatize what had always been public land and waters was questionable, so he rallied the troops and the attempt was defeated. The result is one of the nicest public lakes for fly fishing and other recreation in all of British Columbia. With 5 mi (8 km) of paved road, the north end of Premier Lake is easy to access, but there are no public launches or camping spots because the group did manage to tie up all of the lakefront property. You must travel another few miles over a good Forest Service road to the south end, where there is a well-maintained small boat launch, floating dock, beach area and a very nice campground (rest rooms and water but no showers).

Premier is a big, deep lake, and while you can certainly use a float tube or pontoon boat and stay close to shore, I borrowed a friend's 14' (4.3-m) cartopper and 9.9 h.p. outboard. I launched at the Kimberley Rod and Gun Club–sponsored site about midway down the lake's west side. This cutoff from the Forest Service road has good signage, but it's rough and very steep in places. Don't try it in a low vehicle, even in good weather.

The lake is about 3 mi (5 km) long, at least a half mile (805 m) wide and runs north to south. Strikingly clear, its bottom is easily seen down 25–30' (7.6–9 m). Like most lakes in the region, it features Pennask rainbow up to 24" (60 cm) with an added bonus of brook trout to over 5 lb (2.3 kg). I didn't hook any brookies, but the week before, a friend took an 18-incher (46 cm) nudging 4 lb (1.8 kg) on a No. 16 Disco Nymph. In the picture, I saw it looked like a football with a tiny head and a wide tail. I had to settle for skinny little 3-lb-plus (1.4-kg) rainbow up to 21" (53 cm).

About a third of the way up the lake, I pulled into a small bay where two beautiful homes have been built to within a few feet of the water. A rocky island is in front of one home, and a flat-topped marl shoal about 50' (15 m) across comes within 6' (1.8 m) of the surface in front of the other. It has a steep drop-off all around—a very fishy place.

Anchoring just far enough out to reach the shoal or side of the island with long casts, I started with the same No. 14 black Bead Head Chironomid on my floating line I had used the day before at Echo. Within 20 seconds an 18" (46 cm) rainbow took my nymph and set the pace for the rest of the day. In the next hour, I took six fish up to 19" (48 cm).

At the lake's far end, stretching parallel to the north shoreline about 100' (30 m) out, is a long marl shoal that appears as a white ridge. On one side is a slope plunging into water over 50' (15 m) deep, and on the other is a channel about 12–18' (4–5.5 m) deep between the shoal and shore. Heavy clouds were forming as I anchored just out from the shoal, and I sat and watched as fish after fish cruised along the top of the rise, feeding. It was a slaughter! My chironomid hanging just above the bottom was irresistible, and in addition to four nice 18-inchers (46 cm) and several smaller trout, I took one over 20" (51 cm). This lasted for about an hour before a freshening south wind hit and I had to leave. By the time I got back to the launch site, waves were rolling and rain was coming in sheets, but what a day it had been.

Anyone visiting Premier should launch at the provincial site on the south end. Looking north you'll see a wide, flat shoal immediately in front of the launch. A restricted no-fishing area across here is well marked, so look for it. If you see fish cruising the flats (in the legal zone), use a sinking line and nymph on the bottom or the floating line and long leader method with weighted nymphs. In May and early June chironomids will do it, then damsels from mid-June. Later on, sedges on top and—always—dragons and leeches down deep. A good shrimp (scud) pattern will also take fish there all season, especially in the morning or late evening around the chara weed beds.

Fish in Premier Lake are well fed. A nice average size for rainbow is around 14–16" (36–41 cm) with big ones hitting 24" (61 cm). Brookies are a bit tougher, but once you locate them, you can sit in that spot and take a bunch. They normally eat the same food as rainbow, but for some reason they can be taken on gaudy attractor patterns, small black leeches and, sometimes, chironomids. Brook trout are delicious eating, so don't hesitate to take a couple for camp if you're lucky enough to catch some.

At the bridge just before the turnoff from Highway 95 to Premier, there is an attractive RV site and campground, store, restaurant and gas station complex right on the Kootenay River. The town site is called Skookumchuck, but there is really only the camp and a gas station. My compliments to the memory of Premier W.A.C. Bennett for his foresight in creating such good access to this great fly fishing lake.

Whiteswan Lake

North of Premier Lake, high on the west slope of the Rockies at about 4,300' (1,311 m), is Whiteswan Lake. It is about 3 mi (5 km) long, maybe a half mile (805 m) wide at a couple of spots, and lies east and west. It is stocked with Pennask-strain rainbow but also has Gerrards that can reach 30" (76 cm) and weigh up to 15 lb (6.8 kg). Some are triploids (sterilized females that keep growing until they simply die of old age). I didn't hit any big ones that day but did get one of 23" (58 cm).

After 13 mi (21 km) on a gravel Forest Service road from Highway 95, the first glimpse of Whiteswan is from Pack Rat Point. There is a beautifully maintained provincial boat launch, dock and campground (water and rest rooms, no showers), and I was told the bay right in front has the lake's best fly fishing. I'm not sure where the name was derived, but the second I stepped out of my truck, I was under siege by hungry golden mantle ground squirrels, which look similar to chipmunks but are somewhat chunkier. A handful of Sun Chips held them off until I got on the water. Feeding wildlife may be discouraged by Provincial Parks personnel, but, hey, those critters were in control of the situation.

The bowl-shaped bay is about 900' (274 m) in diameter, sloping out from shore to about 12' (4 m) deep, then suddenly dropping off along the eastern edge into deeper water. The entire area is covered in thick, billowing mats of bright green chara weed, interspersed with bare spots of white marl. In the center is a large depression about 50' (15 m) across that has been hollowed out by underwater springs. Later in the summer, fish go there to lie in the colder spring water.

At about 10:30 that morning, I anchored my pontoon boat just back from the drop-off and cast out over the ledge into deeper water. Since Whiteswan is at a much higher elevation than the other lakes I had fished, ice-off comes two weeks later, so chironomids were the only insects hatching. In another two weeks, the same sequence of damsel, mayfly and sedge emergence would be occurring on the lower lakes, but I used my usual black Bead Head Chironomid, long leader and floating line setup.

The first fish hit within three minutes. I was fishing my nymph dead-drift (no movement at all) and staring off at the mountains, watching a snow-storm develop, when a beautiful Pennask hooked itself, jumped once, then departed in a hurry. I just hung on and let it expend energy with six or seven more great leaps and runs until it finally tired. I spooned its throat, quickly measured it at 22" (56 cm), then revived and released it. It was stuffed with chironomids of several sizes and colors, a few large gammarus shrimp and a small leech.

That sort of feeding is Valhalla for fly fishers. It means fish will take virtually any properly presented pattern that represents natural feed. However, I enjoy chironomid fishing with light floating gear so much that it takes a big club to the head to make me try anything else. But after my third fish of 20-some inches (51 cm) on the Bead Head Chironomid, I switched to a shrimp pattern (all for the sake of you readers, of course, just so I could tell this tale). I quickly took a 15" (38-cm) Pennask, then changed again to a dark green Sedge Pupa ribbed with copper. Again, a fish was quickly hooked, but then a storm hit.

A biting wind rolled down from surrounding snow peaks, whipping the water. I pulled anchor and headed for some heavy firs on the north shore. When rain and flecks of sleet hit just as I jumped under the trees, I was glad for the down jacket under my Gore-Tex outer coat and neoprene waders. The micro-burst lasted for about 20 minutes while I sat and slurped hot coffee. Then the lake went almost dead calm.

Unfortunately, the fishing also had died. It's not uncommon for fish to stop feeding just prior to a storm, when the low-pressure wave preceding it depresses the water column. They often go into feeding frenzies just as a storm opens up and right after it moves through, but this situation was different. The storm had passed and presumably the pressure was off, but the fish were not back on the bite. The explanation came shortly—another storm was just about to hit. Such is fishing, so I packed it in.

About 3–4 mi (5–6 km) back down the main road is a very special treat: natural hot springs. It's well signed and there is an outhouse/changing room. Park and walk about 300' (91 m) down a blacktopped path to the pools, which are beside a glacier-fed stream. The uppermost pool is hottest, the three below progressively cooler. If you wish, you can also sit in the creek with its 34°F (1°C) water. While I had a sumptuous hot soak for nearly an hour, six foreign exchange students arrived, two boys and four girls. They weren't bothered the least bit by signs proclaiming No Nudity—No Alcohol, which made for an interesting 20 minutes while we talked. At least until I was finally warm enough to leave. Well, hey, at my age sitting in water that hot for too long might be dangerous. . . . Only in a hot springs in British Columbia. Whew! By the way, don't worry about the slight sulfur smell you go away with—it washes off in a day or so.

Whitetail Lake

Among fly fishers, Whitetail is one of the biggest and, perhaps, most celebrated of southeastern British Columbia lakes. Just after ice-out and for the month following, the chironomids emerge in clouds. Then comes a fabulous damsel fly emergence that normally starts in June, followed by a grand sedge hatch in late June, both of which I was lucky enough to hit two years previous to this trip. In fact, I picked this particular week, hoping to experience it again, along with the tail end of the chironomid fishing. As it turned out, I was too early for the damsel emergence and a week late for the chironomids.

Of all the hundreds of lakes I have ever fished, this is one of the most beautiful. It is crystal clear, very clean and the entire bottom around the lakeshore is one continuous marl shoal. The shoal at the north end is immense, perhaps a quarter by a half mile (402 x 805 m), with water depths of 10–12' (3–4 m). Patches of high tulles and chara weed beds are dotted throughout, and you can see fish cruising the flats much farther away than can be reached with a cast—even by "wow" casters who can fire out an entire fly line plus a little backing.

In the lake's approximate center is a deep hole about 600 x 1,200' (183 x 366 m). Being spring fed it's a great place for fish to spend hot summer days and to overwinter. Around the edges are dense, dark patches of chara that provide cover for shrimp, damsel, dragon and sedge pupae, leeches and myriads of other aquatic critters. The south end is a repeat of the north end but only a third in size.

Inexplicably, Whitetail's chara beds are disappearing at an alarming rate. What were large tracts a few years ago have dwindled to only a few acres. Locals blame this phenomenon on too many outsiders ripping up the aquatic vegetation with anchors. This could be a partial explanation; hundreds of boats are out there each season. But a fisheries biologist I talked to thinks it might be a plant virus introduced from boats or anchors used in infected lakes. We must remember to always clean all weeds from our gear after each use. Whatever the cause, it's a shame. If the aquatic vegetation goes, so will the insects and invertebrates that provide food for the resident trout.

What trout they are! Whitetail produces some of the biggest rainbow in the region. A 24-inch (61 cm) can eat your lunch, and even 16-inchers (41 cm) sometimes get into your backing. While my favorite rod is an 8', 3-weight, G. Loomis GLX, I don't use it here. On this lake I use a 10', 4-weight GLX with a 5-weight line. The extra length gives me more power to cast long, yet stays soft enough to prevent breaking off the 5x and 6x tippets needed to fool fish that are used to seeing probably thousands of flies thrown at them.

I have a 10' (3-m) Kevlar pram that I row or run with an electric motor. It doesn't do too well in rough water, but it's light, easy to handle and I can stand in it to cast. By the time I ran out about a quarter mile (402 m) from the campground to where two dozen other boats were anchored over the weed beds, the wind was coming in swirls. I anchored front and back to hold the boat in position, then cast downwind with a green No. 12 Bead Head LGF representing a scud or a damsel and probably several other critters. For a while I fished it dead-drift just off the bottom like a chironomid, then like a scud with short strip-strip-strip-stop movements, then like a damsel with slow 6–12" (15–30-cm) pulls and a stop. But no rewards.

At 11:00 A.M. a strong south wind churned down the lake, and the first in a series of rain and sleet storms hit, cold and raw. Half of the boats went in, but the rest of us put on rain gear and turned our backs to it. I settled in under the hood of my parka and watched my line. I had switched to my old standby, the black Bead Head Chironomid and was simply letting it hang back there. Just as the rain quit and the wind went down, an old fellow in a nearby boat hooked a 20-incher (51 cm). It fought for almost 20 minutes against his ultralight rod before it was brought to net and released.

An hour and at least six fly changes later, I still hadn't taken a fish, but the old guy had landed two more. I watched him using a damsel retrieve—long, slow, 12" (30-cm) pulls, then a few seconds rest. About 12:30 the sun peeked through and the wind calmed down, whereupon he yelled over to his friend, "Now maybe the damsels will start moving, and we'll get to see them take."

He was obviously referring to trout takes, so I put on a small, weighted, pale green marabou damsel pattern and emulated his retrieve. After a dozen casts, I finally got a solid hookup. A 20-incher (51 cm) launched itself and made a good run that just showed my backing. Several jumps and short runs later, I had it, a strong, clean fish. I quickly spooned and released it. The contents didn't show much: two shrimp, a few chironomids, but no damsels, which surprised me since I had taken it on a damsel.

Hoping the bite was on, I cast again, but all I did was put myself in position to get into trouble. Storms in this country generally approach from behind the mountains to the southwest, and I hadn't been watching that direction. When boats started heading for shore, I finally looked around and saw black, ugly gloom bearing down on me. I was last in, and by the time I hit shore, whitecaps were churning the lake into froth, and spray blew over my little punt's bow. I climbed into my truck to eat lunch and wait it out, but when sleet and snow started sticking to my windshield, I got the message. It was when I started taking gear out of my boat that I noticed one of my anchors sitting neatly on top of my 10' graphite thunder stick. Mashed. The end of a perfect day.

When I headed up the road at 2:00, there was half an inch of sloppy snow on the ground. Two dozen fly fishers and five fish in five hours. Scandalous statistics for a lake as productive as Whitetail.

Whitetail's provincial campground is not as well laid out or maintained as others I have mentioned. Only a limited number of campsites are level or have tables, outhouses are few and running water is provided by a few spigots. I consider this a "rough" camp. Still, this lake is definitely worth seeing, and the odds of an average fly fisher landing some good fish are excellent during more moderate weather conditions.

Nine Bay Lake

Nine Bay is a wonderful little lake, but you'll need a local map to find it after a two-hour drive from Kimberley to the turnoff at Parsons, then another half hour west on well-maintained logging roads. It's at the end of the Purcells, snuggled under the base of the Bugaboos in the Bobbie Burns ski area. It's a beauty and truly does have nine bays. Every one has wonderful marl shoals set off by islands, rocky points, big pines, huge firs and, in the background, the stunning peaks surrounding Bugaboo Glacier.

A little after 10:00 A.M. I parked at the designated area 100' (30 m) above the lake. Morning started with beautiful bright sunshine, and it stayed hot and calm the entire day. What a change from the previous four days. The only downside occurred while unloading my pontoon boat, when the mosquitoes about sucked me dry. First on the agenda was to slather on copious quantities of repellant. In the clear atmosphere of the mountains, sun screen is a necessity as well. I use Cactus Juice, a combination repellant and sun block, and it's terrific.

I carried my boat and gear down the gradual slope to a tiny dock where, about 40' (12 m) to one side, a dozen spawners were slowly circling the gravel area they had cleaned. While I got into my waders and fins, I listened to three guys, about 600' (183 m) across the lake, who were hooting and laughing as all were into fish.

Nine Bay is about 1 mi (1.6 km) long and, with all of its nooks and bays, shaped like a puzzle piece. Like Whitetail, it is one big marl shoal with beds of chara here and there around the edges and a deep channel up the center. When I finally got out on the water, I muddled along with my chironomid, then a Pheasant Tail mayfly nymph, a damsel and a small, weighted Green Dragon, all without a hit. I could see trout everywhere—big fish—feeding along the marl bottom, but only the odd one looked at any of my patterns. Damsels were in the air, so it was obvious the sun had triggered an emergence. I didn't have any damsel nymphs the color of the pale, watery, yellow-olive ones swimming in the clear water, but I knew that sooner or later I'd hit a fish and get a look at what they were eating.

I headed toward the north end, casting whenever I saw fish working. At one shoal two nice trout were feeding within a foot of shore, and I finally hooked a bright 20-incher (51 cm). Then, as if someone had hit an off switch, they quit. Fish were still moving, and I tried for another 15 minutes or so, but the bite was definitely over for the moment. I've always marveled at how that happens.

I rowed across the bay to a rocky point, then sat on a log in the sun and ate lunch surrounded by stunning scenery.

Back on the water, I went into the farthest bay. Even before I got near shore, I could see fish taking something on or just under the surface in classic head-to-tail arching. I positioned myself out from the fish, and even though I fully expected to hook up, I wasn't ready for such a vicious hit. A very large fish took my damsel, literally, jumped several times, and that was that. It was the last fly I had in that color.

Rummaging through my fly box for something similar, I found an old Bead Head LGF. It was close in color, but the body was scud-shaped. Didn't matter. I eased back toward the shoal and made another cast. A fat 15-inch (38 cm) took solidly, and I landed it a few minutes later. While holding it in the water to release it, I looked down between my knees and noticed the marl boiling up all around as if some giant creature were down there thrashing around. It covered an area about 40 x 100' (12 x 30 m), and everywhere trout swam through the billows as if in clouds of fog. It looked spooky, but then it dawned on me—springs! Here were fish right down in the soft marl bottom picking up all sorts of critters: chironomid larvae (bloodworms) and pupae, damsel and dragon nymphs, sedge larvae, shrimp, leeches, backswimmers, Corixa and other water beetles—you name it. If it was aquatic and lived in the marl, it was being blown out by the force of the springs below, and the fish were having a truly movable feast.

By the time I landed my sixth fish, my Bead Head LGF was in tatters, so I switched to another fly of similar color. It didn't work nearly as well, and to get it down where the fish were, I had to use a small split shot about 12" (30 cm) or so above the fly. That small piece of lead on an 18' (5.5-m) leader caused all sorts of trouble casting with my little 3-weight rod. I shortened the leader a few feet, but it didn't help much. Whenever I did get it right, though, I almost always got a strike.

I stayed on that spot for another hour and landed two more nice, clean fish and lost two. At 9:00 I decided I had to make the break. It was tough, believe me. A person can wait a lifetime to get into a frenzy of big, wild fish like that, and you just don't want to leave. Fish were hitting the entire time I sat on those springs. I had landed a dozen rainbow between 15 and 24" (38 and 61 cm). What a lake! What an ending to the first part of my trip to the Kootenays.

RIVERS

The second part of my Kootenay expedition was in July. Longtime friend Brian Chan and I had made plans the previous fall to meet in Kimberley, then fish four of the most popular rivers in the Kootenays. Since the best way to fish moving water is to drift, we opted to hire guides John Kendal and Kelly Laatsch of St. Mary Anglers in Kimberley. My previous comments about strategies and tactics being much the same in lakes everywhere in the Kootenays holds true for rivers. What we learned can be applied to clear, free-stone streams and rivers everywhere in southeastern British Columbia. Exceptions are the Columbia and Kootenay rivers, which are big and usually off-color. Although fly fishing can be excellent in these waters, the methods are so unique that local knowledge is a must. Besides, these two rivers can be dangerous to those who are not careful or who are unfamiliar with fishing big waters. My advice is to hire a local guide who can show you more in a day than you could find out on your own in several.

Brian and I had four days. We planned day one on the St. Mary River, the Elk on day two, a hike-in to the Wigwam for its legendary "largest west-slopes on the planet" on day three and the upper Skookumchuck on our last day. Things didn't work out quite that way. The St. Mary was in prime shape, so no problem there, and the Elk, while running a little high, was very fishable. The other two were disappointing. The Wigwam was blown out with high water, and while the Skook was running clear, its water was high and still very cold in the upper section we wanted to fish.

St. Mary River

An angler would have to be brain-dead not to catch westslope cutthroat in the St. Mary, which drains the southern Purcell range in the East Kootenays. My fishing log tells me that on my first-ever cast there I took a fat 16-inch (41 cm). I also caught fish on the next dozen casts. And over the next two days of floating and wading a 10-mi (16-km) stretch, I caught and released over one hundred 10–20" (25–51 cm) cutts that chewed up the water to take such highly sophisticated patterns as Muddlers, Hoppers and Hare's Ear Nymphs.

Catching westslope is obviously not very tough. They carefully, deliberately, almost trustingly, look at a wide variety of dry flies and nymphs without showing much concern about how they have been presented. But while that might make a sloppy fly fisher look good at times, it doesn't mean you can get careless. Usually, you get only one good chance at a cutt, and if it doesn't take or if you miss the hookup, don't count on it returning.

Although westslope are strong and hard-bodied, they aren't particularly active fighters—no jumping, no long, ripping runs. Their niche with other native species is such that they have not had to be assertive to survive. As a result, they don't compete well for food, so when nonnative fish like the more aggressive rainbow intrude into their realm, westslope populations suffer quickly.

These character flaws are part of the reason an estimated 90 percent of the original population of Interior cutthroat trout has disappeared—that and the fact they were reefed from every piece of their native water by anglers flinging lures and bait. The St. Mary was no exception until it was realized this classic freestone river contained some of the last pure-strain bull trout and westslope cutthroat in the province. Since then, bait bans above and below St. Mary Lake, single-hook-only, and catch-and-release regulations have brought the St. Mary back from the edge of ruin, making it one of the most productive trout rivers in the country.

It was hot and dry the week Brian and I were there (actually the start of a terrible drought that gripped the west that season), but on that day everything was perfect. I had replaced the 10', 4-weight rod crushed with my anchor a month earlier, using it as a backup to my favorite rod for this river—an 8' (2.4 m), 3-weight. Our first drift was the middle section from the powerhouse at Marysville down to the takeout at Wycliffe bridge—a distance of about 5–6 mi (8–10 km). The water flow along this stretch is moderate with choppy rapids, rock gardens, long flat runs, and miles of gravel banks and sand bars that break the river into braids and channels. Tall pines, firs and aspens grow densely right to the bank edges, and white-tailed and mule deer, elk, bald eagles and all forms of waterfowl are common. Thankfully, manmade structures disappear completely once you push off.

Our first stop that morning was at a long, deep seam where water poured around a small island and rejoined the main river. I tied on an attractor pattern I almost always start with—a high-floating, yellow foam-bodied Deer Hair Hopper—while Brian rigged with a strike indicator and a CDC Baetis Nymph pattern he created. We both used floating lines. As I was using a dry fly, I was allowed first cast. Rainbow are not common in this stretch, but a 14-incher (36 cm) jumped on my hopper before it had drifted 3' (90 cm). Right behind me, Brian caught another nice rainbow about the same size. A great start, but by day's end it would be evident, the floating line nymphing technique was superior to dry flies. While we certainly caught our share on the surface, nymphs consistently accounted for bigger fish at every stop. By the way, the inclination of St. Mary cutts to take nymphs never changes, but as the river clears and drops through summer and fall, fly fishers switch their preference to top water, and the vast majority are caught on small Pale Morning Duns (PMDs) or patterns imitating caddis, summer yellow stones and hoppers.

Our next stop was on a long gravel bar sloping steeply down into the main channel. At the top of the run, Brian was quickly into a cutt in the soft water only a few feet out, indicating that, typical of cutthroat, they were holding tight to the bank. I picked the middle section and had several refusals on my hopper before finally changing to a Prince Nymph and hooking a 15" (38-cm) whitefish. These fish hold in the faster water and think that any small nymph drifting by is simply delicious.

Down below the gravel bar, a long run of broken water formed the section called the Rock Garden—large boulders and slabs of rock that create pockets of holding water down its entire length. We cast from the boat to likely looking spots as we drifted through, but only Brian hooked up on his nymph. At the bottom of the run, Kelly pulled the boat into a backwater, and we got out to wade. The river merged into a narrow channel where the water was fast and deep, so I decided to use a weighted black Marabou Bugger. With the heavy fly and swift water, I used my 10' rod with a 12' (4 m) leader and 12" (30 cm) of 4x tippet. Fish never hit buggers gently, and with my propensity to set up hard enough to fracture a fish's neck (hey, I get excited), the long, soft rod saves a lot of break-offs.

Using weighted flies properly can be tricky. By casting across and slightly upstream, then throwing some slack above the entry point, you can make the fly drift drag-free while sinking. As the current catches your leader at the end of the drift, it will lift the fly and swim it up and across the current—a favorite technique of steelhead fly fishers. If you haven't hooked up during the drift, the hit almost always comes just as the fly starts rising or as it straightens out downstream. On my third cast I had a savage strike. Cutthroat rarely jump, and this one stayed deep, turning sideways to the current and ripping out about 20' (6 m) of line—a solid fish. After a few minutes of give-and-take, I led a beautiful 18" (46-cm) westslope to the shallows. While very respectable, it wasn't the elusive 20-incher (51 cm) that puts you in another class or the 24-incher (61 cm) that vaults you into truly rarified atmosphere. Among fly fishers that is. The size of a fish, though, like so many things in life, only infrequently has a direct correlation to the level of pleasure experienced by the person who caught it.

By early afternoon the intensity was gone from our casting. We'd proved we could catch wild trout on a variety of floating, streamer and nymph patterns, albeit under nearly ideal conditions. We fished the St. Mary again on our fourth day, the lower section this time, and had the same results—trout eager to please. We left with a good feeling about the river and the area in general.

Elk River

The Elk starts its journey at the southern tip of Banff National Park high in the Rockies, then slides down the west slope along Highways 43 and 3, through Elkford, Sparwood, Fernie and Elko before emptying into the Kootenay River at the top end of Lake Koocanusa near Highway 93. As roadside rivers go, the entire length of the Elk is in a truly beautiful setting. Rocky Mountain ridges are so high you almost strain your neck trying to see the tops, wide green meadows are framed by aspen and cottonwood with endless folds of dark pine beyond, and long, jagged rock ledges and gravel bars hold the river to its course. It is home to westslope cutts over 20" (51 cm) and bull trout that can eat them. It also has mountain whitefish up to 3 lb (1.4 kg) or so, which are very impressive on light fly gear. Don't snicker. These are great fighters that have saved the day for more than one fly fisher when the trout weren't active.

The Elk was nearly written off in 1995. Trout fishing had already seriously declined the previous few years due to overkill. Then unseasonably warm weather caused a severe flood of meltwater and heavy ice to scour the entire river channel during spring runoff. Fishing that summer was the poorest on record, and it was feared the resident cutthroat and bull trout populations had been devastated. To allow the species time to repopulate, a two-year no-kill moratorium was imposed on the entire river throughout the 1996–97 seasons, and since then several sections have remained no-kill.

The good news is that both cutthroat and bull trout rebounded dramatically, and populations remain high—even after an article published in *Fly Fisherman* magazine mentioned the Elk and fishing pressure by U.S. fly fishers was excessive during the two summers that followed. The number of river guides also increased from three to about a dozen, along with the usual controversy between local anglers who considered the river theirs and those providing the guide services.

It was in this setting that Brian and I loaded into John's river raft and set out to drift the canyon section of the Elk from Morrisey Provincial Park to the Railroad Bridge takeout below the tiny—don't blink!—town of Elko. From the highway it appears that the river drops down through a steep canyon, but this is an illusion. The river gradient actually stays fairly constant, and it's the road that winds high up along the hillside and then drops down to meet the river at the Morrisey boat launch. The illusion is further enhanced because the river leaves wide, picturesque flat meadowlands, where it is braided and meandering, and becomes compacted between steep hills for several miles.

The water was slightly high and off-color, but as this most-fished section is where the Elk's largest westslope hang out, we wanted to try it. For dry fly enthusiasts, No. 8 and 10 Adams, Elk Hair Caddis, Irrisistibles and low-water patterns like Stimulators and Parachute Hoppers are excellent throughout summer into early fall. While 100-fish days have been recorded along this stretch, a typical day would be 25–30 cutts with a couple over 18" (46 cm) and perhaps a bonus bull trout or two. There also are early hatches of PMDs and blue-wing olive mayflies, spotted sedges and, sometimes, the tiny summer yellow or Yellow Sally stoneflies. There are salmonfly hatches, too, but they are sporadic and normally take place during high water before fly fishers can get on the river.

A neat feature of the Elk is that trout hang right next to the banks, so as you drift, accurate casts into pockets often only inches from the rocks or tight under overhangs are almost always rewarded. Unfortunately for us, it soon became evident that the higher water on this day would preclude that element. We had to stop and wade the pools and runs, which, as far as I'm concerned, is more fun anyway. Another slight disappointment was discovering that the fish weren't interested in dry flies early in the day, so we had to use nymphs to take them.

One of the first places we stopped was at a wide, 100' (30-m) run with a high, gravel bank sloping down into the water on one side and heavy willow growth on the other. We parked our raft at the bottom of the gravel bar and walked back upstream. Brian and I had tried dries earlier while drifting, and even though the odd fish was moving, we determined they were probably taking midges or some other emerger just under the surface.

Brian was first to hook up using his CDC Emerger. As his fly lifted from the bottom on the swing below us, a beautiful 18" (46-cm) cutt followed and grabbed it just under the surface in a huge swirl, then took line in a rush, heading back to wherever it came from. Brian brought it in and pumped its throat, which, surprisingly, was empty. It was about 10:30 A.M. and the fish were probably just starting to feed. I've always smiled at the gentlemanly hours cutthroat trout keep.

I took a nice fish, too, on a weighted Prince Nymph. Then we headed down to the next run, where the river split around a long island. Along the back was a narrow channel that would be dry in summer, but in front the main river moved hard and fast. I hiked to where the current split, then cast upstream so my fly bounced along the bottom out in the main flow. Just as my fly was even with me, a 2-lb (.9-kg) whitefish hit, jumped and threw the hook. Whitefish are built with streamlined bodies to hold in fast water with minimal effort and can be caught in the most turbulent runs. Cutts are lazier, so I picked a seam of water that slowed along the inside edge of the main current. I cast upstream and mended my line so the nymph moved along in a drag-free drift—just as important in nymphing as when using a dry fly.

When drifting nymphs I constantly mend upstream and concentrate on the line just under the surface or on the strike indicator if I'm using one. If I don't feel the fish, I usually see the strike indicator stop and set up immediately. This time, when the line paused, I lifted more by instinct than actually feeling the fish. My line headed straight out into the fast water, then ripped off downstream. I ran down the island past John and Brian until I got below the fish, then finally brought it to shallow water. I quickly measured it against my rod, which later showed it was 21" (53 cm) of beautiful, heavy cutthroat with bright orange slashes on the throat and about as big as river cutts get.

The rest of the day went pretty much the same with nymphs drifted through runs producing the best fish. Late in the day we were able to take a few on large dries—Stimulators and rubber-legged Tarantulas fired into classic lies next to the banks and along the edges of big pools. There are big bull trout in the deep pools here, bruisers that come up from Lake Koocanusa to spend the summer harassing smaller resident fish. Hook a whitefish or cutt over a deep hole and it sometimes disappears in the maw of a monster bull.

It's spooky how big they can be in this river. We didn't hit any on our trip, but later that summer John took a 12-pounder (5.4 kg) that grabbed a little cutt he had hooked, and it wouldn't let go. John netted the bull, weighed it in the net, measured it, kissed it and returned it to the river. I'm sure that fish never even knew it had been kissed.

Two other sections of the Elk deserve mention. From the bridge north of Highway 43 above Sparwood down to the bridge below town on Highway 3, the Elk flows strongly between brush-lined banks with braids and bars. There are many deadfalls and logjams, so drifting this section can be dicey. Westslope hold in the classic runs, and whitefish aren't quite so numerous as in lower sections. There are few sustained hatches in this upper portion, but, as elsewhere on the river, dry attractor patterns like Hoppers, Irrisistibles, Stimulators and Humpies will pull cutts to the top, while nymphs, marabou streamers, Zonkers and weighted Muddlers will take them deep—and sometimes bull trout as well.

Where Highway 3 crosses the river, the country flattens and the river slows. From here down past Fernie to the Morrisey Provincial Park launch where we put in, the fishing is usually good and sometimes borders on outstanding, even though it is heavily fished because of easy access. Much of this segment can be waded, but as with most rivers in the Kootenays, drifting is best, and there are numerous places where small craft can be put in. Just ensure you are near the highway at day's end, so, if you haven't made prior arrangements to be picked up, you can hitchhike back to your car. Car-toppers and inflatables can be used in this section during low-water months and with caution during spring runoff. However, a local guide is recommended, at least on the first trip.

Skookumchuck Creek (River)

The Skook begins far up in the Purcell Wilderness Area's midsection. It's one of those sleeper streams about which little is known. Crystal clear and ice cold, it's one of the area's last rivers to drop to fishable levels, which in some years doesn't occur until early August.

For various reasons I had never fished the Skookumchuck in the 25-plus years I've been going to the Kootenays, so when Brian mentioned it was one of the rivers he wanted to try during our quest, I immediately told John and Kelly, "Too early or not, let's go."

Both said our only chance would be to get as high up as possible, which meant a two-hour drive north to Canal Flats, west up into the heart of the Purcells over various logging roads, then along 4-wheel-drive ruts, followed by a half-hour hike.

Next morning we were at the trail head at 10:00 A.M. I'm not certain of the elevation, but there was still snow, and despite bright sunlight it was cold. A short hike put us next to one of the most pristine freestone streams I have ever seen—even in high water. My first mistake was to assume "what you see is reality." I stepped into water so clear that I still swore afterward it was only a foot deep, but it almost reached my wader tops. Thankfully, John, who has done the same thing on this river more than once, was right there to grab my parka hood and keep me upright, or I'd have been swimming.

Naturally, the best pools were about 30 minutes downstream. The trail along the riverbank was trampled with elk, deer and bear tracks, so we made noise and talked as we walked. The stream was 30–40' (9–12 m) across, flowing swiftly through boulders, broken rock, logs and heavy brush. Looking ahead, the downhill drop in the stream bed was quite definite. Periodically, we stopped and cast to likely looking pockets that would hold trout once the water warmed up and the level dropped a bit, but this early there were few takers.

At the first pool, Brian was given first shot. Kelly said if the cast was in the right spot, the best fish in the pool would normally be the most aggressive and, indeed, this almost always proved to be the case. Brian had barely mended his line when a chunky 14" (36 cm) westslope grabbed his nymph and beat it back into the current. The fight was powerful but quick, the cold water apparently sapping the fish's energy. We pumped it and found numerous tiny nymphs but no significant feed.

I was next. I cast my Hopper to the same seam and was quickly into a cutt about the same size. It headed toward the pool's lower end, where it got off. Right across from where it came loose was a jumble of big rocks. A fish rolled just above them, so I cast to it. My yellow Hopper hadn't gone a foot when the biggest cutt of the day jumped on it and streaked straight toward me, hit the current, then headed downstream. I slogged after it and got into some slack water where I could play the fat 16-incher (41 cm) and bring it in.

The next four hours went pretty well like that. We found only four or five good pools, but they all contained eager little westslope that would build anyone's confidence. Later in the year, larger cutts work their way up from the lower river, along with bull trout that inevitably follow these traditional meals. However, looking at the water's purity there, it doesn't appear it would sustain a very large biomass of trout. Rocks we turned over near shore did have critters crawling around under them—tiny micro-caddis, mayflies and small stoneflies—so there is little doubt that larger nymphs were in the faster water, plus scuds and leeches in the pools. But all in all, the Skook is more suited to smaller fish and smaller numbers of them.

Still, it is a beautiful, fishy little stream that I recommend to those who don't mind driving on a typical, dusty logging road, then making a bit of a hike to get to some very scenic and still pristine country. One caution, though—unless you hire a guide this is not a place you want to try finding without a good, up-to-date topographic map or very clear directions.

AFTERTHOUGHTS

As my friends sat under the massive limbs of an old-growth fir, finishing their lunch and chatting about great rises, jumps, runs and break-offs, I waded into the river to make one last cast. While doing so I contemplated the future. Not of the St. Mary, the Elk or Skookumchuck, for I feel they are safe for the time being with special regulations and more conservative-minded anglers fishing them. Rather, I thought about my own future and that of my young friends. At my age I probably don't have that many more years of this kind of thing left. But that's okay. I've enjoyed my share and for now there are still some westslope cutts and a few rainbow here and there left to be caught. No, the future won't affect me nearly as much as it will Brian, John and Kelly.

My guess is the bull trout will be first to go, their required pristine spawning streams ravaged and violated by logging and forestry mismanagement. While bulls are not really that exciting to catch, to lose the opportunity is sad. Next will be the westslope, those willing trout that make all anglers look good. They will be displaced by the same bottom-line mentality that will spell the end of bull trout. Along with that will be the aggressive, nonindigenous species like the rainbow, which will assert itself into the remaining cutthroat habitat and drive them away until they have no place left to survive. We lost 90 percent of our wild westslope cutthroat during the century just ended, so what is the measure of their future? British Columbia will most likely continue to have tremendous fly fishing, but not for pure native westslope. I fear their future is on a parallel with my own—their time gradually waning until it finally just runs out.

A 12" (30-cm) westslope nailed my nymph, rolled at the surface and quickly came in. It lay quietly as I remove the barbless hook from its mouth, its trusting innocence punctuating my earlier observations about this species. Then it was gone with the current, and I realized that living long into the future was not the real issue here. I agonized then—as I do now—that these beautiful wild trout may be history even before I am.

Elk River rainbow are suckers for high-floating dry flies.

The Kootenays offer fly fishers a wide range of wadeable trout streams.

Lake fishing in the Kootenays can provide fast-paced action for trophy-sized trout.

Chapter 8

Welcome to the Thompson–Okanagon & Cariboo–Chilcotin

JIM CRAWFORD

BEFORE COVERING THIS REGION, which is renowned for its trout lakes, let's pause for a moment to clarify just what constitutes a Kamloops trout. In scientific terms, Kamloops are not a separate genetic species; however, they do have traits that set them apart from other rainbow—physical appearance, behavior, fighting stamina and rapid growth rate—all of which are proved to be the result of unique ecological and environmental conditions exclusive to their native waters. If removed from this environment, Kamloops trout lose these distinctive characteristics, whereas rainbow placed into it will take on these traits. So even though stocked lakes in Kamloops country might actually contain Pennask, Blackwater, Tzenzaicut or other strains of rainbow trout, thanks to prime environmental conditions, these fish develop all of the qualities that anglers happily associate with Kamloops trout, the collective name by which we will continue to identify them.

At Hope the Trans-Canada heads north, following the Fraser to its confluence with the Thompson River at Lytton, continues beside the Thompson to Cache Creek, then east along the river through Kamloops and the northern boundary of the fabulous Thompson–Okanagan fishing region to Shuswap Lake at Salmon Arm. There the Trans-Canada meets Highway 97, which runs due south through Vernon and Kelowna, along Okanagan Lake, then down through the heart of the Okanagan Valley, where it connects with

Highway 3 at Osoyoos on the U.S.–Canada border. At this point it's about 150 mi (241 km) west back to Hope. Within this 21,000 sq mi (54,386 sq km) rectangle is some of the greatest fly fishing on the planet.

Also from Hope, Highway 5 (the Coquihalla) provides fly fishers a straight shot onto the Merritt Plateau, considered the center of the Kamloops lakes region. Between Merritt and Kamloops, along Highway 5A, virtually every lake is stocked with Kamloops trout. Magic names like Roche, Peterhope, Plateau, Jacko and Hosli conjure images of big fish taking sedges on the surface. East of Merritt, off Highway 97C (the Okanagan Connector) are two famous lakes, Pennask and Hatheume, plus dozens of others, all of which have rainbow that come eagerly to the fly. On 97C north of Logan Lake are Lac Le Jeune, Tunkwa and Leighton lakes, and Island Lake (also known as Big OK), where a fly fisher has an honest chance at a 10-lb (4.5-kg) Kamloops trout. North of Kamloops, more or less off of Highway 5, are Pass, Paul, Knouff and Heffley lakes.

Another approach to Kamloops country is Highway 5A where it connects from Highway 3 (the Crowsnest Highway) at Princeton. Lakes along this route—Courtney, Corbett, Lundbom and many others—are loaded with rainbow that can reach 5 lb (2.3 kg) or more. Great fishing country, this.

Between Kelowna and Vernon in the Okanagan, Highway 97 touches the shores of Wood and Kalamalka lakes, both with kokanee and lake trout that can be caught on flies, especially in the spring. As well, Okanagan Lake itself has excellent dry-fly fishing for rainbow and lake whitefish early in the year, then again in late fall. Farther south down Highway 97, near Oliver and Osoyoos, lakes and ponds, including Osoyoos Lake and the oxbows of the Okanagan River just above the lake, are full of smallmouth and largemouth bass. The hills along both sides of the highway harbor numerous small lakes stocked with Kamloops trout that never let a fly fisher down.

Combined with such good fishing are great beaches, swimming, boating and biking opportunities, which make the Okanagan a perfect place to consider for family vacations.

The geographic transition between the Thompson–Okanagan and the Cariboo–Chilcotin is subtle, but the lakes and fishing tactics remain similar. There are two approaches: Highway 97 (the Gold Rush Trail) from Cache Creek, and Highway 5 (the Yellowhead Highway) from Kamloops. Both climb to the Bonaparte Plateau, where the terrain flattens out somewhat and is more heavily treed. There is also an approach eastward from Bella Coola via Highway 20 (the Freedom Highway) to Williams Lake, some of it on a well-maintained gravel surface. This trip requires ferry passage from Port Hardy, on Vancouver Island, then a drive up "The Hill"—a 6-mi (10-km) stretch that climbs about 4,950' (1,509 m) through a series of switchbacks and grades of up to 18 percent.

Over 600 lakes in this region provide everything from easily accessible fishing to remote fly-in wilderness locations. Coastal lakes are teeming with cutthroat trout and Dolly Varden, and countless saltwater inlets and estuaries offer summer and fall fishing for chinook, coho, chum, pink and sockeye salmon.

Visitors are pleasantly surprised to discover that this region's top-quality fishing for trophy-sized rainbow trout, char and kokanee is uncrowded. Catch rates are among the highest in the province for rainbow ranging from pan-sized to 20-pounders (9 kg). Consider Sheridan Lake near Lone Bute, where a 16-lb (7.3-kg) rainbow was taken on a dry fly in the summer of 2000, or Dragon Lake near Quesnel, where several rainbow to 16 lb have been reported over the years.

Kokanee in some lakes reach 5 lb (2.3 kg), and this region has the world's healthiest population of bull trout. Lake trout of up to 40 lb (18 kg) have been recorded, as have introduced brook trout to 7 lb (3.2 kg). Large summer-run steelhead return each year to the Chilcotin and Chilko rivers, providing exciting action for anglers. Many fly fishers consider the Blackwater River, northwest of Quesnel, one of the finest available for rainbow trout.

With such an abundance of excellent, uncrowded fishing, it is little wonder that year after year, visitors from around the world return to the Cariboo–Chilcotin to experience some of the finest fly fishing available anywhere.

Chapter 9

Fly Fishing the Thompson–Okanagan & Cariboo–Chilcotin

RALPH SHAW

HISTORY IS INTERESTING STUFF if taken in small doses. When Bryan Williams wrote about Kamloops in 1919 in his book *Rod and Creel in British Columbia,* he mentioned that there were three lakes of note in the area where you could get good fly fishing for rainbow trout: Paul, Pinantan and Fish (Lac Le Jeune). When W.F. Pochin wrote *Angling and Hunting in British Columbia* in 1946, the close-in lakes had been expanded to include Knouff, Leighton, Stake and McConnell.

In the mid-1960s, "Sandy" Sandiford from the Kamloops Chamber of Commerce talked about the great fishing in the area, claiming there were 200 pure culture lakes within a 25-mi (40-km) radius of the city. In the introduction to this book you learned that there are over 30,000 lakes in British Columbia, and that the B.C. *Freshwater Fishing Regulations Synopsis* tells us there are approximately 23,000 lakes of 12 acres (5 ha) in the province. It is a very safe bet that a few thousand of them are located within the Thompson–Okanagan and Cariboo–Chilcotin regions. Along with them are some great rivers that cut across the Cariboo Plateau and intersect the Thompson and Okanagan valleys. This is all rainbow trout country, and because the denizens of these lakes and rivers in the Interior reach near perfection as members of their race, they are known collectively as Kamloops trout.

Along with revealing the fishable lakes in this area, those early writers mentioned tackle. As a result, we know that there has been little change in the reels we use. But believe it or not, double-tapered silk lines were part of the tackle Bryan Williams wrote of in his chapter on tackle. Rods of choice were split cane, and to cast with one all day was a challenge, even for those with strong arms and wrists. Leaders were made of gut that had to be soaked before tying flies onto them, and they were subject to breakdown from sunshine and weather conditions. Trout flies of that period were largely developed from patterns originating in the British Isles and Europe.

Probably the biggest changes since the turn of the century have been in rods, first with the introduction of fiberglass in the late 1940s, then the lightweight graphite rods that now dominate fly fishing. There have also been dramatic changes in fly patterns, resulting in a wide variety of match-the-hatch patterns invented by fly tiers from the late 1950s right up to the new millennium.

One of the most staggering changes from those early days is the incredible increase in the number of lakes with trout fishing. This great explosion of trout waters came about as a result of improved transportation and increased accessibility to various lakes, vigorous stocking programs from provincial hatcheries, and the development of water storage dams for irrigation and electrical energy. Statistics tell us that trout lakes provide a prime example of a resource that has been much enhanced and increased since the days of our early settlement, and when you think of the good old days (at least as far as lake fishing is concerned), we are reminded that we actually have much greater fishing opportunities now than our forefathers ever dreamed of.

The primary species in these waters is the world-famous Kamloops trout, which was named in 1892 by D.S. Jordan, an American scientist who discovered many new species of fish in North America. He called this new variety of rainbow trout *Oncorhynchus kamloops* after specimens he collected in Kamloops Lake. He separated this new trout from *Salmo gairdneri,* which was the sea-going rainbow identified by J. Richardson in 1836. From this simple beginning, the romance of the Kamloops trout has continued to grow in the minds and hearts of all fly fishers who pursue this perfect creation of a trout in the lakes it inhabits.

Over the years, to cast a fly for Kamloops trout in their home waters—the Thompson Basin, the Cariboo Plateau and the Okanagan Basin—has been the Holy Grail for millions of anglers throughout the world. Over the years, brook trout and other varieties of rainbow trout have been introduced into these waters, but the prime species is still the Kamloops trout, which reigns supreme in the minds of anglers who pursue this magnificent fish.

INTERIOR PLATEAU RIVERS

While plateau rivers are not as well known as the lakes, some offer exceptional fishing opportunities, and many are at their best during the hot days of summer, when lakes are in the doldrums. One that surely qualifies for world-class status is the West Road (Blackwater) River west of Quesnel. It is one of the few Class II waters in the plateau region, meaning it is a quality fishery with special regulations concerning access. Basically, this regulation ensures there will be no crowding on the river. For a complete description, refer to the provincial freshwater fishing regulations.

The Blackwater is a small stream that lends itself to using a canoe, but it can be waded quite easily throughout the summer. There are not many access points, which adds a quality of solitude to the experience. When I first fished it in the early 1950s, all I had to do was drop a fly into any pool and I instantly had a taker. There is still superb fishing for rainbow that run up to 3 lb (1.4 kg), occasionally larger. According to Brian Smith, a noted fly tier in Prince George, the following patterns work well: Black Stonefly Nymph, Caddis Pupae, Tom Thumb and Cinnamon Sedge. If you are fishing deep with pupae patterns, expect to have good action on whitefish, as there is a healthy population of these sporty little fish.

The main stem of the Blackwater River doesn't open until June 15 and closes on October 31. The fish are migratory, and early in the fall most move out of the river into feeder lakes. Blackwater rainbow are a popular strain because of their size and strength, and many hatchery trout planted farther south in the Thompson–Okanagan are of this origin.

Another river of note for fly fishing includes the Thompson from below the Savona bridge on the Trans-Canada Highway to Ashcroft. This is a big river with some excellent resident rainbow up to 5 lb (2.3 kg). Fly fishing shops in the area can recommend local patterns, but good dry flies for summer are stonefly and grasshopper imitations, and large Tom Thumbs.

A late-summer run of magnificent steelhead appears in the Thompson system around early to mid-October, and they are noteworthy for rising to dry flies. Popular patterns include the Riffle Dancer, Bulkley Mouse, Purple

Bomber, Cigar Butt, Air BC, Disco Mouse and variations on Atlantic salmon Bombers.

There is also some excellent fishing for rainbow, bull trout and mountain whitefish in the Clearwater River, which runs out of Wells Gray Park into the North Thompson River at the town of Clearwater.

The Cariboo–Chilcotin is blessed with several rivers containing winter- and summer-run steelhead, but most are remote and lightly fished. In the Bella Coola region, we find the Class II Bella Coola River with a good population of resident rainbow, Dolly Varden and cutthroat trout, winter-run steelhead from November to April, an early run of chinook salmon in May to June and coho in September to October. Its major tributary, the Atnarko, is also a Class II river and has similar species and run timings.

The Chilcotin's most famous river is the Dean, which, in effect, is like two rivers. The upper river is road accessible from the Freedom Highway 20, but the lower river is approachable only by water or air to Kimsquit, near the head of Dean Channel. This is a Class I and II river with so many restrictions and special closures that they require a full quarter page in the *Freshwater Fishing Regulations Synopsis.* Despite its remoteness, you won't be lonely on the Dean, for it attracts fly fishers from around the world who arrive eager to test their skills (and luck) against summer-run steelhead to 20-plus lb (9 kg). The best period is July to September. Chinook also are available in July and August, and coho in August and September.

INTERIOR PLATEAU LAKES

When all is said and done, most of the fishing pressure throughout the Interior plateaus is directed at rainbow, brook trout and kokanee dwelling in lakes. Lake fly fishing is spread across spring, summer and fall. Variations in what constitutes the beginning of a season is directly related to lakes' altitudes. Those situated in major valley floors at low elevations of 1,500–2,000' (457–610 m) above sea level open as soon as the ice goes off, regulations permitting, sometimes by early April. Mid-elevation lakes at around 2,000–4,000' (610–1,219 m) are usually ice-free by mid-May and high-elevation lakes—anything above 4,000'—by the first week of June. By way of example, three typical, well-known lakes in the Kamloops region are classified as follows: Jacko, low elevation; Roche, mid-elevation; Lac Le Jeune, high elevation. I must point out here that while I allude to the elevation of lakes affecting the start of a fishing season, there is no hard and fast rule dictating this because in some cases micro-climates within specific lakes may also affect their life systems.

In the fall this process reverses. High lakes freeze over by October, and some lower lakes occasionally remain ice-free until the end of November. The effect of these variations produces a wide spectrum of fishing opportunities from April through November. By starting your season in the southern parts of the Cariboo–Chilcotin and then working north, it is possible have continuous fly fishing for upward of 240 days in any given year. Throughout this period you will be able to follow the cycles of various insects, offering inspiring challenges for fly tiers who seek to match the hatch and develop new patterns.

Connected to the elevation of lakes and the chemical makeup of their waters is a condition in trout referred to as a "muddy" flavor. As the water warms in shallow lakes during the summer, trout take on a downright unpleasant smell and taste. It doesn't happen in all lakes, nor is it restricted only to those at low altitude, but it is quite rare in high-elevation lakes. During the period when this condition is prevalent, you should practice catch-and-release, unless you wish to keep a trophy-sized fish for mounting. By late fall most lakes are free of the condition, and it will clear up entirely over the winter.

Possibly more than any other activity we do, fly fishing stands out as one that puts us in continual contact with ecosystems and what makes them work. To be a successful fly fisher, you must learn about life cycles, whether it is the simple life cycle of an insect or the infinitely more complex ecological life cycle of an entire, living lake system. As we cast our flies and catch fish in a lake, we become part of that cycle. It is legitimate to take some fish home to eat; it is also legitimate to release some for another day. It is not legitimate to regard fishing as an endless source of protein or to regard catch-and-release fishing as an endless activity whereby we can catch as many as time and conditions permit. These are ethical considerations that have little to do with successfully fly fishing the plateau lakes—or anywhere else for that matter—but I thought I would toss them in, anyway.

One of the frustrations about working for a living is that you must forego this exciting madness until weekends or holidays. During the nearly 30 years that I shared lakes and fishing time with the legendary Jack Shaw (no relation), he used to drive me nuts at times. For example, we might be talking in the evening after I had finished work, and he would say, "I took a drive up to Six Mile Lake this afternoon, and the west end is clear of ice. I guess I'll give it a try tomorrow."

Sure enough, the next day he would drop by with a nice trout and tell me that small green shrimp patterns produced well just off the old Trans-Canada Highway. The problem was that Jack was 10 years my senior, so he got to go fishing from Monday to Friday a few years ahead of me. This situation persisted for years, and in the process I always got to know where the fishing was hot and what patterns to use. The major benefit, of course, was that when the weekend came around I knew where to go and what to use.

Jack was a master angler and innovative creator of fly patterns who single-handedly did more for this form of angling than any other person in British Columbia. In my estimation he was the pioneer who led the way for the rest of us. Those of us who follow in his casting shadows are building on the foundation he laid.

Normally, just after the ice goes off a lake there is a window of opportunity for some good fishing before the lake goes into turnover. The water is clear, and trout will move well into on the shallow shoals at depths of 5–15' (1.5–4.6 m). This is wet-line fishing where you can frequently see a fish take your fly. If you are anchored along a favorite shoal and observe trout cruising the shallows fairly rapidly, then pausing to take something before moving on, it is feeding on shrimp or scuds, which are fast-moving little critters. The trick is to lay a suitable shrimp pattern far enough in front of them that it is near the bottom when the trout passes by. The take on this type of fishing is very positive, and unless you are skillful at setting the hook without breaking the leader, you will lose a lot of flies and fish—but have lots of fun in the process.

The trout are firm and silvery during this opening of the season, and their bright red flesh is of superb flavor. This marks the perfect beginning to six months of an insatiable madness that occurs on thousands of still waters, which is what makes this region an angler's Mecca.

Irrigation Lakes

Fishing irrigation lakes in the Okanagan Basin is primarily a springtime activity. The tea-colored water in many small impoundments isn't too warm and the fish are still in good condition but tend to be of a darker hue than we typically associate with Kamloops trout. It is important to get well out onto the lake's main body to avoid catching a lot of spawners that are attracted by the moving water near the shore or off the dam itself. If an irrigation lake has a major draw-down during the summer, the trout are put under a lot of stress and are somewhat slimmer than fish found in stable bodies of water. On the positive side, trout in irrigation impoundments are less species-selective about what they feed on, so you are pretty well assured of good action without having to match the hatch precisely. In the past, we used traditional fly patterns like the Carey Special, Doc Spratley, Royal Coachman, Deer Hair Shrimp and others. However, fishing these waters today, I use match-the-hatch patterns that have become so much a part of our fly fishing techniques.

In the early 1950s, Glenn Ashcroft and I built log rafts on each of six irrigation lakes we hiked into over six consecutive weekends. We used a Swede saw to cut the logs and carried wire and nails to keep things together while we fished. It was a sort of Huckleberry Finn approach that two grown men thoroughly enjoyed, while our wives thought we were nuts. We did it early in the spring to avoid the radical draw-downs to which these lakes are subjected during irrigation. One thing I remember about these trips was that we never met any other anglers. I suspect that even today you can find the same kind of solitude on any small, secluded lake that requires some effort to reach.

Traditional Punts versus Float Tubes

Today, fishing these same impoundments, we would hike in with float tubes and save a great deal of work. Fishing from float tubes is something I have done only in moderation. There are several reasons for this, but among the most important are mobility on the water, remaining warm while fishing and the problem with frequently getting rid of morning coffee or a lunchtime beer. These have convinced me that my 8' (2.4 m) Springbok aluminum punt is the most comfortable for my style of fishing. To get rid of excess liquids, I use a small can discreetly from my seat without standing up. (I realize that the ladies who practice our form of madness have a different problem, and short of suggesting going ashore whenever necessary, I don't have a solution.)

To further my case for small punts, consider the following: I can carry four rods completely set up for any conditions I may face on the water in a given day. My graphite rods are all nine-footers. There are two 5/6-weights and two 7-weights, one of each weight with a slow-sink line, one 5/6-weight with a floating line and the remaining 7-weight with a sink-tip. I also carry a spare reel with a fast-sink line. The use of floating line is obvious. The sink tip is used for fairly shallow waters and water boatman falls. The slow-sink is used for chironomids, leeches and dragonfly nymphs. The fast-sink is used for fishing leeches in deep water and also for making steep retrieves with chironomids in water over 20' (6 m) deep.

My large wooden fly box has spaces for several hundred flies, plus supplementary items like leaders, small scissors, pliers, a sharpening stone and a testing spoon to see what the fish are feeding on. In recent years I've begun to use small fly boxes to separate my flies by type, while I carry the other items in my fly vest. Also forming part of my gear are a Thermos of hot tea, a lunch box and a small insulated box with ice packs to properly care for any fish I choose to keep. When going on the water, I frequently plan to be there most of the day, so my little punt also has room to store my rain gear in case of a shower. After more than 65 years of knocking around in the outdoors, I completely understand the wisdom of the adage, "Old farmers and fisherman dress for the weather."

Essential elements of my boat's equipment are two anchors that are attached to small locking rollers, one at the stern, the other at the bow. These can be lowered or pulled in from the center seat while remaining seated. Since fishing is a leisurely pursuit, my boat is rowed up and down the lake, and aside from the pleasant exercise, it is quiet, nonpolluting and a fortification for the soul.

My boat is modeled after Jack Shaw's well-known punt, which now rests in the fly-fishing section of the Kamloops Museum. An important innovation I picked up from Jack is the comfort of sitting on a raised seat, which puts your knees at about 90°. It is simply a plywood frame about 3" (7.6 cm) high with a sheet metal lip hanging down front and rear so it slides down over the seat and remains in place. The top of the frame is drilled with a series of holes, through which is laced a crisscrossing web of nylon parachute cord or similar small diameter rope. On top of this are stacked two flotation cushions, which raises me a total of about 6" (15 cm) while seated. This little trick makes it possible to sit in my boat for long periods without suffering from leg cramps or knee pain. Another recent modification was to have 18" (46 cm) cut off the bow. It now nestles in the box of my pick-up, allowing the tailgate to be closed and the canopy locked, providing security for all my gear.

Now, after this long discourse, you know why I think fishing from a punt is superior to fishing from a float tube. How the new pontoon boats stack up against my old-fashioned punt is yet to be determined.

THOMPSON RIVER VALLEY

While driving out of the Okanagan Valley from Vernon on Highway 97, you enter an elevated valley that wends its way through ranching and farming country toward the Thompson River. As you approach the Salmon River bridge, a small paved road bears to the right toward Salmon Arm. If it was near the middle of May, you might be inclined to take a detour down this road and spend a day or two fishing White Lake, located off the Trans-Canada Highway between Salmon Arm and Sorrento. This lake is home to some very big trout, and you can see them take your Dragon Fly Nymph in the clear waters at depths of 10–20' (3–6 m).

If you stay on Route 97, watch for MacDonald's Fly Shop on a sweeping curve of the highway between Falkland and Westwold. Take time out to drop in for a short visit. Staff will have up-to-the-minute information on local flies and might possibly give you some tips about Jimmy, Todd, Pratt or Monte lakes.

After leaving the Okanagan, you enter the first of a series of plateaus, hills and low mountain ranges that are cut by two major river systems: the Thompson and the Fraser. This area has thousands of lakes with good populations of trout, and if you worked your way from the Okanagan through the Thompson region into the Cariboo, you could fish every day for years and never see the same waters twice. While there are certainly other species of fish in these waters—natural and introduced—this is predominately Kamloops trout country. Many of the lakes are fairly large, but the most popular with fly fishers are the smaller ones.

Depending on the winter, fly fishing for real addicts starts around early April in some lower lakes in the Thompson region. Perhaps this is a bit of an exaggeration, though, because what really happens is that those dedicated souls start prowling the edges of lowland lakes, trying to get the ice melted sooner than nature intends. As soon as one end of a lake opens and they can get a boat in the water, they will be fishing. One year, while fishing a good-sized lake with a companion, who also suffered from fly-fishing addiction, I felt the wind shift and saw our open water quickly being covered by drifting ice. We pulled our boat out and watched the ice grind against the shore. However, as I recall, we took several nice trout on shrimp patterns before the ice moved.

THE CARIBOO

In my experience, if you plan to do serious fishing before the Victoria Day weekend in May, you are pushing your luck on all but low-elevation lakes. While doing some research for this book, I traveled through the Cariboo during that holiday weekend, and I met several glassy-eyed fly fishers who were trying desperately to find some quiet little lake out of the wind, snow and rain where there might be some action. The problem with rushing the season in the Interior is that the lakes could be in turnover or the weather could turn so cold that the fish simply take a holiday from feeding.

Anglers who live in these regions have choices that are much more generous than those unfortunate souls that have to build their fishing time around family holidays and special weekends. When you study the fishing regulations, you will notice that many of the popular lakes are open to fishing from May 1 to November 30. In effect, this covers the ice-free period for these lakes in most cases but not all.

If you have a good network with local residents who can tell you when the lakes are out of turnover, you are definitely on the way to success. Failing any such source, a good substitute is to go into any reputable fly-fishing shop. The staff are usually only too happy to supply you with up-to-date information.

Assuming the ice is out, fly fishing any lakes in the Cariboo during early May calls for wet-line techniques. It would be most unusual to find a situation where you could take fish on a dry fly. I use three lines in early May: a sink-tip, a slow sinker and a high density fast-sink. Because I fish from a small punt with rod racks along the gunnels, I have a selection of rods rigged and ready to meet any situation, not unlike a golfer changing clubs for different situations.

Early Season Flies & Tackle

My choice of flies will depend in part on the water clarity and type of bottom over which I am fishing. I usually start with a small green, blue or pink Marl Shrimp pattern on a tapered leader up to 12' (4 m) long. I use at least

6-lb (2.7-kg) test tippets to survive the hard strikes of large fish. Shrimp and scuds are fast-moving little critters, so you must be prepared for hard hits when your line is fairly straight out.

I fish shrimp with moderately short casts if in deep water of 20' (6 m) or more. If on a shoal with depths of 8–12' (2.4–4 m) of clear water, I use long casts but always remain seated. This is primarily for the sake of safety, and while this reduces my casting distance accordingly, my lower silhouette reduces signs of movement and the possibility of casting long shadows on the water.

If fishing fairly deep water, I would choose a Black Leech or Blood Leech. A Bloodworm also is a good pattern for early May, especially if there has been some mild weather. Doc Spratleys in various colors offer another good early fishing alternative.

Leeches are important trout food, and modern materials make it possible to imitate them very accurately. When fishing leech patterns, I use sinking lines and let the water depth be my guide. Get into the habit of using your wristwatch to time the descent of your fly in seconds. This will pay big dividends if you do much wet-fly fishing. Retrieving a leech is an acquired skill that takes a little getting used to. When trout take a leech, they tend to do so gently at first, before really setting up on it. What I think they do is nip a live leech to make it ball up, then gulp it down.

Leeches are a very good prospecting pattern. If the lake is unknown to you, a good way to locate feeding fish is to slowly row, paddle or drift along the shoreline or drop-off and mooch a leech well out behind your boat. A word of caution: Many fine fishing rods are lying around the bottoms of lakes because some trusting angler didn't secure it against a heavy strike and resulting hook-up. While there are many nice fly-rod holders available, I simply lay my rod on the seat and place a folded sweater or similar article of clothing on the handle, which is heavy enough to prevent it from being dragged out. I have been doing this for over 50 years and have never lost a rod, so I see no real reason to change my ways.

Chironomid Season

After the middle of May comes the glory period of chironomid fishing, which starts in the low-elevation lakes and moves through the others depending on their elevation and daytime temperatures. Virtually all of the thousands of lakes in the plateau regions have healthy populations of chironomids, making them a universal food in these trout-rich environments.

Throughout the lakes you will find hundreds of species of small flying insects whose greatest mission in life seems to be supplying hungry fish with a bountiful food source. There is a direct correlation between the appearance of these all-important insects and the weather. For many anglers, me included, fishing early hatches of chironomids represents the peak of the trout season. Depending on how you follow the hatches, you can stretch this highly skilled form of wet-fly fishing over a period of at least two months, and by progressively moving to higher elevation lakes, it can be extended to three months. There are two distinct methods of chironomid fly fishing. One calls for floating lines, long leaders and strike indicators. The other, to which I am addicted, is wet-line fishing with slow-sink, sink-tip or fast-sink lines, depending on the circumstances. I learned my trade under the tutelage and encouragement of Jack Shaw, whom many consider the father of chironomid fishing. About 90 percent of my chironomid fishing is done with slow-sink lines.

Through this early part of the season, when the weather turns warm, chironomids are the number one fly for trout. The last count I heard identified over 1,200 different species of chironomids in British Columbia's waters. They range in size from minute little creatures too small to represent with a fly pattern to large specimens that in rare cases will be the size of a No. 10 hook. It cannot be overstated too often that matching the hatch in chironomid fishing is critical to success. They come in a wide range of colors, so matching a hatch can be a real challenge at times. However, when there is a hatch of brown insects coming up from the bottom, that is what the trout want. To be successful you must use a brown fly to match that hatch. The size of the insects will dictate the size of hook to use, although it is not quite as critical as matching the pattern.

Inside the Fly Box

My lake fly box contains hundreds of patterns, and they are mostly chironomids. Before this gets too complicated, I will point out that there are combinations of colors that will get you into fish most of the time. For example, if you have 100 chironomids in your fly box, you want the following spread in hook sizes: 10 No. 10 Black and Gold Tunkwanamids, 30 No. 12 (six Black and Gold, six Brown

Pheasant, six Turkey with Silver Butt, four Dark Maroon with Gold Wrap, four Two-Tone Green and four Brown with Silver Wrap); 30 No. 14 (six Black and Gold, six Brown Pheasant, four Brown with Wide Tinsel Wrap, four Turkey with Silver Butt and Red Tail, four Light Green with Brass Wrap and Yellow Tail, four Brown Pheasant with Gold Wrap and two Dark Brown with Wide Copper Tinsel Wrap); 20 No. 16 (four Black and Gold Wrap, six Light Green with Brass Wrap and Yellow Tail, four Brown Pheasant, four Light Yellow and two Dark Green); 12 assorted No. 18 hooks in similar natural colors, but, because of their small size, without wrappings on the body. These patterns may be tied on traditional Mustad 9671 hooks or the new chironomid-style hooks.

While this selection will get you started, you should be warned that once you get addicted to this glorious form of wet-fly fishing, you will need plenty of hooks available if you are hitting many big fish. The largest trout I have landed on a chironomid was 9 lb 2 oz (4.2 kg) taken in Plateau Lake. The best I have ever seen landed was 14 lb (6.4 kg) from Pass Lake, northwest of Kamloops. Dragon Lake, near Quesnel, and Stump Lake, south of Kamloops, are two others that regularly give up some huge fish on these tiny patterns. Many lakes in the plateaus produce trout in the 6–8-lb (2.7–3.6-kg) range, prime fish that are similar to coho salmon in their aerial displays. But for my money they are stronger than coho.

Tactics & Techniques

The wet-line chironomid technique is one of the simplest of all forms of trout fishing to master if you follow a few simple rules. I belong to a group of anglers who range in age from their early sixties to early nineties, and they have used this technique with great success. In the spring of 2000, I sat beside Everett Irwin while he landed three nice trout in the 3–4-lb (1.4–1.8-kg) range, and he had just celebrated his 93rd birthday. In August of 2001, Everett crossed the bar to that fishing pond in the sky where the fish always bite. My point is that if these guys can master wet-line techniques, so can you.

Here are some simple rules will help you in learning this addictive type of fly fishing.

1.   Watch for hatching chironomids in waters up to 20' (6 m) deep. A good tip for locating an area where chironomids are emerging is to watch for swallows as they swoop down over the water in their feeding forays. Whenever they concentrate over an area, take it as a good

indication that there is a hatch in progress. When you find a spot where chironomids are emerging, carefully and quietly lower the anchors with your boat lying to the breeze if there is one.

2. Use two anchors, one at the stern and one over the bow.
3. Use a 5- or 6-weight fly rod with appropriate lines.
4. Use a No. 2 slow-sink line.
5. Use tapered leaders about 12' (4 m) long with 4–6-lb (1.8–2.7-kg) test tippets.
6. Match the hatch from your collection.
7. Make reasonably short casts of 40' (12 m) plus or minus.
8. When you make a cast, let the line sink for at least thirty seconds.
9. Time the descent of your fly with your wristwatch.
10. Take as long to retrieve your fly as it took to sink.
11. Hold your rod so it points straight back at the line with the tip 6" (15 cm) off the water.
12. When you see the line make any unusual movement, set up and look out.

Follow these simple rules and I am certain you will soon be taking trout on chironomid flies with a wet line.

The other popular method of chironomid fly fishing is even simpler. It calls for using a floating line, a long leader and a colored strike indicator (fly fishers don't like it if you liken it to bobber used for fishing steelhead).

1. Use leaders of up to 20' (6 m).
2. Fasten a strike indicator where the leader joins the line.
3. Make fairly long casts and let the fly sink straight down.
4. When the strike indicator moves, set up quickly.

As long as you continue matching the hatch, that's all there is to this second method.

Wet-line chironomid fishing takes the same kind of intense concentration that you associate with a chess player deeply involved in a challenging match. The insects have a very slow vertical migration through several feet of still water, so you must watch your line very intently for the slightest movement that tells you a fish has leisurely gulped your fly. It is a general rule that if you feel the strike, you have missed the fish. Learn to tighten the line, then set the hook; otherwise, you will break off a lot of big fish because of their swift, violent reaction when they feel the hook. A word of caution here about when to start a conversation with a chironomid angler: Wait until he has completed his retrieve so you don't break his concentration.

One of the nicest things about chironomid fishing is that it takes place during the warmest periods of the day, which is why it's often referred to as "banker's hours fishing." This exciting fishing will last from a month to six weeks before the fish seem to get tired of eating these little insects and are ready to switch to other food. But don't worry—some of the best is still to come.

Action On and Under the Surface

Following close on the chironomid hatches are the mayflies, sedges, damsels and dragonflies. During the heady days of June and early July, the fly fishing just seems to get better and better. Lakes of the Interior Plateaus are trout factories fed by a rich ecological balance of insect life that emerges on a regular set of schedules, keeping fly fishers in a state of continuous bliss as they move from one lake to another, meeting new hatches along the way.

While most chironomid fishing is done with a wet line, there are times when you can have great dry-fly fishing with these important insects. When you observe trout slurping an emerged insect from the surface, it may be time to switch to a floating line and tie on a No. 16 Tom Thumb. Cast ahead of a moving fish and wait for it to take your fly. This works best when there is a gentle breeze on the water. I have occasionally witnessed small schools of trout cruising together and feeding on concentrations of flies, which were probably adults that had just laid their eggs and were floating on the surface. At these times trout can be very selective, so your presentation should match the floating insects as closely as possible.

Sometimes you may find the breezes blowing insects against a marl bed, lily pads or weeds, and the trout will be working the edge. This can create some dry-fly situations that make for legendary fishing with small Bivisibles or Tom Thumbs.

Close on the wings of chironomids come the mayflies. There is nothing finer than a mayfly hatch over a clear shoal or bed of marl weeds in depths of 3–8' (.9–2.4 m). There you can watch large trout cruise the shallow shoals as they slurp emerging mayflies. This is heady stuff. When a little riffle is on the water, it is easier to cast your fly without frightening shy, line-sensitive trout. Then comes a soul-shaking rise as a trout takes your fly—oh my, but it's great.

When fishing a mayfly hatch on the lakes, you may have a couple of choices about how you approach the scene. For dry-line fishers it's a dream come true as trout aggressively swirl and gulp down a resting fly before it can take flight. It is some of the most exhilarating fishing imaginable because all the action happens right in front of you as you cast to moving fish. Need I remind you that matching the hatch with the appropriate color and size of mayfly becomes important?

A second approach to a mayfly hatch is to match the emerging nymph rather than the adult. This calls for mayfly nymph patterns tied on 3x and 2x hooks of the right shape and color. A mayfly nymph bears some similarity to a chironomid, except it has a forked tail, a longer shell case and is fuzzier. Tie nymphs on No. 14 and 12 hooks for most situations. When a mayfly comes out of the weeds to make its migration toward the surface, it travels quite rapidly in a fishlike motion at an angle of about 45°. When trout feed on them, they must move quickly, as opposed to when they feed on chironomids, where the situation is the opposite. Trout hit the fly aggressively, and if your line is straight off the rod with nothing to cushion the hard strike, you end up breaking off. A little frustrating when you run short of the correct patterns.

In the Kamloops area, Paul Lake still has great mayfly fishing right in front of the provincial park despite all of the activity going on there. It is a place where you can enjoy a family picnic, the children can play along the created beach and anglers can enjoy some great fishing in full view of all of the action. This is possible because most of the productive marl bed is still intact. Marl beds, wherever you find them, are treasure troves of productive insect life forms. You will find dragonfly nymphs, damsel fly nymphs, shrimps and scuds, mayflies, chironomids and leeches all sharing this rich environment. These are the types of place where you can run a variety of patterns through and get action on all of them at times.

Depending on the elevation and where you are in the plateaus, the traveler starts around the middle of June and moves into the summer months. The term *sedge* refers more to their method of moving across the surface than to a particular species. One might wonder how paradise could get any better, but traveler sedge hatches set off a fishing event that must be experienced to be appreciated. The excitement is sizzling and the challenges heart-stopping. The hatches will start around midday and continue right into evening darkness.

I shall always remember my wife, Elaine, on the shallow shoals in Hyas Lake. She was casting a Tom Thumb in the approaching darkness when she exclaimed, "Oh, my God! I've hooked the beaver!" We had seen a beaver off and on during the evening, so it may have been a logical assumption. Except it turned out to be an 8-lb 9-oz (4-kg) Kamloops trout, probably still the largest to come out of Hyas in the last 40 years.

Another sight I fondly remember was the late Bob Allen, an outstanding fly caster, making long, smooth casts over the shoals of Blue Lake with his 9 ½' Ogden split cane rod, which was his pride and joy. His shouts of elation rang out over the water whenever one of those very large trout took his Green Sedge or Black O'Lindsay dry flies.

One of the most exciting components of fishing trout with sedge imitations is the attack methods of the large rainbow feeding on them. Traveler sedges scoot across the surface of a lake at surprising speeds as they try to get airborne. It is reminiscent of some water birds that paddle like hell before they get into the air. What happens when a large trout targets a traveling sedge is that it first comes up, makes an impressive splash and swirl that confuses the sedge and then returns to gulp down the befuddled insect. If you take your fly out of the water at that first attack, you miss the real strike. Believe me, it takes courage to leave your fly alone until the second charge, especially when a 7–8 lb (3–3.6 kg) trout is involved. It is undoubtedly one of the most exciting forms of fly fishing, and you can quickly become addicted to the exhilarating challenges of traveler sedges.

Sedges—particularly big traveler sedges—have a group of dedicated anglers who follow their hatches in much the same way others follow chironomid hatches. When you include both forms in your fishing repertoire, life is that much richer. Just as some flies seem to be designed for the wet-fly fisher, sedges were put here especially to make the hearts of dry-fly purists happy with their lot in life. I have no knowledge of how many species of sedges live in our waters, but they must number in the hundreds. Sedges are also found in streams as well as still waters, so they have much potential to add happiness to your life as an angler.

While the most popular form of sedge fishing is with dry-fly imitations, there is also a very effective wet-fly method for trout that are feeding on these large insects. Very concentrated sedge hatches frequently occur in small areas on shallow weed beds or rocky shoals. It's as if a multitude of eggs have been laid in a particular spot and they all start hatching and coming off at the same time. If you happen on such an event, you might notice that large trout are feeding beneath the surface and not paying much attention to the insects on top. What is happening here is that they are targeting sedge pupae as they come out of the weeds on their way to the surface. For this situation use a sink-tip line and cast a sedge pupae pattern into the melee. Then watch out. One of the best sedge pupae imitations is the Knouff Lake Special. The key to this wet fly is making a two-tone striped body of wool in olive green or light yellow. Jack Shaw made the best sedge pupae I have ever seen, and I swear they would confuse even another sedge. Tie sedge pupae patterns on No. 12–8 hooks with at least 2x shanks.

Some of the most popular sedge dry-fly patterns are the Dexheimer Sedge, Mikulak Sedge, Black O'Lindsay, Nation's Sedge, Green Sedge and Brown Sedge. There are many more, which gives you an indication of this insect's importance in our still waters.

Does it get better? Well, I'm not certain, but there is still much good fly fishing to be had with the dragonfly clan. These large insects are rather unique in that they remain predators throughout their lives. In the nymph stage, they cruise around the bottoms of lakes—in some cases for three or four years—looking for unwary shrimp and other small critters, even small fish. When they emerge as adults, they continue to eat other insects until they get on with the business of procreation.

Where trout are concerned, flying adult dragonflies are of little interest as food. However, their long developmental period as nymphs is of great interest to wet-fly fishers who understand the predatory role these large insects play. One of the most common dragonflies in the plateaus is the gomphus *(Gomphidae)*, the nymphs of which can be over 1" (2.54 cm) long. They crawl around the lake bottom wherever there is a suitable habitat for prey species. To match this, the nymph imitation is fished with a sinking line and retrieved slowly just above the bottom or, at times, right along the bottom. Fishing gomphus nymphs over submerged islands in a clear lake is a heart-stopping activity, especially if there are many big trout cruising the shallows. Strikes will be solid and with immediate action, so use about 6-lb (2.7-kg) test tippets.

One of the best gomphus nymph patterns is made from tightly spun and trimmed-to-shape deer hair with a few pheasant tail fibers angling out from the sides to simulate legs. Being fairly buoyant, they will actually ride slightly off the bottom while being retrieved with your line right on the marl or surface of a weed bed. Although gomphus patterns are usually fished over marl shoals, there are times when you can cast from shore and take trout feeding on emerging nymphs. When these large insects are emerging along the shoreline, move in close to shore, cast out and make your retrieve back up the slope—and be prepared to hit some trophy trout.

Damselflies are smaller members of this group, and for brief periods when you hit the right conditions, you can have some truly great wet- and dry-fly fishing. The nymphal stage is somewhat similar to a large mayfly nymph, only bigger. It is a slender creature about 1" (2.54 cm) long and a somewhat challenging pattern to imitate. You can fish the nymph stage over weed beds throughout late May, June and into July, depending on the lake's elevation.

Damselfly nymphs' colors vary with their bottom environment and lake of origin, so matching the color is important. As they approach maturity and are ready to emerge, they migrate from deeper water to the shoreline, then crawl onto standing patches of tules and bulrushes growing from the lake bottom. At times they emerge in the millions. When you run across this type of hatch, there are two ways to fish it. If you see trout splashing in the weeds in order to knock emerging nymphs off the vegetation, stay back and cast a damselfly imitation into the feeding frenzy, and be prepared for some dramatic action. If fishing before the hatch, anchor in shallow water and cast out along the sloping weed bed, then bring your fly up the slope with a moderately rapid retrieve using short, erratic 6" (15-cm) pulls with occasional stops.

What with all of the fall colors and migrating flights of waterfowl flying overhead, September and October are two of the most glorious months to be fly fishing around the Interior plateaus. If it is a mild fall, you can still hit good hatches of chironomids and sedges, or you can always fall back on leeches and shrimps. There are, however, two insects that can make an autumn fishing trip absolutely frenetic. I refer to that small bug known as the water boatman, and its lookalike cousin, the backswimmer. If the surface of a small lake appears to be pockmarked by raindrops, but there is no rain, you are probably observing water boatmen fooling around on their nuptial flights. Associated with this disturbance, you may notice swirls of feeding trout that don't quite break the surface. This is the time to put on a water boatman imitation and use a sink-tip line if you have one. Cast out, and then let your fly sink so that your line and leader curve down from the fly and up again toward your rod tip (think of the letter C tilted on its back). Then make a rapid retrieve. Be prepared to have some fast, exciting action and lose a few flies from the violent takes. These insects are speed demons in the water, so the strike is hard and downright vicious. In the event that you don't have a water boatman pattern in your collection, you can make a suitable substitute by clipping a ubiquitous Tom Thumb very short and fishing it with a wet line.

FALL FISHING

Fall fishing is best enjoyed during the bright afternoons and early evenings as the ecosystem starts shutting down for the winter. I recall one afternoon in late October on a high-elevation lake. The sun was warm, and in the skies overhead, sandhill cranes traveled south, trumpeting their high, musical calls to the hills below. Later that evening, an amorous cow moose issued her love call to any listening bull that felt up to the challenge. With frost in the air and life systems preparing for seasonal change, it was a glorious time to have a fly rod as a companion on those still waters.

During the fall season, fishing around the edge of water lily patches is a good bet. Use sedge patterns, Tom Thumbs and Badger Hackle Bivisibles on No. 12 or 10 hooks. Another technique that pays dividends is fishing from shallow to deep water with shrimp, leech or dragonfly nymphs. This technique imitates the outward migration of insect life from the shoreline areas as these aquatic creatures prepare for the coming winter.

Trout are very selective about what they eat on occasion, and we know how critical it is to match the hatch. Size, color and image are all important. Some species of creatures are present on the feeding grounds at all times, and as such they are important trout food the year round. Two main sources of trout fare throughout the fall season are leeches and shrimps or scuds. There are times when, if nothing else works, imitations of these creatures can make the difference between a good day of fishing and a day spent watching clouds, birds or, worse yet, other anglers catching trout. As suggested previously, these are dependable early season patterns, but as trout feed on them throughout the year, you should carry a few representational patterns in your fly box to use when things are slow.

PREPARING FOR THE UNFORESEEN

Success in fly fishing is not very mysterious when you understand something about the various food sources available to trout. Consider this simple fact: Virtually all insects that make up the diet of Kamloops trout spend 99 percent of their lives swimming around the lake as nymphs or pupae before emerging as adults. In most cases the adult version is available for only seconds as a floating insect. This tells me that when you go on the lake to fly fish, you should take at least two outfits—one rigged with a sinking line and one with a floating. If you want to make contact with many fish, plan on using the sinking line most of the time; however, be ready with the floating line to take advantage of those spellbinding periods of excitement when surface hatches occur. This type of preparation is called preparing for the unforeseen.

When I go on a lake with my collection of four rods and several hundred flies, I'm prepared to cover virtually any situation in which I find myself. In fact, it is unusual to not catch fish. I got into this habit from my association with Jack Shaw, and I recall one day when we were sitting on a lake doing more casting than catching. Jack looked at me and said, "Ralph, when we aren't catching anything we are learning something." This is true, because once you find the correct fly, the learning is usually limited to errors in judgement while attempting to land the fish.

I have frequently referred to matching the hatch as the most common way we fly fish today. This perfection in copying insects is a relatively new approach, at least in the plateau waters. The legendary flies of Bill Nation were, by and large, duplications of British and European attractor patterns that usually bore little likeness to real insects, which raises the question of why they were successful so much of the time. The answer, I suggest, was that these imitations had the color, size and shape that, along with presentation, made them close enough to the real things to satisfy the trout. We still have many flies that fall into this category as part of our collections, and at times they are successful when all else fails. A few patterns that fall into this group are the Royal Coachman, the many variations of Carey Specials and Doc Spratleys, Badger Hackle, Woolly Worm, Zulu, Silver Doctor, Professor, March Brown, plus many others. If you have some of these patterns in your box and are not into buying a lot of new flies, there are things you can do with a pair of small scissors that can make credible match-the-hatch illusions. For example, clipping the long hackles on a Woolly Worm makes a credible caddis larva and clipping the long wing on a Doc Spratley comes close to a dragonfly nymph. A clipped Tom Thumb or Humpy—both dry flies—can pass for a shrimp that is fished wet. It pays to be innovative when the fish won't bite, and never be afraid to experiment—for you may learn something new.

Many large plateau lakes contain natural populations of kokanee, which are nonanadromous sockeye salmon. In addition, many smaller lakes have been stocked with these very popular game fish. There are some excellent kokanee lakes in the Cariboo region, and Stump Lake, located beside Highway 5A between Merritt and Kamloops, yields kokanee to 5 lb (2.3 kg). While it may seem sacrilegious, many anglers claim they actually fight harder than rainbow. And, being a sockeye salmon, their bright red flesh is of the highest quality for eating. An interesting thing about kokanee is that in large lakes they tend to be schooling fish that are primarily pelagic and zooplankton feeders, but when introduced into small lakes, they become somewhat more troutlike and readily adapt to feeding on chironomids and other aquatic invertebrates. As a result, whenever you cast your fly into water containing rainbow and kokanee, you can never be sure about which will bite. Kokanee have a softer mouth than trout, so they can come unstuck in a hurry if you try to horse them.

Another popular species with fly fishers is brook trout, which have been stocked in several lakes throughout the Thompson–Okanagan and Cariboo–Chilcotin regions. Brookies reach weights occasionally exceeding 6 lb (2.7 kg), and their bright red flesh makes for excellent eating. They are actively sought during the winter months by ice fishermen, and a somewhat unique way of catching them is to dangle a brightly colored fly through a hole in the ice. This isn't fly fishing per se, but it certainly is fishing with a fly. This is not to detract from the fact that brookies are popular among open-water fly fishers, where the same patterns and tactics used for rainbow work well to take these strong, colorful fish.

A FEW WORDS ON BASS

Other species that take flies on a regular basis are mountain and lake whitefish, squawfish (now a politically incorrect name), smallmouth and largemouth bass, and yellow perch. Both species of bass readily take flies on the surface and offer good fishing prospects when many low-elevation lakes are in the summer doldrums. They go for fairly large, bushy patterns incorporating deer hair or closed-cell foam to keep them floating high in the water. Included are any of the Atlantic salmon Bombers, Madam X, Tom Thumb and Stimulator, plus small bugs and mouse imitations fashioned from tightly packed and clipped deer hair. The best-known bass lakes are Osoyoos, Vaseux and Skaha.

AFTERTHOUGHTS

The still waters of the Thompson, Okanagan, Cariboo and Chilcotin regions have important transportation routes transecting them from all directions. Highway 97 leaves the Okanagan and runs west along with Highway 1 to Cache Creek, then north to Williams Lake and beyond. This is the main route running north and south through the western portion of the plateaus. Highway 5, running north from Kamloops, is the major eastern route.

As you travel along these two main highways and all the little roads branching from them, you will pass through towns and cities and find routes leading to hidden fishing resorts and camps. And almost everywhere you travel you will discover specialty fly-fishing shops dedicated to your service, places like FLYS-R-US on Route 97 at Lac la Hache, The Legend in Williams Lake or the Little Fort Fly Shop over on Route 5 in Little Fort. These are only a few of the many facilities dedicated to the well-being of fly fishers throughout the Interior plateaus and just part of what makes them a fly-fisher's paradise.

Imagine, if you will, the flaps on a cardboard box as they fold outward. Think of these flaps as part of the extended plateaus on either side of the highways. In this large lake and river wonderland that is densely carpeted with forests, grasslands and parks, you have an area approaching many small countries in size. Now, pick a clear night and lie on your back, and look up at the stars overhead in the sky. The stars you see are like the lakes scattered throughout this rainbow trout Valhalla. You can try counting them, but before long you will probably be overwhelmed. You might just as well give up and go to bed for a good night's sleep, so in the morning you can awaken refreshed and look forward to some of the finest trout fishing in the world.

Ralph Shaw has his hands full with a high-jumping Kamloops trout.

Ralph and Elaine Shaw pose with her 8-lb 9-oz (4-kg) Kamloops trout taken on a Tom Thumb dry fly at Hyas Lake.

Kamloops trout are noted for their high-jumping antics.

Ralph Shaw with a fine Kamloops trout, the result of an oh-so-slowly-retrieved chironomid on Heffley Lake.

Everything in this well-loaded punt belonging to the late Jack Shaw had a specific use.

Fly-fishing guru Brian Chan tussles with a frisky Kamloops trout on Heffley Lake.

The late Jack Shaw is considered the father of chironomid fishing, which he is shown here practicing on Heffley Lake.

Chapter 10

Welcome to the Lower Mainland

JIM CRAWFORD

THE TRANS-CANADA runs for about 100 mi (161 km) through the middle of the Lower Mainland from the ferry terminal at Horseshoe Bay to Hope. Along the north shore of Burrard Inlet, across from Vancouver, it crosses the Capilano River with its runs of coho, chinook and a few steelhead. After Ironworkers Memorial Bridge, the highway passes numerous small lakes and ponds that are stocked with rainbow trout and warm-water species like perch and crappie—some right in the middle of cities like Surrey and Abbotsford. Farther out in the Fraser Valley is Cultus Lake, which has a population of large bull trout, and the Chilliwack–Vedder River with the best runs of winter steelhead and coho in the Lower Mainland. Near Hope, the Skagit and Coquihalla rivers support resident rainbow trout and summer-run steelhead. The Skagit also offers bull trout and Dolly Varden.

The best fishing is found on the north side of the Fraser River along Highway 7. From downtown Vancouver to Hope, Highway 7 crosses scores of streams and skirts many small lakes, providing access to big lakes like Pitt, Stave and Harrison, plus their rivers, which lead to the Fraser itself. Most species of game fish in British Columbia can be found along here—even a few lake trout left over from a test introduction into Alouette Lake many years ago.

North of Horseshoe Bay, Highway 99 winds toward world-famous Whistler ski resort and the high mountains of Garibaldi Park. Along the way, the Squamish and Cheakamus rivers still support fair runs of coho, chum, pink and chinook salmon. Here there are lakes, too, some with native coastal cutthroat and stocked rainbow. Farther north at Pemberton, the Lillooet River has a good trout population, and a few salmon and steelhead get up there as well. Beyond Mount Currie on the way to the historical gold rush town of Lillooet, Highway 99 runs past Duffey Lake and along Cayoosh Creek. Both offer good fly fishing for rainbow trout, but this highway might better be called a "trailway" as it tapers to a very narrow, winding, albeit paved, road. Not dangerous, but large campers and motor homes are not recommended for those inexperienced at handling them.

Chapter 11

Fly Fishing the Lower Mainland

GEORGE WILL

IMAGINE YOURSELF in a large cosmopolitan city with all of the amenities one could possibly dream of: beautiful scenery, first-class restaurants, trendy stores. Now, imagine that within this city's boundaries are many waters, both still and flowing, containing several species of fish that look favorably upon cast flies. We are not talking about silly little sunfish and bluegills here, but five species of Pacific salmon, steelhead, rainbow and cutthroat trout. During the warmer months, you can charter a boat right at your hotel and head out a few miles to cast flies at milling coho and feisty pink salmon. Just a short drive across a narrow neck of ocean are two rivers that once were the stuff of legend but are now merely good producers of salmon and trout. Just to the east, again within the city limits, are two small lakes that produce surprisingly large trout early in the season. There are even a couple of small mountain tarns with native cutthroat that come readily to a fly on hot summer evenings. You could conceivably spend a few hours on the water, then be back at your hotel in time for that business meeting or dinner engagement.

If that's not enough, there are hundreds of other great fishing destinations within a two-hour drive. To the north, along a famous stretch of pavement known whimsically as the Sea to Sky Highway, are numerous small lakes, all containing trout. This is in a place where most visitors go to enjoy wintry downhill pursuits, but in the springtime those heavy snowpacks start melting into lakes and streams, which, in the summertime, are a virtual heaven to fly fishers.

To the east of this fabled city are dozens of lakes and streams. All contain fish—some very large—and a few are spoken of in hushed tones. One of this continent's greatest rivers empties into a saltwater estuary on the edge of this city. Each year, millions of salmon swim up this river: huge chinook, voracious coho, silvery sockeye and surprisingly strong chum. All take a fly, and, best of all, fairly recent regulation changes have made them fair game to recreational anglers. Another salmonid swims among them: the much-treasured steelhead. Many tributaries of the main river have small annual runs of steelhead, some of which may seize the fly of a knowledgeable angler during the winter months, others in late summer.

There are also native rainbow and some amazing coastal cutthroat trout in a few of the tributaries. Some lowland lakes are fishable in the early spring, a few in the mountains produce during the heat of summer and some of the large lakes have flats and tributaries that are rarely fished. Last but not least, there is a stream less than a two-hour drive east that may some day be as well-known as the Ausable, Madison or Bow.

Is this city a figment of wishful imagination? No. Vancouver is real—a truly beautiful, exciting, interesting, cosmopolitan city—and the waters alluded to do exist. All of them. In the following pages, you will learn the when, where and how of fishing them. So if you are visiting the Lower Mainland, even for only a day or two, bring a fly outfit. There are some nifty four- and five-piece rods, which, when combined with a reel, a box of flies and lightweight waders, will hardly fill up a pocket in your carry-on luggage.

Fly-fishing season on the Lower Mainland is year-round. By the time winter steelheading ends, lakes in the lower Fraser Valley are usually fishable. I have often fished Mill, Whonnock and all of the Greater Vancouver lakes by late February or early March, and by April the chironomid fishing is in full swing.

Virtually every body of water I will cover can be regarded as a day-trip from Vancouver. There is not a lake or river that can't be reached in less than three hours, and most are within an hour. I often fish the Skagit River and return on the same day so, obviously, the Whistler, Vancouver and Fraser Valley lakes can all be viewed as single-day efforts. The other advantage of having so much opportunity nearby is that you can move around so easily while prospecting for fish.

A few comments regarding fishing regulations: Look for information about your chosen destination and pay particular attention to requirements such as the need to use single barbless hooks or follow catch-and-release practices. Even the tiniest fly should have the barbs flattened when fishing any stream. I know of two anglers who were zapped on the Skagit for using hooks with barbs. Both were using No. 16 Adams—hardly meat hooks but still illegal.

Three places of interest to anglers should not be missed. The first is the Granville Island Fishing Museum, which has a great collection of Hardy fishing reels and lots of memorabilia related to the history of sport fishing in the region. Another is Ruddick's Fly Shop, located near the Fishing Museum on Granville Island. It is a great place to stock up on flies and other tackle, and to ask about local angling opportunities. The Capilano Salmon Hatchery on the North Shore is worth a visit in the late summer and early fall, but not on weekends when there are dozens of tourist buses in the lot.

SQUAMISH AREA LAKES

You can find supplies and accommodation at the town of Squamish, about 30 mi (50 km) north of Vancouver. The lakes in this area are located a short distance north of town. Alice Lake is 8 mi (13 km) away in Alice Lake Provincial Park. This 30 acre (12 ha) lake is very accessible and provides a fairly typical rainbow fishing experience. The park contains 95 vehicle campsites with picnicking and day-use areas, a boat launch and hiking trails leading off in every direction. This park is extremely popular, so finding a site on most summer weekends is iffy at best. Three nearby hike-in lakes—Edith, Fawn and Stump—provide much better fishing. It only takes a couple of minutes to carry in a float tube, and there is usually a chironomid show with black the favored color. Stump is the best bet in my opinion.

A little to the north, Brohm is right beside the highway and loaded with fish. If you are into serious hike-in fishing or have the money to pop for a fly-in, Lake Lovely Water is worth the effort. This beautiful, high-altitude lake is appropriately named and contains some sizable trout.

WHISTLER & PEMBERTON AREA LAKES

This area has a number of lakes, some, like Alta, right in the Whistler town site, others, like Garibaldi, high in the mountains. Of the many lakes within this region, these two are typical. Alta is stocked with rainbow, kokanee and Dolly Varden. It fishes well from ice off, right through the summer months.

The village provides lots of accommodation, but be warned that it is on the pricey side. Accommodation at Pemberton, about 20 mi (32 km) north, is a lot more reasonable and two nearby lakes provide excellent fishing. In addition to Alta, there are several alternatives close by. Alpha Lake is about 1 ¼ mi (2 km) south, and Nita is located between Alta and Alpha. Both have loads of small rainbow. Green Lake is beside the highway about 3 mi (5 km) north of Whistler. It holds decent rainbow, and some very large Dolly Varden have been reported.

The best bet for trophy-sized fish is Ivey (Horseshoe) Lake. It is managed as a quality (catch-and-release) water and has been known to give up rainbow in the 10-plus-lb (4.5-kg) range. Located about 4 mi (6.5 km) northeast of Pemberton and 2 mi (3 km) north of Mount Currie, it gets a fair amount of pressure, especially from Vancouver area fly flingers. Launching boats or tubes is tough, and the lake is somewhat lacking in ambience (read ugly), but in this case size does matter. Leech patterns and Woolly Buggers seem to produce well, and I suspect Nick's Bead Head Leech would also do the trick. This is an early season producer with a narrow window of opportunity, so ask for updates at local fly-fishing shops.

Garibaldi Lake is a relatively large lake by mountain tarn standards—2,456 acres (994 ha)—and considered the crown jewel of Garibaldi Provincial Park. It is also incredibly deep at 2,760' (841 m). The lake is located just off the scenic Sea to Sky Highway about midway between Squamish and Whistler, and the route is well marked, so simply follow the directional signs. The hike to the lake is a scenic and not especially challenging 3.75 mi (6 km), and there are glimpses through the forest of massive peaks, sprawling meadows and shimmering ice fields. The hike alone is worth the visit, but the fishing for rainbow during the heat of summer can be amazing—and with little competition from other anglers. There is a great campsite at the lake, and you will find full services and accommodations in Squamish or Whistler Village. Fishing does not usually start until early July, but it remains good right through until fall. Chironomids will always produce, and there are great hatches of small mayflies and caddis in the evenings, for which a small Adams will suffice. As these fish have not seen a great many artificials, they are not jaded, so virtually anything you throw at them produces strikes. I remember one great mid-July camping trip with fresh-caught trout as the meat course in our menu. I also remember that it snowed that night, so be prepared for anything.

VANCOUVER AREA RIVERS
Capilano River

A few miles up Capilano Road from Marine Drive in North Vancouver, the Capilano River provides a surprising urban fishery. A federal fish hatchery just below the dam produces tremendous numbers of fish, especially coho salmon. These "wind-ups" were intended to supplement the commercial fishery, but quite a few return to the river each year in late summer and autumn. Depending on water levels, these fish either mill around at the mouth or they move upstream rapidly. Upstream from the highway bridge, there are limited opportunities for fly casters, largely due to steep canyon walls and lack of access. For an angler willing to do a little hiking and rock scrambling, there are a couple of runs near the pipeline bridge, where a cast fly will produce; however, watch out for the kayakers and other crazies drifting downstream. They are easy to hook but real buggers to land in that fast water.

My favorite spot on the Capilano is the estuary. I have had reasonable success there from an anchored boat, though I have endured the taunts and comments of some from the local aboriginal band, which annually occupies the spit right at the mouth, and shags salmon for sustenance and ceremonial purposes. I usually fish during the time around high slack and try to intercept moving fish. Most often I use a brightly colored streamer pattern like a Mickey Finn, but lately I've been trying Clouser Minnows and epoxy flies with some success. Color seems to be the key with red, orange and yellow over silver bodies working best. The trick is to try triggering an aggressive strike, so getting your fly close to the fish is imperative. A large flotilla of boats ranging from 10-footers (3 m) to large cruisers vie for position in the outer part of the estuary. They begin gathering in July and remain until the fish move upstream to the hatchery. It is often difficult to find a spot, what with anglers heaving Buzz Bombs from shore and dozens of boats either trolling or anchored up. The surroundings are almost surreal at times, especially when I glance up and to the east and see seemingly endless streams of vehicles whizzing over the Lions Gate Bridge.

The Capilano also supports a small run of steelhead, and if and when the season for them opens, strict catch-and-release rules apply. As a general rule, if you intend to fish above tidal waters, consult the fishing regulations and watch for closure signs along the river.

Seymour & Coquitlam Rivers

The Seymour empties into the saltchuck just east of the Iron Workers Memorial Bridge. It is slightly longer and a lot wilder than the Capilano, which it resembles. The lower section is difficult to access because of private property, but there is a great section of fly-only water in the upper river and reasonably good access at the mouth. There is a hatchery operated by the Salmonid Enhancement Program just below the dam and a very scenic spawning channel a half mile (805 m) or so from the upper parking lot. The upper section is very scenic and has some great hiking trails. The Seymour is very fishy-looking, and with successful enhancement and some creative habitat reconstruction, it could once again be a memorable angling river. The run of winter steelhead is slightly larger than the Capilano's, and there is some wonderful water in the fly-only section. I prefer fishing small runs between the boulders, so I often look for fish while hiking the trail, then drop a fly on them. This technique works even better for the coho, which tend to lie directly behind boulders. At the time this is written, pressure on the upper Seymour is still relatively light, possibly, I suppose, because the hike discourages a lot of the physically declined.

The mouth of the Seymour is the scene of some amazing action every odd-numbered year when the pink salmon arrive. They mill around the estuary in the thousands, waiting for a rise in water level to allow them to continue their upstream migration. The schools of jumping fish bring out hundreds of "anglers," most of whom use thinly disguised snagging techniques to catch fish. Space for fly casting is limited unless you have a boat or floatation device of some kind. I must admit that at times it's kind of fun to watch fish hogs beating the crap out of each other or getting dragged away by the police for various infractions. Again, high tide seems to be the best time, and your fly simply has to be pink or chartreuse.

The Coquitlam River upstream above the gravel operation has some pretty good coho fishing, but frequent problems with settling ponds have kept the fate of salmonids in this river in limbo. It might be worth a look, but there are better bets.

VANCOUVER AREA LAKES

A lot of folks have a low opinion of the lakes located within the city limits, regarding them as either lifeless bogs or duck ponds. On the contrary, all are full of fish and can produce some tension-releasing, early season action. I am not suggesting that local fishing is in any way comparable to that found on the Douglas Lake Ranch, but I have caught some huge trout in Deer Lake early in the spring. For the short-term visitor, it is possible to get in a couple of hours of fishing within a cab ride of downtown. Of course, as the temperature heats up, the action (for trout) declines. Other good bets include Rice Lake up in the Seymour Demonstration Forest, Latimer Pit out in Surrey, which takes a tremendous pounding but still produces good chironomid action, and Buntzen Lake just north of Port Moody. Buntzen Lake is located 2 ½ mi (4 km) north of Ioco on a paved road that gives way to good gravel. It is fairly large at 375 acres (152 ha) and has both shallow and deep areas. Cutthroat have been stocked since 1986, and BC Hydro has since introduced a permanent floating spawning facility. The cutthroat are usually around 2 lb (.9 kg), but larger fish have been reported, while rainbow tend to peak in the 1–2-lb (.5–.9-kg) range. There are some nice shoal areas in the bay on the southwest corner and at the extreme north end, and fishable points are scattered up and down the lakeshore. I have not fished Buntzen much of late, and when I did I caught mostly squawfish. But it's a pretty place and the stocking program has been a success. Sasamat Lake is just south of Buntzen, and while it does contain rainbow and cutts, the main attractions these days are the park and beach.

SEA-RUN CUTTHROAT TROUT

Once common along the beaches of Burrard Inlet and Indian Arm, sea-runs are now a little more difficult to find. They still do frequent the mouths of small feeder streams, and once in a while you can find them slashing baitfish along the beaches. There is one area in Port Moody, namely Old Orchard Park, where you can still find reasonable numbers of fish during the fall months, especially October. The steep beaches and complex tidal channeling at the east end of Burrard Inlet provide almost ideal habitat for sea-runs. Most of my success has come on an incoming tide and high slack, and I almost always use a Murray's Rolled Muddler. This is a very fragile fishery, and I suspect one chemical or oil spill will end it. WARNING: Stay off the tide flats! They may look wadable at low tide, but when the tide starts to come in, they liquefy and turn into quicksand.

FRASER VALLEY LOWLAND LAKES

Mill Lake in Abbotsford is typical of the dozen or so shallow, low-elevation lakes in the Fraser Valley. It's hidden in a little municipal park behind the Seven Oaks shopping mall, just off the Fraser Highway. The lake is surrounded on three sides by housing, but there is a parking lot and boat launching ramp (motors prohibited).

The Mill is very weedy along the edges, which makes casting from shore difficult. Wind is seldom a problem, so this is a good candidate for tubing. Less than 900' (274 m) across and about 1,950' (594 m) long with the long axis southwest–northeast, Mill Lake is about 50 acres (20 ha) in area. It is shallow, and the bottom is fairly dark with tea-colored water. It produces good insect hatches, especially chironomids. Rainbow trout predominate, but there are also black crappie, which readily take flies.

There are a few trout in Mill Lake that can make even the most ardent Interior lake devotee salivate. Each spring finds some brood fish from the Inch Creek Hatchery included in the tens of thousands of 10-inchers (25 cm) used to restock the lake. Local anglers have photos of trout in the 8-plus-lb (3.6-kg) range, which, alas, most often fell to worm drowners, but I know of several whales that were hooked on flies.

Successful angling on Mill Lake requires a boat or float tube. Fish close to the weed beds, and know how to fish chironomids just under the surface. Grease your very long 12–20' (4–6 m) leader right up to the fly so it hangs just under the surface film. Closely watch the movement of the schools of trout. Fish of the same size tend to hang together. If you spot a large fish, it is likely more of similar size will be in the school. Cast a chironomid in front of them and wait. A strike indicator is useful when hunting trout (here or anywhere else for that matter).

The trout in Mill Lake are very active in the early spring. By early summer, weeds and warm water make the fishing lousy, but it picks up again in late fall. Insect hatches are irregular, and when the trout feed, it's usually voraciously and in quick bursts. You must observe these feeding patterns closely and be ready to change flies in an instant. Carry a range of chironomid patterns in No. 14–10, ranging from orange through shades of brown to black.

Whonnock Lake is north of Whonnock on Highway 7. In addition to rainbow and cutthroat trout, there are some huge black crappie that can be enticed out of the vegetation along the edge with a yellow and white Crappie Basher bucktail. One late spring day a few years back, my daughter and I caught over 70 in a couple of hours. I don't care where you are from—that's action! My late father caught a dinner-plate–sized crappie that weighed around 4 lb (1.8 kg). Oh yeah, I almost forgot—crappie are delicious to eat.

Other nearby favorites include Alouette Lake and, just south, Mill Lake. Alouette is a little too large for my liking and is often drawn down, but I have heard that the cutthroat fishing for fairly large fish can be excellent at times. I have had some excellent dry-fly action on Mill Lake when the ants are on the move. It meets the definition of a perfect tubing lake. Rolley Lake, about 11 mi (18 km) north of Mission, is heavily stocked. Lots of early season action there, but the fish tend to be on the small side.

There are several other lakes north of Mission, but one deserves special notice. Sayers (Cedar) Lake is in a restricted area that is open only from 6:00 A.M. to 6:00 P.M. except weekends and holidays. To get there you must sign in at the Stave Falls Prison Camp, during which procedure your vehicle might be searched. Why put up with this hassle? This small lake offers cutthroat, Dolly Varden, a few brook trout and rainbow. And not just any rainbow but dropouts from the Fraser Valley Trout Hatchery net pens located in the lake. They are obviously well fed, for trout to 17 lb (7.7 kg) have been reported.

Harrison Lake is huge at almost 54,000 acres (21,853 ha). Weather-wise, it is very unpredictable, and the wind can make boating extremely hazardous. There are zillions of fish in this lake, and a variety of species, but they can all be very hard to find. In fact, this is a classic case where hiring one of the local guides might be the best way to home in on those fish. There are numerous feeder streams up and down the lake, and trout tend to congregate at their mouths.

Being a popular recreation area, Harrison Hot Springs has an abundance of accommodations and restaurants. More important from our point of view is the fact that there are at least a dozen small lakes that are home to cutthroat and rainbow trout. Deer Lake is located in Sasquatch Provincial Park about 7 ½ mi (12 km) northeast of Harrison Hot Springs. It can be reached by car on a decent gravel road. Other lakes within the same park include Trout and Hicks, both of which produce loads of medium-sized trout and the odd monster. Dark chironomids are the usual fare, but when the carpenter ants are flying, the dry-fly action can be awesome. West of Harrison Hot Springs and north of Harrison Mills off Highway 7, the Morris Valley road leads to a half dozen small lakes. Weaver is arguably the most popular and productive. Good camping and easy boat launching make this lake a magnet for locals, especially on weekends. If you have a 4x4 vehicle, you can reach several other very fishable lakes like Francis, Grace and Wolf. As with most lakes in the region, small, dark-colored flies are your best bet. Consult the fishing regulations as almost all of these lakes have special restrictions.

After a tough day of fishing, you can soak your troubles away at Harrison Hot Springs. Several spas are open to the public, and there is a huge complex at the Harrison Hot Springs Resort. This town is well worth a visit simply because of the good eateries and funky shops.

FRASER VALLEY MOUNTAIN LAKES

There are a number of small, higher elevation lakes located in the eastern portion of the Fraser Valley. Lindeman Lake, one of the most accessible, is fairly typical. Like most alpine lakes in the region, the fishing kicks in by June and continues through until freeze up. To get there, turn right off the Trans-Canada at Sardis, proceed south to Vedder Crossing, then turn left along the Chilliwack Lake road. After about 23 mi (37 km), keep your eyes peeled for a small road leading off to the left to Post Creek Campground. Sometimes there is a sign, sometimes not. Parking is often at a premium, especially on hot summer weekends. Follow the trail north past the bathrooms. It's a steep trek in places, but because it's only about 1 mi (1.6 km), you should make it in about half an hour if you are in reasonable shape. If you don't haul in your float tube or some other craft, the best fishing tends to be at the north end, where avalanches have cleared out the vegetation.

The first time I visited Lindeman Lake was on a hot July day in the mid-1970s. While making my way along the rocks, I could see a few fathoms down into the depths and immediately noticed the cruising shapes of numerous trout. I set up my gear, beginning with a Black Bivisible dry fly, and you would think those poor starving trout had never seen food before! I switched to a small, dark caddis imitation, and they swarmed it, too, several trying to grab it at the same time. To cut a short story even shorter, I had a field day.

On other occasions, a green caddis nymph retrieved slowly worked well. Carry and use some general searching patterns like Doc Spratleys and Carey

Specials. Tips: Pack out your garbage, watch your back-cast and take a camera.

About 2 mi (3 km) farther along , and maybe 600' (183 m) higher in elevation, the trail takes you to Greendrop Lake, which offers more of the same rainbow fishing. Even farther along is Flora, which is the best lake in terms of fish size, but it requires a two-hour–plus trek and should probably be treated as an overnight.

Another accessible Fraser Valley mountain lake is the Jones (Wahleach). It is one of those rare commodities—a high-elevation lake at about 2,000' (610 m) that you can drive to. It is actually a 1,135 acre (459 ha) BC Hydro impoundment located approximately 15 ½ mi (25 km) southwest of the town of Hope. Turn south off the Trans-Canada at the community of Laidlaw and follow the signs about 5 mi (8 km) to the lake. Beware, however, that the Jones Lake Forest Service Road is not really car accessible. The last time I drove there it was very rough, so forget trying to get in with a motor home or low-slung vehicle of any kind. There is a BC Hydro Recreation site with a boat launch, a picnic and day-use area, approximately 20 campsites and hiking trails. Unfortunately, depending on hydro requirements, the lake is periodically drawn down, which leaves the shoreline littered with dead trees. However, the fishing usually remains anywhere from good to hot. The stocked rainbow are usually in the 1-lb (.5-kg) range, but the real attraction are the abundant kokanee that readily take flies on a chironomid or maggot patterns fished fairly deep.

FRASER VALLEY RIVERS

If you are interested in tossing flies at huge cutthroat trout, then the place to be is the area around the mouth of the Harrison River from October through to the end of the year. There is a launch ramp and campsite at Kilby Park. Harrison Bay and the mouth consist of large shallow flats that are braided with meandering channels. The cutts roam these channels looking for minnows and smolts. The V-shaped wakes as they slash at bait reveal their locations. In a way, fishing in the late fall is like bonefishing: You roam the flats looking for schools of feeding cutts. When you spot them, cast a smolt pattern, like a Rolled Muddler, ahead of the school and rapidly strip in your line. The hits are incredible and the fight long and strong. This huge strain of cutts truly meets the definition of game fish. An added bonus when fishing at this time of year is that once in a while a coho, chum or even a chinook salmon will grab your fly. Memorable.

A mile (1.6 km) or so upriver from the mouth, the Chehalis River joins the Harrison. There is a very productive hatchery a short distance upstream, but the area from the fishing boundary provides some excellent, albeit crowded, fishing. The real attraction is the strong run of winter steelhead, but the angling for coho is not too shabby. Large attractor patterns tend to do the trick with simple yarn flies becoming almost the rule. You will want to scale up your tackle to 8- to 10-weight outfits and stick to 2x leaders. Be prepared to do some wading if you want to get away from the mob.

The Fraser River, while one of the continent's great rivers and chock-a-block full of fish at times, has been little known to fly fishers until recently. Some anglers have fished the backwaters and sloughs for cutthroat trout and even crappies, but the main runs of salmon and steelhead were largely left alone. Recent changes in federal regulations have made salmonids above the tidal boundary fair game. Between Mission and Hope are sections of braids, channels and islands that contain thousands of fish at times. Obviously, with schooling fish like salmon, when you find one you find them all. The trick, of course, is to find them. Judging by the concentration of vehicles, the area around Laidlaw is one of the hottest spots. Again, big tackle, yarn flies or large attractor patterns are the rule—as is a big net. There are miles of fishable water, and a patient "prospector" will always find fish during the late summer and fall fishery. To find out what patterns and colors are working best, ask at local tackle stores. Fred's Custom Tackle in Vedder Crossing is a great place to ask questions, especially about their "home water," the Vedder River.

Easily the most productive and heavily fished river in the Lower Mainland region, the Vedder River has runs of both wild and enhanced salmonids. There are also Dolly Varden and mountain whitefish in the deeper pools. The hatchery upstream pumps out incredible numbers of salmon and steelhead. When these fish are in the river during the late fall and winter, space can be at a premium. Popular stretches like the Peach Run near the former army base, or the Allison Pool farther upstream, can get pretty crowded. Fly fishers usually have a little trouble finding elbow room among the bottom-bouncers and hardware-tossers. It might be wise to fish during the week or do a little bush bashing to find some open water. The strong flows in this river mandate the use of heavily weighted flies and sink-tip lines. If you are not touching bottom, you are not down in the fish zone, and because it is fairly snaggy, be prepared to go through lots of tackle. Have a look at some of the pocket water that is often ignored by other anglers, and don't neglect the "canal zone" upstream from the Trans-Canada Highway.

The lower Skagit Valley almost became a hydroelectric impoundment because of some short-sighted government decisions. Outraged outdoors lovers lobbied ferociously until, in 1985, the valley was protected from flooding. Thankfully, because this is one of the most beautiful places I have ever seen, and to think of it being destroyed is almost beyond comprehension.

The Skagit starts as a mountain creek in Manning Park east of Hope. It joins Sumallo Creek beside the Hope–Princeton Highway, where it doubles in size and continues flowing southeastward. From Sumallo Grove right to Ross Lake, the river and surrounding forest are protected. The stretch of water from the confluence of Sumallo Creek is about 9 mi (14.5 km) in length. There is a hiking trail the entire distance from Sumallo Grove to the 26 Mile Bridge. This water is not fished much, but it does contain a lot of small fish. About a half mile (805 m) below the bridge, the Klesilkwa River joins from the north, doubling the river's size yet again. Below this confluence, the Skagit becomes a fantastic trout stream with long stretches of pools and rapids often totally arcaded by gigantic moss-covered trees. One long series of pools that I often fish reminds me of a gothic cathedral. There are over 9 mi (14.5 km) of water to fish with access from the Silver–Skagit Road. Two tips: Take lots of bug repellant as the mosquitoes on the lower section are voracious, and make sure you have decent chest waders and are a fairly strong wader. I have seen guys knocked down even in knee-deep water, and to reach some of the better beats, you normally have to go waist deep. A wading staff is a very good idea, as is an inflatable Personal Flotation Device.

The river is closed to fishing from November 1 to June 30, and catch-and-release is the rule. Spring runoff usually makes the Skagit too dangerous to wade (or boat for that matter) until July. Some of the best fishing occurs during August and September. The evening hatches can be awesome during this period, with mayflies, caddis and stones coming off at various times. Just be ready to change flies quickly.

Skagit trout tend to be very selective about fly size and color. When mayflies are in the air, it may be necessary to go down to a No. 16 or even 18.

An Adams in the appropriate size seems to be effective, and there is also a hatch of small caddis that can be matched with a No. 12 Deer Hair Caddis. Larger flies are available at times, like bigger versions of the caddis and western green drakes. Both dry versions and emergers work in light-colored shades. By late season, the trout move up to the heads of pools and gorge on nymphs. Bead Head flies like a Hare's Ear Nymph work well then. There will still be rises, but often just as the light fades. A larger Adams comes into its own at this time, but be ready to change patterns in an instant.

FAVORITE FLIES

Flies I always carry are Doc Spratley, Carey Special, Murray's Rolled Muddler, Adams, Mikulak Sedge, Gold-Ribbed Hare's Ear (Bead Head and standard versions), Nick's Leech, black and cinnamon ants, and chironomids in a variety of colors and sizes. Following are a few patterns that are useful in the region. They are not standard ties but meant for specific applications.

The Crappie Basher is a very simple fly to tie and is essentially a yellow and white bucktail over a Mylar body. Use a full floating line and cast it shoreward as close to the weeds as possible, allowing it to sink briefly. The retrieve is long and slow. Don't set the hook too hard as crappie have very fragile mouths.

I have caught well over 90 percent of my decent trout from Mill Lake using a black No. 12 Mill Lake Chironomid. Early in the season I have used a gray-bodied fly with a red rib to good effect, but most of the time I use the same black chironomid hung just below the surface. To achieve this result, use fine wire hooks and grease your leader to within 2" (5 cm) or so of the fly. When you see a head-to-tail rise (indicating that the fish are taking chironomids just below the surface), try to hit the ring with your fly. Wait a couple of seconds and the fish will usually hit on its return. If you don't get a hit, begin a very slow hand-twist retrieve, watching your leader for the slightest twitch.

Gloria's Green/Pink Skirt is a simple pattern to tie, which is a good thing because you will tend to go through them. This heavily weighted fly obviates the use of sinking lines, which are a pain to cast, and it casts well on an 8- or 9-weight outfit. For a leader, use 10-lb (4.5-kg) test monofilament—a maximum of 10' (3 m) long.

The Harrison Minnow, the pattern I use most often, was given to me by

Harry Penner, a local angler and guide who has fished the eastern part of the Fraser Valley for most of his life. He knows every dip and flow on the Harrison. A simple silver Mylar-bodied fly that is intended to imitate a salmon fingerling, it is fished as close to feeding cutts as possible and retrieved quickly with small jerks. Try to imitate the movement of a wounded baitfish. In the early morning I have often found schools of cutthroat right along the beach near the launch ramp at Kilby Regional Park, but they can be located in virtually every slough and backwater on the Fraser system. Cutts tend to move around a lot, and it is very important for an angler to be constantly in search mode. If you find a school try to follow them. I have spent hours rowing around at the mouth of the Harrison following a feeding school of cutts.

Nick's Bead Head Leech was developed by my nephew, Nick Soloman, who lives in Kamloops. One of the key ingredients is brown dubbing gleaned from his wife, Karen's, sweater (don't even ask). The pattern was originally based on Jack Shaw's leech pattern, but with the addition of a bead head and some other changes, the fly has become much more than a hybrid. Nick looks for cruising or feeding fish and throws his leech at them. The strike is usually immediate.

Martin Lamont with a typical sea-run cutthroat trout.

Most rivers located along the British Columbia coast and offshore islands are easily wadable.

Playing a cutthroat, Ian Forbes uses a canoe to test the waters of a coastal lake.

Thanks to an excellent stocking program, most lakes throughout the Lower Mainland and Sunshine Coast offer good trout fishing.

Getting off the beaten track may lead to peaceful solitude amid spectacular settings on some smaller streams.

The Coast & Islands

Chapter 12

Welcome to the Coast & Islands

ROBERT H. JONES

FOR A GRAPHIC ILLUSTRATION of why British Columbia offers so much potential for saltwater fly fishing, simply study a map of the province. A straight line from Washington's Olympic Peninsula northwest to the southern tip of the Alaska Panhandle is slightly over 500 mi (805 km), but all of those bays, sounds and long, narrow inlets cutting deeply into the British Columbia mainland increase the actual shoreline to well over 7,500 mi (12,070 km). By adding the shorelines surrounding the 6,500 or so islands and islets scattered along the British Columbia coastline, the total increases to around 17,000 mi (27,358 km). That's a lot of structure around which to cast a fly. And flowing into these bays, sounds and inlets are thousands of trickles, creeks, streams and large rivers, most of which attract anadromous fish like coastal cutthroat trout, Dolly Varden, steelhead and runs representing up to all five species of Pacific salmon: chinook, chum, coho, pink and sockeye.

FERRIES & FLIGHTS

The southern mainland coast and Vancouver Island offer several excellent fresh and saltwater fishing locations, most of which are road accessible. Major destinations are well served by scheduled flights from Vancouver and, in some cases, from ßSeattle, Washington. BC Ferries operates daily from Horseshoe Bay, northwest of Vancouver. There are scheduled sailings to the

Sunshine Coast on the mainland, and to Nanaimo on Vancouver Island. South of Vancouver near the international border, BC Ferries also has runs from Tsawwassen to Nanaimo and to Sidney, near Victoria. Travelers departing for Vancouver Island from Washington have the option of taking the Black Ball Ferry between Port Angeles and Victoria's Inner Harbour, the Victoria Clipper between Seattle Harbor and Victoria's Inner Harbour, and the Washington State Ferry between Anacortes and Sidney.

GETTING AROUND BY ROAD

On the Sunshine Coast, Highway 101 meanders about 75 mi (121 km) northwest from Langdale to Lund, a trip requiring a second ferry crossing from Earls Cove to Saltry Bay. There is also a ferry crossing from Powell River to Comox, on central Vancouver Island. Beyond Lund, further access to points north and west is by aircraft or boat. The only roads leading to the central and northern mainland coast are Highway 20 from Williams Lake to Bella Coola, Highway 37 off Highway 16 from Prince George to Kitimat and Highway 16 to the Prince Rupert area. Ferries operate between Prince Rupert and Skidegate on the Queen Charlotte Islands, and between Prince Rupert and Port Hardy on northern Vancouver Island. The Discovery Coast Ferry runs between Port Hardy and Bella Coola on the Central Coast, with scheduled stops at McLoughlin Bay, Shearwater, Ocean Falls, Klemtu and Namu.

On southern Vancouver Island, Highway 14 runs west from Victoria to Sooke, then 45 mi (72 km) to Port Renfrew on the southwest coast. Highway 19/19A extends about 300 mi (483 km) northwest from Victoria to Port Hardy, bordering the eastern shoreline for much of the way until well past Campbell River. Those in a hurry to reach northern destinations can use the new Inland Island Highway 19 from Victoria to Campbell River, but they will miss an interesting drive through several small communities and towns situated along the Oceanview Island Highway 19A, a few of which offer good fishing potential. All west coast destinations on Vancouver Island are reached by branch roads from Highway 19/19A. These include Port Alberni, Bamfield, Ucluelet and Tofino, all via Highway 4; Gold River via Highway 28, then onward by gravel road to Tahsis; Zeballos and Fair Harbour via gravel road; Port Alice and Coal Harbour by paved roads; and Holberg, Cape Scott Park and Winter Harbour via gravel roads. All these roads lead to saltwater fishing destinations and pass over or beside many lakes, rivers and creeks, all with healthy populations of game fish.

Accommodations range from none at all to rustic British Columbia Forest Service campgrounds to fully serviced RV parks to various levels of motels and hotels to luxury resorts that cater specifically to anglers. My only words of warning: When it comes to popular saltwater fishing destinations like Pender Harbour, Port Alberni, Tofino, Campbell River and Port Hardy, it pays to book your accommodations well in advance—at least three months.

Chapter 13

Fly Fishing Coastal &
Island Lakes

ROBERT H. JONES

THE TACKLE, techniques and fly patterns described in previous chapters are identical for coastal lakes on the mainland, Vancouver Island and the Gulf Islands, so I will concentrate primarily on where and when to go.

Largest of the thousands of islands offshore from the British Columbia coast is Vancouver Island. At just under 300 mi (500 km) long and about 65 mi (105 km) at its widest point, its land mass is over twice that of the state of Hawaii. Located throughout its landscape are 699 lakes, tarns, ponds and bogs, most of which contain trout, some of trophy proportions.

The major is one great difference between coastal lakes and those located farther inland is that lakes at lower elevations (some are very close to sea level) seldom freeze over. This is especially true on Vancouver Island, the Gulf Islands and the Sunshine Coast, which traditionally experience short winters (November through February). As a result, it's not unusual on occasional warm, sunny days during these four winter months to see fly fishers bobbing around on lakes in their punts and pontoon boats, even in float tubes, probing the waters with a leech or chironomid pattern. Honest!

THE FISH & WHERE THEY ARE

Coastal cutthroat trout, rainbow, kokanee and Dolly Varden are native to most coastal regions, but on Vancouver Island introduced brown trout and smallmouth bass do surprisingly well in all of the lakes where they are stocked. Brook trout are also available, but only in Spectacle Lake northwest of Victoria. Three of the most popular bass lakes are St. Mary on Saltspring Island, Quennell south of Nanaimo and Spider west of Qualicum Beach.

The best periods for fishing low-elevation lakes are mid-March through June, then September through October. The shoulder periods vary from one year to the next, but seldom by more than a week or two. When lowland lakes start into their summer doldrums, which usually last from July until early September, the mountain tarns will have warmed up enough that the aquatic bugs and trout are active and begin providing good action, and those lakes containing smallmouth bass will continue offering good fishing prospects all summer.

NORTH VANCOUVER ISLAND

For wild trout and uncrowded conditions, it is hard to beat the lakes on northern Vancouver Island and along its west coast. Many of the latter can be reached only by floatplane or helicopter, or by boat through an often confusing maze of islands and channels, then by hiking in from tidewater.

Several lakes throughout Vancouver Island have "quality regulations" in effect, meaning only artificial flies can be used and only one fish can be retained daily. Some small lakes where stocks of Dolly Varden appear to be declining are strictly catch-and-release during all or part of the year. These lakes are relatively few in number, and there are plenty of others where anglers need not hesitate to keep a few trout to eat. Management practices such as these help ensure the abundance of fish, and by reducing the harvest they increase the potential for catching trophy-sized trout. In addition to good fisheries management, fertilization projects on various lakes with low nutrient levels have provided a much-needed boost in the food chain, which has also increased the number and size of fish.

CENTRAL & SOUTHERN VANCOUVER ISLAND

Central and southern Vancouver Island anglers also enjoy good fishing, that (thanks again to good planning and management over the years by the fisheries branch) can be outstanding in some cases. While wild fish still dominate the catch in North Island and west coast lakes, yearling cutthroat from the Vancouver Island Trout Hatchery at Duncan are used to supplement wild

stocks in small, high-use lakes around Nanaimo, Cowichan Valley, Victoria
and the Gulf Islands. In addition, about 40 small lakes are stocked up to
three times annually with catchable-sized hatchery rainbow, which provide
great family fishing opportunities. Areas with one or more such lakes include
Victoria, Duncan, Chemainus, Cassidy, Nanaimo, Courtenay, Campbell
River and Gold River. Some of these trout survive and grow to impressive
sizes, which is always an incentive, even for fly fishers who might normally
shun stocked urban lakes.

Anglers seeking big cutthroat trout to 10-plus lb (4.5 kg) must go deeper than we can ever contemplate with standard fly fishing tackle, which usually means employing saltwater salmon trolling tactics on large lakes like
Buttle, Upper and Lower Campbell, Comox, Sproat and Great Central on
Vancouver Island, and Powell Lake near Powell River on the Sunshine Coast.
However, as interest in saltwater fly fishing continues producing improved
tackle and new, innovative techniques, perhaps it's only a matter of time
before we see some dependable tactics developed for tempting these deep
water lunkers.

While South Island anglers have more crowded conditions than those
found in less populated northern areas, they also have the added attraction of
brown trout and smallmouth bass. Lakes containing browns include Cowichan, Somenos and Cameron. Despite yielding occasional trophy browns
nudging 15 lb (6.8 kg), Cameron Lake, right beside Highway 4 about midway between Parksville and Port Alberni, remains lightly fished.

Smallmouth bass fishing in South Island lakes surpasses many highly
touted central Canadian waters, and thanks to some sensible regulations, it
should remain that way for the foreseeable future. There have recently been
some illegal movements of bass into unauthorized lakes, so even the fisheries
branch is unsure of how many lakes now contain them. Suffice it to say that
of about 18 to 20 lakes with bass, several are small and located in urban areas,
yet smallmouths—some well in excess of 5 lb (2.3 kg)—seem to thrive in
them. All of the lakes stocked with bass also support rainbow and/or cutthroat trout, which offers anglers excellent mixed-bag opportunities.

In high-use urban settings, daytime angling in bass lakes during the summer months means sharing the water with swimmers, water skiers and pleasure boaters. As a result, many anglers go out between midnight and early
morning, and do quite well with small poppers and deer-hair bugs. This, by

the way, is also a highly recommended tactic for brown trout in those lakes mentioned previously.

Then, after a night of fishing, as the sun peeps over the eastern mountain tops, if our erstwhile fly fishers feel like it, rather than go to bed they can trundle down to the nearest dock and head out for some salmon fishing, find a beach and cast for sea-run cutthroat trout or head for the closest river with a run of summer steelhead. That's truly Island living at its finest.

THE MAINLAND COAST

Coastal lakes in northern climes are somewhat harder to access, but many are well worth the effort. One of my favorites is Link Lake at Ocean Falls. Getting there requires flying from Vancouver or Port Hardy, or booking passage on the Discovery Coast Ferry from Port Hardy or Bella Coola. On our first trip to Walls Fish Camp in 1999, my wife, Vera, and I flew through snow squalls over Link Lake in mid-May, but by that afternoon I was catching wild coastal cutthroat to 18" (46 cm) on a Carey Special. They were in the shallows at the base of several spectacular waterfalls cascading from the steep mountain bordering the eastern shoreline. High up on the sheer face were slide areas where barely discernible white dots proved to be mountain goats casually munching on whatever it is that mountain goats eat, all the while defying gravity. We counted 11 on one face alone. During a trip in 2001, Jim Walls and I spotted a huge billy feeding within 200' (61 m) of the lake. Adorning its shaggy head were horns that Jim, an experienced goat hunter, guesstimated at over 11" (28 cm).

There is so much of interest to see around Link Lake that it's often hard to concentrate on the fishing, but I always manage to force myself. After all, like in many other large coastal lakes, Link's cutthroat grow to impressive sizes—certainly over 10 lb (4.5 kg)—which is always an incentive to keep casting.

Whether wood, aluminum or fiberglass, small punts are often the choice of fly fishers testing coastal lakes.

A typical, beautifully marked coastal cutthroat trout from Link Lake near Ocean Falls.

Noted Japanese photographer Noboru Takahashi with his first rainbow trout caught on a fly at Quennell Lake on Vancouver Island.

Fly fishing on coastal lakes can mean doing so in the rain—so be prepared.

Chapter 14

Fly Fishing Coastal Rivers

RORY E. GLENNIE

F REE-FLOWING RIVERS are a demonstration of water in its loveliest form. The same simple beauty is there, too, in streams, brooks, rivulets, trickles and seeps—miniature renderings of grand rivers. Largely, the geography and geology over which water flows determine its characteristics. High-gradient, boulder-strewn pocket water; deep, rock-walled canyon pools; and broad, meandering flows cutting through low-gradient alluvial gravel are but three types of water one might encounter. With a number of variations on these common themes, often within the course of any given river, anglers confront seemingly unending puzzles of water types. Upon closer investigation, however, there are a limited number of recurring themes. Given the confining laws of physics, water and gravity in combination can perform only certain physical tasks. Understanding those limitations aids in your quest of catching fish.

I won't dwell on major rivers like the Fraser, Skeena and Nass, or significant tributaries like the Thompson, Bulkley and Meziadin. Those flows have been well documented in volumes focused on fly fishing for various species, so my words here are aimed at the comparatively smaller, usually shorter, often tumbledown waters draining the mountainous coastline of British Columbia. Most rivers I will mention are relatively easy to access, well-known producers of the species highlighted and representative of the water types described. Bearing in mind that there may be some shift in species distribution as a matter of geography (numbers and variety differ somewhat with regard to north–south latitude), you will find that most streams with similar characteristics will likely fit somewhere into the fly fisher's picture.

DECIPHERING WHAT TO LOOK FOR IN A RIVER

No matter where anglers wander or which rivers they visit, there are always commonalties between new, unexplored streams and more familiar home waters. The differences can be interesting to explore, but familiar waters are usually more productive in terms of locating fish. Natural laws governing the way water flows play a large part in determining where we find fish. If, for example, you regularly chase coastal cutthroat trout in white-water pockets on your home stream, look for similar situations on unfamiliar streams as a starting point. Most likely, the same types of fish frequent the same types of water. If you pursue trophy-sized chinook salmon at home, search for those same types of heavy waters that they may frequent on other rivers. Dolly Varden will haunt the same sort of deep, slow-moving pools on a river 200 mi (322 km) away as surely as in the stream next door. This sounds straightforward because it is. Confusion arises when seeking unfamiliar species on unfamiliar waters, but a little study of fish habits and habitat can pay big dividends in understanding the fishing on such streams. Combine your education with observation and emulation of anglers who are consistently productive, and you will be on a shortcut to fly-fishing success.

BEFORE YOU START

First, factor in the species you want to catch, the amount of traveling you wish to do, the limits of your budget and time, and the extent of your physical abilities when it comes to hiking, clambering up and down steep banks and wading about in the river.

You also need to do some other groundwork before setting off. If exploring a nearby stream, simply do a quick mental check to make certain you have the necessary equipment. But when a major journey is involved, make a much more detailed reconnaissance before departing.

Some resource materials are available to help in planning trips. A current B.C. *Freshwater Fishing Regulations Synopsis* is an important tool in understanding the complex regulations governing anglers and freshwater fisheries.

Obviously, you must obtain and carry with you a valid nontidal waters angling license, along with the appropriate species stickers necessary for the type of fish you wish to catch. In our case this includes steelhead and salmon. Before going off on your much anticipated river sortie, study those regulations, which can save you a lot of grief and frustration later if the waters you choose to fish have angling closures, species nonretention, boating restrictions or are a Classified Water that requires purchasing an additional permit. A good working knowledge of the regulations brings more than the comfort of simply knowing you are fishing legally. On occasion prime fishing spots are found hidden within the restrictions. If, for example, a river has a Classified Water restriction for part of the year, it may have better-than-average fishing during the restricted time and probably offers the opportunity to catch a specimen fish. Streams with a size restriction above the standard baseline length often do so to protect the large adults found there. These slot-size limits denote big fish, and big fish equals big fun.

Another useful planning tool is the *BC Freshwater Fishing Directory and Atlas* published by *BC Outdoors.* Available at sport shops, tackle stores and booksellers, it is updated annually and encompasses a wide range of fishing areas. The directory includes dozens of maps, cross-referenced listings for thousands of waters, plus information on access, species, facilities and methods. This book is a basic tool for exploring new waters and a good way to jump-start your quest. If you have a certain river in mind, simply look it up in the index, which refers you to a short description with an informative commentary, including the fish species present. If you'd rather look for likely streams by perusing the maps, just let your fingers do the walking, determine the stream's name, then return to the index. Afterward, check the fishing regulations synopsis for further pertinent advice.

Another great source of information is the Internet. A little searching yields a few fly-fishing-specific sites that provide river reports and other useful information. An especially useful website is Canada's National Weather Office (weatheroffice.com), which provides up-to-date forecasts for various coastal areas. Besides the obvious merits of knowing the weather predictions before you leave, the site also has links to water-level charts specific to many rivers. Automated sensing stations collect the water level and discharge information, then relay it via satellite to a central agency. Hourly updating of data gives an almost real-time picture of what is happening in that river. Checking on specific or neighboring streams will assist in planning your fly-fishing strategy and may help avoid some disappointments.

Once you decide where you will be going, what you will be fishing for, and have acquired the appropriate licenses and permits, your next step is to assemble the tackle and other gear required to help make the trip proceed as planned.

GEAR & FLY TACKLE

If you have some fly-fishing tackle and other essentials, lay it out and see what might be missing and what can be jettisoned as superfluous. British Columbia coastal anglers should prepare for specific weather conditions: hot, cold and wet. Some anglers praise synthetic materials for their breathability and light weight. Others prefer the dependability of rubber bonded to sturdy cloth. Each material has positive and negative points, so I leave this selection entirely up to you.

For the most part, a mobile river fly fisher operates on foot. This usually means a good pair of chest waders to keep you dry and warm, and properly fitted boots—preferably with thick, nonslip felt soles attached—to provide ankle support and protection on uneven terrain. A belt cinched around the waist (on the outside) keeps water from filling the waders should a dunking occur. A wading staff—either the handy collapsible variety or a solid version—acts as a necessary third leg when crossing heavy water.

Fly boxes, tippet spools and other oddments needed throughout the day are best distributed throughout the multiple pockets of a vest or close-fitting chest pack. This way everything is at hand no matter where you are, and your hands are free to assist in wading, climbing stream banks, swatting mosquitoes or whatever. Additionally, a vest provides a layer of clothing to your upper body, which helps keep some of the natural elements at bay.

Good quality polarized sunglasses help you see into the water by reducing surface glare and are useful for spotting fish, their lies and the bottom in general. They also provide much-needed eye protection from errant hooks, poking branches and such. Although seemingly optional, a hat is actually a necessary piece of gear for river anglers. Other than the obvious ability to keep natural elements from beating on your noggin, a proper hat accentuates the benefits of using polarized sunglasses by shading your face and keeping light from reflecting off the inside of the lenses.

This is really about all you need for necessary gear. Not overly simplistic, merely Spartan. Too many river fly fishers carry around more tackle than necessary with the idea that one thing or another may come in handy. By developing a minimalist attitude and paring your tackle back to essentials, you are less burdened with dead weight.

Tools, gadgets and doodads have a way of multiplying within the confines of vest pockets, so to lighten your load stick with a few basic implements. A small, fine-cut file is essential for properly pointing-up hooks. Combination scissors–pliers serve as a line/fly trimmer, hook remover, barb crusher and split-shot crimper. Attach these to a pin-on retractor cord so when tucked away inside a pocket, they remain within easy reach at all times. This is all you require.

Fly boxes are the most commonly carried item. An angler knows his destination and desired catch can limit the number of flies required at any given time. Leave extraneous fly boxes in the vehicle or packsack, where they will be at the ready should changing conditions warrant. Two reasonably good-sized containers with an assortment of appropriate patterns should keep any stream angler in flies for at least a full day.

Leaders and tippets—those inexpensive, nearly invisible links to expensive flies—are best made up as pre-tied units and carried in a sectioned leader wallet. Fumbling to tie good knots with cold, wet hands at streamside is a chore that often results in less than stellar results. Before venturing out, take time to tie up a selection of leader and tippet combinations while you can work in good light and a relaxed atmosphere. A Triple Surgeon's Loop at the end of the desired length of monofilament provides a near-perfect connection between line and tippet. For the most part, loop-to-loop connections allow building a leader system as the situation dictates. Pre-looped sections of monofilament are easily strung together to form any practical combination of leader length and line strength. Simply place one loop over the other, then thread the tag end of one through the loop of the other, feed it through, and pull tight to form a strong figure-8 connection.

Tying a permanent loop at the end of your fly line can be easily accomplished by simply folding the line's tip-end back on itself, winding over the doubled section with a tying thread, then coating the thread with rubber-base cement for durability. Alternatively, you can install a commercially made braided loop over the line's end following the instructions provided with the package. Either produces the foundation for building a series of strong, dependable leader–tippet connections.

An almost endless list of secondary, nonessential items may be necessary on specific occasions—dry-fly floatant, split-shot, spare spools of monofilament. These small items can be tucked into vest pockets until a situation warrants its use. Other nonessential items can include a pocket-sized multi-tool, measuring tape, note pad and pencil, a small first-aid kit, toilet tissue, matches, whistle, flare gun, sun screen, bug spray, ad infinitum, up to whatever you feel comfortable carrying. My experience suggests that the planning stage of a trip is the time to decide which secondary items you may need and which can be left behind. Often, less is more.

RODS, REELS & LINES

Almost any size and type of fly rod, reel and line will suffice for some types of river fly fishing. The key word is "some." There are many overlaps between various water types and the fish species sought, and while your current outfit may work in a general way, there will be situations where a more specialized setup will be more efficient and effective.

Unless you become a specialist seeking a single species in limited types of water conditions, another rod is required. You needn't be overburdened with a bagful of rods, but a second or third purpose-built rod will extend your pleasure and lower your frustration.

Fly fishing for large anadromous species like chinook or chum salmon, winter steelhead and some races of coho and summer-run steelhead requires a hearty fly rod. The rod strength required to subdue large fish efficiently is often underestimated. The often-heard argument that light rods can subdue big fish as well as heavy ones is sound—but only sometimes. It is a given that we should be actively fighting a fish, not just worrying it to death by simply letting it tow the line around until it goes belly up. That goes for any fish we catch, not just the monsters. More often than not, there comes a time during the battle when your rod—fighting butt jammed tightly into your abdomen—provides needed leverage as you pour on the power to turn a fish from a hazard or to keep it from resting in heavy water. Without entering into an interminable discussion on the constituents of rod strength, suffice it to say that fly rods rated for heavier line weights offer the strength needed to subdue large fish. Modern, good quality fly rods of 9–10' in the 9- to 11-

weight range are best suited to large fish and the sometimes heavyweight sink-tip or sinking lines and big flies frequently used.

Smaller sea-run fish found in some streams—coho, pink and sockeye salmon, cutthroat trout, Dollies and "half-pounder" summer steelhead—are best handled with 6- to 8-weight tackle, with rods of 9–10'. However, a lot more than a fish's average size plays a part in determining what size rod to choose. Heavy, fast flows seemingly magnify the strength of any fish, and many seem to know how to use this to their advantage. Hence, depending on the type of water being fished, a fly rod on the heavier side of the scale may be more appropriate.

Lighter rods—3-, 4- and 5-weight—are fun to use for resident rainbow found in smaller coastal streams and for cutthroat trout, which may be resident or sea-run. Fishing small waters usually requires stealth and finesse rather than brute strength and often sees an angler ranging over a goodly distance. At the end of a long day astream, the lightness of these wee rods is a blessing. These lightweights can vary greatly in length depending upon individual tastes, casting skill and the size of the stream. They are manufactured in the preferred 7–10' range, which should fit anyone's taste or skill level.

TWO-FISTED FISHING

While on the subject of fly rods suitable for river fishing, I must illuminate the attributes of a two-handed fly rod as a line-control tool. During the 1980s and 1990s, a surge of interest from coastal river anglers led to the rediscovery, refinement and practical application of the old British weapon known widely as the Spey rod. That upswell of enthusiasm continues today. Simply, the two-hander is a purpose-built fly rod for assisting an angler in efficiently managing the fly line in areas with limited or nonexistent back-cast room and, most importantly, for effectively controlling the fly line and fly after a cast is made.

Quality Spey rods are currently manufactured for many line weights (most commonly 6- to 12-weight) and range in length from 11–18'. Selecting one that suits your preference for the species pursued and the waters you intend to fish is about as easy as going to a good fly shop and chatting with the sales staff. How to use a Spey rod effectively and pleasurably can be learned in short order by consulting a good instructor. Again, the fly shop should be your best source for locating one. After that, competence comes with repeated practice on your part. Beyond the different form of casting required, a fly fisher quickly learns the ease with which the waters are efficiently covered using a two-hander. This lesson can only be learned and fully appreciated through repeated practice on flowing water—preferably with fish in it.

While a Spey rod is not a cure-all for every demanding situation, it has its place on most flowing waters at some time or another. When you get used to using one in certain circumstances, it quickly becomes evident that fly-fishing horizons have broadened, and then, quite naturally, your long rod will find more time on the water in more situations.

Whether seeking a single- or two-hander, you should find that a good fly shop handles a variety of makes and models from which to choose, usually enough to suit most tastes. The quality of rods these days is top notch and a real dog is hard to come by, but be prepared to pay handsomely for the quality that is worth it in the long run.

FLY REELS

Fly reel construction is subject to far less debate than it was a few short years ago. The burgeoning aerospace industry with its attendant drive for perfection in materials and machining not only left its mark on fly-rod manufacturing, but it accelerated the level of excellence in building fly reels. Many small jobbers who cranked out bits and pieces for building space toys were also anglers who focused their engineering expertise on producing better fly reels. As established, big-name business played catch-up with these advances, the industry overall began producing better products. As a result, one would have to make great effort to find a poorly constructed fly reel these days. The staff at a good fly shop also can accommodate your desire for the proper reel. After explaining the type of fishing you will be doing, the size of rod on which it will be fitted and, of course, your budgetary limitations, you can then select with confidence following their advice.

FLY LINES

In the wake of fly-rod and reel advancement, fly lines have also improved rapidly in quality, durability and variety. Much of this progress was spurred by the broadening of fly-fishing horizons and the exploration of almost boundless fishing venues. These days there is scarcely a fish species that is not pursued by fly fishers. This is good news for river anglers because as improving technology becomes focused in one area, there are spillover benefits in others. Suffice it to say that even among experienced river anglers, there is ongoing experimentation with different line configurations in changing water conditions. In short, no one line or line type will do everything needed to present your fly properly to a fish at all times.

There are, however, advancements in fly-line technology that comes close. Several line manufacturers offer an Interchangeable Tip System (ITS) that relies on interchanging various tip sections, which attach easily to the base casting portion. For many years anglers had cut and spliced portions of various fly lines in an effort to obtain the casting and fishing characteristics they desired. The sinking "shooting head" configuration provided an increase in distance casting and in sinking a fly to the bottom, but it failed miserably in line control following the cast. Homemade sink-tips often hinged during casting and delivery, then collapsed on the water in a messy heap. Improvements in quality control, fly line design and engineering, coupled with new line coatings gave rise to lines better suited to the needs of anglers.

By choosing an ITS, you save money by not having to purchase a large variety of full-length lines in the configurations desired, and in the number of spare reel spools required to hold them. Initially, the cost of an ITS is significantly more than a single or even two full-length fly lines, but considering its versatility, the savings become substantial. An added benefit comes when a worn-out section or tip must be replaced; the cost is minimal compared to buying an entire new line.

Again, seeking advice from knowledgeable fly shop personnel is a wise move when choosing a fly line. After that, time spent on the water will be your best teacher. Experimenting with various ITS configurations, along with a few distinct fly types, will soon demonstrate the versatility of this setup in getting your fly to the fish.

THE HABITS & HABITAT OF FISH

Sometimes one can't help but feel that it would it be nice if all of the various fishes we cast to always fell prey to one fly pattern and one kind of presentation. All we would need to do is find places where fish hang out, cast to them, then wind in our catch. Thankfully, such is not the case; if it were, fly fishing would get boring in a hurry. One good thing is that, for the most part, a particular kind of fish will take a particular kind of fly presented in a particular fashion. Repeat that scenario often enough and a specific technique for catching those fish evolves. Luckily, much of that groundwork was laid out ages ago, and most of the specific techniques are now well known. Consistently successful fly fishers study those established methods and techniques, then apply them to their own fishing.

Free-rising trout—brown, resident rainbow and cutthroat—are taken as a matter of course by using dry flies or small nymph patterns floated on the surface. While this is a standard approach for catching trout, it is not considered a worthwhile method for tempting chinook salmon. Depth-charging heavy-water chutes for chinook with a fast-sinking line and leaded fly will scarcely ever catch a pink salmon—unless your line swings widely at the end of its drift and snags one. A polar bear hair streamer retrieved rapidly through a riffle for fresh-run coho is a poor technique to employ while chasing winter steelhead, which hug the bottom in a near comatose state. Scouring the bottom of a pool with a slow-rolling egg pattern would probably pay off with a Dolly Varden before a summer-run steelhead got excited about it. Dead-drifting a mayfly on the surface for brown trout will hardly impress its pool mate, a late-running winter steelhead. Do you see what I mean? The need to use proper presentation techniques geared for particular species in specific water types cannot be over emphasized. As a general rule, the following proven tactics are fish producers and will typically work well, but, fishing being fishing, sometimes nothing works.

Chinook Salmon

Boulder-strewn heavy-water riffles, pools with a substantial surge running through them and white-water chutes characterize good chinook water. Bright, fresh-run fish seek these heavy flows for protective cover and oxygenation. Dark, ripening spawners are found lower down in moderately fast water and tailouts. Chinook quite often reveal their presence by rolling porpoiselike up to the surface or by jumping clear of the water for no apparent reason.

The world-renowned Campbell and Toquart rivers, both on Vancouver Island, have logging road bridges spanning prime chinook holding water. The turbulent head of the Campbell's big Sandy Pool and the Toquart's deep, streamy Canyon Pool can be viewed and studied from the elevated perch of their respective bridges. The opportunity to scope out the water beforehand aids in preparing a plan of attack when seeking chinook.

Use high-density or lead-core sink-tips with short leaders and weighted attractor fly patterns to get well down where the chinook hold, which may be closer to midwater depth than right on the bottom. Cast upstream of the suspected lie, and use a dead-drift, deep-nymphing approach. Steer your fly into the hot spot by mending your line to achieve the desired slow, head-on presentation. Watch where your line enters the water, and if it tightens at all, set the hook. Usually, chinook simply stop a fly without really striking it, but after the hook is driven home there will be no mistaking what it is. More often than not a chinook will head directly upstream through the heaviest water, then turn and make a beeline down or across the stream again. Surprisingly enough, these large fish often take a relatively small fly better than they do the extra-long streamer types.

Chum Salmon

There are times when it seems that if you tossed out your key ring a chum would snap at it. They are usually quite visible in streams as they roll and cavort in shallow riffles and tailouts. Two examples of places that hold chum for the duration of their spawning cycle are the quick, riffly flats downstream from the Condensory Bridge Pool on the Puntledge River in Courtenay and the shallows around Dove Creek bridge on the nearby Tsolum River (both are tributaries to the Courtenay River). These same areas are literally windrowed with chum carcasses after spawning is complete, usually around Christmas.

Chum often chase after a fly swung through the holding area; other times a deep-sunk, dead-drift presentation is required. Use sink-tip lines to achieve the desired result. After being hooked, a chum usually likes to duke it out by holding in place and bearing down with the odd head shake. The real fun begins after it becomes tired. That's when river currents become its ally and put the utmost strain on tackle.

While there have been a few patterns developed especially for taking chum in rivers, most of the flies used for other anadromous species will hook their fair share of fish. However, one pattern currently in vogue on some northern rivers may warrant further trial on southern streams: the surface-chugging Pink Polly Wog. Fished on a floating line, this spun deer-hair and marabou concoction is fished on a tight-line swing over top of the salmon, creating quite a surface commotion. For some inexplicable reason, chum salmon sometimes charge after and clamp down on this weird-looking intruder. Watching such a dramatic take can be awesome.

Coho Salmon

When they first enter a river, silver-bright, fresh-run coho can be found in heavy-water areas similar to those preferred by chinook. As coho acclimatize to their new surroundings, they quickly drop out of those heavy flows and into fast-flowing riffles and runs more typical of good steelhead water. At times they are found in slower water and pools, where they mill about while ripening in preparation for spawning. When coho are in a river, they can be located through a little streamside reconnaissance. Like chinook, they often break the surface with porpoiselike rolls and jump repeatedly for no apparent reason.

These extremes can be seen when you compare the smooth lower section of the Tlell River, downstream of the Yellowhead Highway bridge on Graham Island in the Queen Charlottes with the brisk pocket water around the Courtenay Fish & Game Protective Association property on the Puntledge River. They are quite different in nature, but both are good places to intercept coho with a fly.

Although coho are not known as bottom huggers, use a heavy sink-tip to get your fly down far enough in the water column to interest fish suspended in midwater. Both a deep-sunk, dead-drift nymphing approach with small attractor flies and a swinging-retrieved streamer fly will work on coho. Which one they choose seems more dependent on their mood than anything else I can figure out. That same Pink Polly Wog used for chum has a similar effect on coho on some streams and warrants further experimentation—if not for its efficacy at catching fish, then at least for the sheer fun of using a floating line and surface presentation. Regardless of how they are tempted, coho go ballistic at the hookset and give their all before coming to hand completely exhausted.

Sockeye Salmon

It's funny that in this land of great salmon runs there are more rivers that don't host a fishable sockeye run than those that do. For the most part, silver-bright sockeye are often caught in the lower portions of rivers that do host substantial runs. Shortly after entering fresh water on short coastal rivers, sockeye begin ripening toward spawning with the attendant change of body color from silver to bright red and a garish, emerald green head. When one sockeye is found, usually many more are close by. Whether in small groups of a few dozen or in schools exceeding a thousand, they may be found holding in, or moving upstream through, smoothly flowing runs and glides. They often rest on or beside submerged midstream gravel bars.

Oktwasht is a native word meaning "place of the smoking salmon." A derivation, *Oktwanch,* is the name of the river flowing into Muchalat Lake, near the town of Gold River on central Vancouver Island. Nearly joined in the headwaters with the Oktwanch, the opposite-flowing Nimpkish River also hosts a run of "smoking salmon." Once again, logging road bridges allow easy viewing of some holding water and access to other areas.

Sinking lines, or at least sink-tips, present a typically small, sparse fly at the level sockeye hold. A slow, swinging drift over the area brings the best response. Occasionally, persistence with a deep, dead-drifted fly elicits a strike, and reduces the chance of foul hooking. A fish hooked in comparatively soft, sensitive body tissue will go squirrelly, and it's easy to tell the difference between this activity and the quick, dogged fight of a sockeye fairly hooked in the mouth.

Pink Salmon

Despite having the smallest average body size of all salmon, these fish are worthy adversaries on appropriate tackle. Like sockeye, pinks start turning from silver-bright to darker spawning colors soon after entering a stream, and more often than not they are found groups ranging from small to large. Broad, smoothly flowing riffles from 2–4' (.6–1.2 m) deep hold pinks for quite some time before they spread out into shallower spawning areas.

Two excellent places for finding pinks I recall fondly are Roderick Haig-Brown's bouldery Line Fence Pool on his home stream, the Campbell River, and the riffles around the logging road bridge crossing the lower Deena River on Graham Island in the Queen Charlottes. Both are examples of prime holding areas for pinks.

Small, bright attractor patterns, usually with a preponderance of pink, work best. Swing them slowly through on sinking or sink-tip line. These salmon simply stop your fly on its drift—a definite take but not quite what would be called a strike. Once hooked, they run long distances and repeatedly jump clear of the water, and they know how to use the current to their advantage. Their fight is relatively shortlived, but they come to hand with enough reserve strength to dart away strongly upon release.

Dolly Varden

This much maligned, rascally char is not often pursued by fly anglers. More are hooked incidentally while fishing for other species than on purpose. The first encounter with a Dolly is often at the expense of a small trout's or salmon's life when the poor little fish just hooked is suddenly engulfed by a Dolly as it is being brought to hand for release. At the surface, the Dolly lets go of the now mortally wounded fingerling, and it is clearly seen who perpetrated this evil deed as the char slinks off into the depths. This is the kind of behavior that has branded Dollies a menace. They eat baby sport fish! Taking a cue from that habit, good fly patterns for Dollies represent baby trout and salmon, as well as sculpins and sticklebacks—in a word, fish.

Deep, slow-moving water, preferably with some large, woody debris for cover, is a favorite Dolly hangout. Near the town of Sayward on east coast of northern Vancouver Island is the Salmon River, and a bit farther north is the Eve River. Both host good-sized Dollies in their lower reaches, fairly close to tidewater. It is a matter of conjecture whether these are a sea-run variety or resident homebodies.

Sinking lines or sink-tips with good-sized, meaty flies sunk to the bottom, then moved in an enticing wounded, hapless fashion will hook Dollies. Unless the fish you hook is an outsized creature, it will put up a respectable bulldogging underwater tussle but will come to hand quite quickly. Larger specimens, as with most big fish, use their size to advantage and put your fly tackle to a good test.

Sea-Run Cutthroat Trout

If there is one fish that has spawned a cultlike following amongst fly fishers, the sea-run cutthroat trout is it. Enigmatic, elusive and ephemeral are words often used in reference to the lifestyle habits of those fine little fish. Cutts seem to come and go on their own timetable and say to the devil with everyone else.

Two fine examples of sea-run cutthroat streams, especially in their lower reaches, are the Oyster River, which drains into the Strait of Georgia midway between Campbell River and Courtenay, and, on the opposite side of the Island, the Toquart River, which flows into Barkley Sound a bit southeast of Ucluelet. Kootowis Creek (Indian River), which spills into Grice Bay near Tofino, offers a true upstream setting for chasing cutts.

Sea-run cutthroat are springtime spawners and have to be in certain spawning areas at specific times. Other than looking in these waters, watch for sea-runs in all but the heaviest cascades (although the small, calm slot alongside such waters may also be a good place to find one or two). Gravelly tailouts where insect nymphs are abundant usually hold a cutt or two. Pools 3–4' (.9–1.2 m) deep, preferably with some large woody debris anchored alongside or overhung with tree branches, are often juicy spots for sea-runs. Good lies can be found in the tiny white-water pockets behind boulders or downstream from ledge rock. In well-shaded, medium-fast riffles and runs with submerged boulders, cutts often range about in search of morsels. Lazy Susan back eddies of big pools attract feeding cutts to the endless smorgasbord of food items circling about there. True to their mystique, sea-runs can be found everywhere—and nowhere. Cutts will hang downstream of spawning salmon, patiently waiting to gobble up the odd egg drifting loose,

Fortunately for fly fishers, sea-run cutts are aggressive feeders and take a poke at just about anything that looks like it might be good to eat. This may be the best way to find them—simply run a fly through likely-looking water and see who's home. Unless the water temperature is dead low, a surface fly will often bring a response. Even if not hooked, or if they are unresponsive a second time, they give away their presence. Then a more appropriate technique can be used with confidence. Buggy-looking nymphs, small Muddlers and various Woolly Buggers are the medicine. Bright little attractors, single egg, and bushy dry flies also produce fish well. Name a fly pattern and it has probably caught a sea-run cutthroat at one time or another. That is the real beauty of these marvelous trout—their willingness to participate in our fishing.

Brown Trout

This import to the province, circa 1933, has a limited distribution but a small, loyal following. In the few coastal streams hosting browns, springtime offers the best crack at them. Being fall spawners, brownies have a good appetite after a winter of comparatively meager rations, so feeding rather than procreation is the driving force then.

Only three well-known coastal rivers host brown trout, and all are on Vancouver Island: the Cowichan and Little Qualicum rivers to the south and the Adam River on the North Island. Not all reaches of these streams hold brownies. Those that do include the middle section of the Cowichan, well downstream from Cowichan Lake to Skutz Falls and somewhat below the falls; the top end of the Little Qualicum where it spills out of Cameron Lake (as well as the lake's outlet); and 1 mi (1.6 km) or so stretch downstream from the Highway 19 bridge on the Adam are notable brown trout havens. Reports of brownies below the falls on the Adam, near its juncture with the Eve River, have also been substantiated by fisheries branch snorkel surveys of that area.

Insects make up a large part of this trout's diet, and the spring emergence of mayflies, caddis and stoneflies is a good time to be on stream with small nymphs and dry flies imitating these insects. It was found that a brown trout's diet roughly consists of 80 percent mayflies and 10 percent caddis with the remainder being other food organisms. As is often the case on Vancouver Island, that ratio of insects consumed often changes when stoneflies become the predominant hatch. As well, the spring emergence of salmon fry from spawning areas plays a big part in feeding brown trout. When the water levels recede to normal summer height, browns tend to migrate to the deeper holes and become highly reliant on sculpins, crayfish, other salmonid parr and bottom-dwelling nymphs as mainstay food items. Brown trout are thermotropic to a high degree, meaning that as a stream warms beyond their tolerance level, they seek more comfortable water temperatures by moving to areas with cool water springs, even if the current is less than they usually desire or the food base is less than optimum. Find these spring-holes in summer, and you will find browns.

It might be ancient advice, but it bears repeating: Fishing for browns is better in low light and even best in the dark. Unless nymphs and dry flies are catching fish, it may be best to put on a sink-tip and slowly swing a big, fishy imitation like a Muddler or Woolly Bugger through the depths.

There is empirical evidence that some brown trout will make brief journeys downstream to an estuary, where they feed on the high-caloric chow available there. Over time, enough outsized browns have been caught to support this theory. One great thing for those of us who fling flies is that even large browns never really abandon their liking for insects and may rise to snatch our offerings without warning. They are the ones that will put your light trout tackle to a severe test.

THE CHALLENGE OF SUMMER-RUN STEELHEAD

Over and above the prolific runs of salmon, it is summer-run steelhead that really made fly fishers sit up and take note of the rich rewards coastal rivers have to offer. A summer-run steelhead is a type of supercharged rainbow trout fattened on the great bounty of the ocean and willing to rise to a stream's surface to bite a feather and fur bauble in broad daylight. Almost limitless prose and several exhaustive tomes have been penned in honor of this great game fish, and I can add little. Search out the literature, study the methods and techniques, pore over maps to locate prospective waters, talk to anybody who has been to those streams—and not just the fly fishers; others can provide a wealth of knowledge, too. Above all, listen.

Linking-up with a skillful fly fishing guide your first time out can be a shortcut that pays enormous dividends in the knowledge gained. After that, do-it-yourself adventures will likely be more productive, and their skill level and knowledge base will broaden accordingly. For determined, self-reliant fly fishers—at least those whose understanding of steelhead has been kicked up a notch by studying the greats—the best approach may be to simply get onto a river known to have a good run of summer fish, and start exploring.

Two well-known waters, favored and written about by the late Roderick Haig-Brown, are the Campbell and Heber rivers. The historic Islands Pools in the fly-fishing-only section of the Campbell have attracted summer-runs and fly fishers for a long time. Of late the runs are diminished, but the hope is that they will rebuild to former glory. The Heber, a tributary to the Gold River, hosts a strong run of wild, naturally produced summer-runs. There is good access to the river from Highway 28, which runs right beside the river for several miles. Beware! These steelhead are spooky. The water in the Heber is so clear that those fish can see you coming when you pull out of your driveway to leave home.

As a base, start searching out riffles and runs with boulders on the bottom, preferably from knee- to armpit-deep, and flowing at what could best be described as a comfortable walking pace. Cover each area with consecutive arcs of a sunken fly swinging slowly across and downstream. Then try a bushy dry fly swung over the same water. Or vice versa. Present the fly to any summer-runs you may see holding beside boulders or rolling at the surface. Should that fail, go to Plan B: Seek out a competent fly-fishing guide.

THE AGONY OF WINTER-RUN STEELHEAD

In my opinion, these are simply the toughest fly-fishing challenge offered on coastal streams. Period. If there is any form of fly fishing that requires anglers to pay their dues by putting in countless long hours before finding grace with a hook-up, winter steelhead fly fishing is it. The extraordinary concentration necessary to detect a steelhead subtly mouthing your fly before the hook-up is often thwarted by harsh natural elements: a sullen monochromatic backdrop of black, white and shades of gray lulls the eyes; frozen fingertips and icicles hanging from your nose make physical reactions sluggish; flat-lighted flowing water fixes your mind in a near hypnotic trance; and your feet are like lead from hours in frigid water. Then, all of a sudden, this all becomes history with an electric jolt sent via the line to your body when a steelhead is suddenly on. That is the beauty and reward of winter steelhead fly fishing—resurrection.

Three fine Vancouver Island rivers with good access to winter steelhead are the Cowichan, Gold and Salmon. Sadly, several other easily accessed rivers suffer from depleted runs, and many are subsequently closed to angling. Hopes are that these runs will rebuild, and fly fishing on them can again be pursued. Both logging road and highway bridges cross each of these streams in a few places. Scoping out the flows from them can help you plan your trip, either farther upstream or down, depending on the clarity and quantity of the water.

As with summer-runs, there has been much written about taking winter-runs with a fly rod. It would pay a prospective winter fly fisher to study the literature available. Generally, I don't recommend starting out on your own by stumbling about blindly on a winter steelhead stream, but I guess you have to start somewhere. Linking up with an experienced steelheader helps kick-start the process.

A good grounding in the basics of winter steelheading, plus an understanding of specific run timing, will undoubtedly save much useless flogging of water. Many of the same water types that hold summer steelhead also hold winters. The main practical difference between the two is that winter-runs are notorious for hanging tough near the bottom. With the heavy flows of winter, one wonders how a steelhead can hold so easily in such strong currents. The physics of the combined hydrodynamic shape of the fish and a thin layer of slower-moving water down along the bottom help it hold in place. To elicit a strike, you must drift your fly almost into its face. Heavy-weight sink-tips coupled to weighted flies (although not necessarily large ones) are dead-drifted with the assistance of multiple line mends. Once it sees the fly, a winter steelhead may follow it for a brief moment as it swings and then take it.

The biggest single factor in determining whether steelhead can be expected to move very far to take a fly is water temperature. Generally, warmer winter flows mean more active fish. Even when the water is quite low, they occasionally follow a fly right into thin water before grabbing it—or spooking themselves back into deeper or more turbulent cover water. When the fish seem more willing to move a bit to intercept or chase your fly, use lighter density lines, even floaters.

Much has been written on this subject, and it is required reading if you wish to aspire to proficiency in winter fly fishing. Should you become a winter steelhead devotee, you will have joined a minority. When you hook onto your first winter-run, you may well become an enlightened convert. After that, your fly-fishing perspective will never be the same.

A fly fisher about to practice steelhead catch-and-release on the Big Qualicum River.

Jim Omori laying out long casts for summer steelhead on the world famous Campbell River.

Dr. Robert Bailey with a fine pink salmon caught and released in the Campbell River.

Inflatable boats allow fly fishers to quickly cover long stretches of even modest-sized rivers such as the Oyster.

Barry Thornton with a pink salmon from the mouth of Black Creek near Courtenay.

Ralph Shaw landed this prime October-run coho in the Puntledge River near Courtenay.

Chapter 15

Salmon Feeding Grounds &
Spawning Migration Routes

ROBERT H. JONES

THE MOST PRODUCTIVE PLACES to locate salmon are major feeding grounds, spawning migration routes and staging areas near the mouths of rivers, especially those with successful federal salmon hatcheries like the Conuma River in Nootka Sound and Robertson Creek on the Stamp River system, both located on the west coast of Vancouver Island, and the Qualicum and Quinsam rivers on the east coast. In addition to federal hatcheries, there are smaller community hatcheries scattered throughout the entire coast. Many are operated on the proverbial shoestring by volunteers, but some are very successful.

During the winter months, "feeder" chinook are found in areas with ample populations of herring, anchovy, sandlance, krill, shrimp and squid, but this type of fishing is strictly weather controlled. Bluebacks (immature coho) are often present in these same areas, but they are usually too small to be of interest to anglers until the late spring of their final year, when they suddenly start adding size and bulk.

Upstream migrations from saltwater usually start about one month earlier in northern rivers, and many of the larger systems have two distinct runs: early and late (usually spring and fall). Generally, early fish are those which run to the upper reaches of a system, while late runs spawn closer to the mouth. Early chinook start entering rivers in late May to early June, while late runs often stage in the estuaries until fall rains raise river levels from their summer lows, usually in mid- to late September. On the other hand, early coho start running up the Skeena River around early August, while late coho may enter the Fraser system as late as the following March. Thus, while late November to early December normally signals the end of the coho spawning season in most rivers, some traditionally continue for much longer periods.

Depending on location, "northern coho" (thought to be offshore ocean feeders) usually start arriving from late summer to early autumn and average somewhat larger in size than inshore local stocks. They are also darker (more a burnished pewter than chrome silver), indicating their advanced maturity.

Pink salmon appear around July and taper off in September. Some populations are relatively stable, while others follow a two-year cycle. Strait of Georgia returns are more abundant during odd-numbered years, but some enhanced rivers also have good returns on even years.

Although sockeye salmon are found in most waters, the largest populations are present along the western and northeastern coasts of Vancouver Island, and from the Island's southern tip over to the Fraser River estuary. Sockeye start appearing in inshore waters during the latter part of June and continue until September.

Chum salmon show in August and continue until well into winter in some areas. Anglers willing to dress for cold, often wet, weather, can experience good fishing into November, by which time West Coast weather generally gets a bit much for even the most die-hard anglers.

THE PECKING ORDER

Before ichthyologists decided to muddy the waters by reclassifying rainbow and cutthroat trout from the genus *Salmo* to *Oncorhynchus,* there were five species of Pacific salmon: chinook, chum, coho, pink and sockeye. Okay, six if we count the masu or cherry salmon of Asia, but their range in the Pacific is limited and nonexistent in North American waters. Despite this official designation, anglers—and virtually all fisheries biologists—still refer to rainbow and cutthroat as trout. As will I.

For the better part of the 20th century, chinook and coho were considered game fish, while the remaining three species were only of commercial value. There were several reasons for this: A high percentage of immature chinook and coho often remain close inshore to feed and grow, meaning they are available to anglers all year round. Pink, sockeye and chum all head elsewhere in the ocean, returning inshore only for the relatively short period it takes to make their way along migration routes, stage off the estuary of their home river and travel upstream to spawn and die. During this same period, of course, swarms of mature chinook and coho also move inshore, feeding heavily as they migrate southward along the coastline toward their natal rivers.

In the early days of European settlement on the West Coast, anglers learned how to catch immature chinook and coho. Then, as the much larger mature fish passed by on their spawning migrations or arrived to stage off their home estuaries, these became the prime targets. Thus, even though the other three species of salmon became available, anglers were too busy concentrating on chinook and coho to notice, and pink, sockeye and chum showed up in their catches only by accident.

There also was the misconception that pinks and sockeye did not fight well. This came about because these species don't attain anywhere near the size of chinook and so could not perform very well against heavy trolling tackle. Coho anglers, at least those using medium- to lightweight tackle, gave them a bit more credit as fighters, but there was never much effort devoted to fishing for them specifically because anglers could not catch them with any consistency.

The story was a somewhat different for chum salmon. As most chinook anglers had quit fishing for the season by the time the chum arrived, they had little to do with them. Coho anglers who tangled with them were usually impressed with their often respectable sizes, some well over 20 lb (9 kg), and the aggressive battles that resulted after hooking one. Nevertheless, these anglers were actually after coho, so they seldom made any effort to learn how to catch chum consistently. Now that they are aware of this chance to extend their sport well into the finger-numbing winter season, many fly fishers welcome the opportunity to target late-running chum.

Chapter 16

Down to the Sea with Fly Rods in Hand

ROBERT H. JONES

A T SOME POINT NOW LOST IN HISTORY, freshwater anglers followed streams and rivers down to their estuaries and discovered that at certain times of the year virtually all anadromous salmonid species could be taken while casting from shore, including sea-run rainbow (steelhead), cutthroat trout and Dolly Varden. A few even tried flinging flies and were fairly successful at times. Their greatest problem was trying to keep the metal components on their fly rods and reels from corroding to the point of destruction through contact with salt water.

Cessation of the Second World War saw some dramatic improvements in fishing tackle and associated equipment, including the reintroduction of open-faced spinning reels from England and France, truly anti-backlash Ambassadeur casting reels from Sweden, and fiberglass rods, nylon monofilament lines, dependable outboard motors, and mass-produced boats of fiberglass and aluminum from the United States. Soon, more people than ever were fishing, and, as entry-level anglers gained knowledge and experience, they sought more challenges, which, for many, meant taking up fly fishing. For the most part this remained in the realm of freshwater fishing, but a few of those who had fished the beaches and inshore waters began venturing back to them with their fly-casting gear.

This was also about the time that anglers without preconceived ideas and prejudices began looking at those other three salmon species as game fish.

Around 1957, commercial trollers developed a method for consistently taking pinks on artificial lures. This attracted recreational anglers, and the most productive tactic to evolve, which works coast-wide, is to slowly troll in a straight line at depths ranging from subsurface to 100' (30 m) with small hootchies or lures in various shades of pink or red, trailing them 22–28" (56–71 cm) behind a Hot Spot, O'Ki or Gibbs flasher trimmed with red or pink. Note those colors, for when fly fishers took up the challenge, they found their most productive patterns were euphausiid and shrimp imitations in shades of red, pink and orange, fashioned on hooks ranging from No. 10–4.

In the late 1960s, anglers in northwestern Washington discovered that sockeye would take small, red-colored plugs and spoons trolled slowly at depths of 35–90' (11–27 m). Since then, fly fishers also have learned that patterns and colors that work for pink salmon do just as well for sockeye.

These same basic setups and trolling tactics also attract chum salmon, but as these fish seldom appear until after anglers have stopped fishing for sockeye and pinks, the correlation was never widely recognized. One group of anglers who started intentionally targeting chum were those using drift jigs. When Comox Valley resident Rex Field introduced his now famous Buzz Bomb back in the mid-1960s, it was discovered that a 50/50 model (light gray on one side, dark gray on the other) would consistently take chum that were staging near the estuaries. While unscrupulous anglers found it faster to snag the fish, those who played the game fairly found chum quite willing to bite. Doug Field, who now runs the operation in Courtenay, told me that each year he still makes up a small run of 50/50 Buzz Bombs specifically for chum salmon anglers. However, feedback from other customers over the years indicates that these fish are also partial to brighter colored Buzz Bombs, especially those finished in chrome, green, yellow and in some cases yellow or green with the paint scraped off one side. I mention their preference for swinging wildly between dark and bright colors because the same holds true for fly patterns.

What really sparked interest in chum salmon was the decline of Strait of Georgia coho stocks during the 1990s, when the West Coast experienced a closely spaced series of El Niño events. In 1994 coho that normally migrated southward down the Inside Passage veered around Vancouver Island and traveled down its western coastline. The upper Strait of Georgia, which once boasted some of the highest coho catch rates on the coast, was suddenly devoid of them. No one was more shocked than the Campbell River resort owners and fishing guides who had bookings for the season. The guides met this challenge by heading north up Discovery Passage to fill the void with pink and sockeye salmon. Then, as the fall season approached, they started intercepting chum salmon. Many kept fishing right into November, and in so doing they discovered new techniques and tackle for increasing their chum catches. Although chum are attracted to the standard colors of pink, red and orange, fly fishers in particular have found they also turn on to purple, blue, green, chartreuse and black. Some winter-run steelhead fly fishers simply pluck patterns like the Skunk, Purple Peril and Popsicle from their boxes and do quite well with them.

In the great scheme of things, saltwater fly fishing is still a relatively new frontier, a facet of the sport that offers challenges, excitement and plenty of opportunities for experimenting with new tackle, techniques and fly patterns.

Well-known fly-fishing guide Rory Glennie with a small lingcod taken from Clayoquot Sound.

When coho appear off the beaches during late fall, fly fishers are there to meet them.

Dave Lornie watches as Jim Crawford releases a chinook, guesstimated at 23 lb (10.4 kg), which fell for a pale brown squid pattern.

Chapter 16

Fly Fishing Coastal Beaches & Estuaries

NEIL CAMERON

I HAD COME TO THE BEACH six days in a row. On this, the seventh morning, the calm waters lapped at my feet as I looked across the Strait of Georgia toward the Coast Mountain Range, about 30 mi (48 km) in the distance but only a reflection's breath away. The late summer breeze carried the sweet, pungent aroma of the rising tide, and a slight gust lazily flicked my tie over my shoulder. My gaze swept the waterfront, darting here and there at tantalizing rings on the surface before I realized they weren't made by fish but by diving waterfowl surfacing momentarily. I had started wondering if the coho would ever come at all, but I held onto the hope that with each passing day the chance of my being first on them was becoming more and more a reality.

But the beach and the fish seemed as reluctant as they had been on the previous days. I glanced at my watch, tossed down the cigarette and twisted it into the gravel with the toe of my dress shoe, then turned toward the Jeep. My fingers were already buttoning up my suit jacket as I took that first step, but they suddenly locked into place. Did I hear what I thought I heard? A second later came the confirmation. I smiled and turned around.

I saw two rings, then a third as a fish broke the water. Then a fourth and fifth. I spotted the backs of two others, porpoising leisurely near shore. There was increasing movement and signs as I watched. This is what I had invested my time in. This was the annual ritual—to be first on the first in.

I had been close before, perhaps a day, even only a tide away, but never had I been onto them when they first arrived, which these apparently had. Just. The losing hands of the previous six days had suddenly turned into a royal flush.

I wheeled and ran to the Jeep, hurriedly tearing off my jacket. I opened the driver's door and hastily flung the coat inside, then grabbed a small plastic Ziploc bag containing a couple of new flies and some tippet material and stuffed it into my shirt pocket. Hearing more splashes behind me, I ripped off my tie instead of undoing it, threw it inside, slammed the door shut and rounded quickly to the hatch. I thought I had misjudged the handle in my haste because my fingers slipped free as I yanked. I grabbed it again and pulled. It was locked.

In the chilling stillness that followed I vividly recall two things: my Sage SP 690, 9'6", 6-weight rod gleaming at me through the tinted back window, and the splashing sound of coho frolicking no more than 50' (15 m) away. I slowly approached the driver's door like a safe cracker, flexed my fingers, reached out, closed my eyes, and tried the handle. It was locked. So, of course, was the passenger door.

Splash-splash-splash. . . .

I kicked the front tire. I slammed my clenched fist on the hood. I kicked the tire. I cursed. I, well, kicked the tire. Then, unable to figure out some way to blame my wife, I became even more frustrated. I scrambled atop the low embankment between my Jeep and the beach for a better look. The entire goddamn bay seemed alive with coho! There were feisty jacks of up to 3 lb (1.4 kg), slender torpedoes between 5–8 lb (2.3–3.6 kg) and regal bucks of 9 lb (4.1 kg) and more. This was once-in-a-lifetime stuff. Being first on the first in is difficult to describe. Maybe like being a kid turned loose in a candy store. But this was bittersweet.

Splash-splash-splash. . . .

That's when I saw the rock. I picked it up and hefted it, noticing how good, how natural it felt in my hand. Smooth, round, solid, heavy . . . If I whopped the passenger window once I could be fishing within five minutes. I looked around and pulled it back. Then a brilliant idea came to me. Dr. Larry Reynolds is a fellow Rotarian. What's more, he is a fellow Rotarian who lived just down the beach. Even more importantly, he fly fishes. I could use his phone, then borrow his gear! I dropped the rock. It had barely touched the ground before I was ringing Larry's doorbell. Ten minutes later there was still no answer.

I started walking back toward the car to look for that rock but decided to take a chance on Larry's neighbor, whose house also fronts the beach. It turned out to be another fellow Rotarian, Roy Parker, the founder of Parker's Marine in Courtenay. I quickly explained that I had locked my keys in the Jeep along with my fly rod and waders. "Could I possibly use the phone?" I asked. He not only invited me in; he phoned the locksmith himself. His wife, Barb, put on some tea, then we sat at the table and chatted, while outside their window the coho leapt and laughed at me.

"Lots of them, it looks like," Roy said with the faintest hint of a smile.

"Yes, it does."

"They must be just fresh in," he added.

"I think they are."

"Looks like some really nice-sized ones."

"You got that right."

"And close to shore."

The locksmith had said he would be 20 to 30 minutes, so I finished my tea, thanked Roy and Barb for their great hospitality, and returned to the Jeep. When it started raining a few minutes later, Barb walked down the beach to invite me back to the house. I took her up on the offer, but while I could see my car from their dining room patio, I worried that the locksmith would miss the turnoff, so I went back out after 30 agonizing minutes.

An hour passed and the rock had magically leapt in and out of my hand a half dozen times. I began carrying it around, talking to it. "If I made the insurance claim," I reasoned aloud, "would having called the locksmith give me away?" The rock didn't answer. One thing about being publisher of the local newspaper is that it's tough when you have to put a friend's name in the court report, but it's even tougher when you have to put in your own. To make things worse, I had a meeting scheduled in another hour. The rock remained silent.

Splash-splash-splash. . . .

Just when I decided that I might be better off using the rock on myself, the locksmith pulled up. My Jeep is a 1998 model, so I figured it would be a quick, simple job with a Slim Jim. But the locksmith looked at the door, frowned, then thoughtfully pursed his lips and whistled. He studied the door from several different angles before finally slipping a Jim in to try opening it, but to no avail. He tried the driver's door. He tried the passenger door. He went through three different instruments. On each door.

Splash-splash-splash. . . .

"Well," he said, retrieving yet another wand from his truck, "if this one doesn't work I'm afraid we're out of luck."

Just when I thought I might use the rock on him, he succeeded. I handed him my Visa and had my waders on and my rod strung before he handed me back the receipt. My hands were shaking as I felt the tippet: 6-lb (2.7-kg) test; perhaps too light, but there was no time or patience to change. A couple of quick casts, and I could still make the meeting.

It was tempting to just wade in and have at it, but I've seen what that will do to near-shore salmon. Instead, I stripped out some line, and my first cast was made while standing 5' (1.5 m) back from the water. My fast, stripping retrieve kept the medium-sink Cortland 444 Clear Tip from bottoming out in the shallows. Not that I noticed, however, because my entire attention was wired to the V-shaped wake that had turned instantly and gatorlike, behind my fly.

It took all of my self-control to maintain the even pace of my strip. I have hurried it before, and I have slowed it down, and I have missed fish almost every time. The reason is simple: A fish is attracted to whatever strip I was doing to start with, so why change it? In this case, the strike came a second before the wake turned into a noisy swirl. My rod bucked up and down as I released slack line between thumb and forefinger. There was a satisfying *whap* when the coho's run slapped the line against my rod and the fight went to the reel.

About five minutes later a 7-lb (3-kg) buck with a Jimmy Durante nose and sides the color of polished pewter came begrudgingly to the beach. More through good luck than anything approaching skill, I had managed to check its runs and keep the fight away from where the other salmon seemed to be congregating. I quickly released the fish and watched it dart away toward deeper water. While running my fingertips lightly over the leader, I looked up and down the beach and smiled. Not so much smiling at the fish swirling and leaping within reach of even my rather modest free-throw, line-casting distance or even at the fact that I had them all to myself. No, with dress pants tucked into dress socks and a freshly ironed dress shirt stuffed haphazardly into my waders, tie and suit jacket back in the Jeep, I smiled at the meeting I was going to miss.

IN THE BEGINNING

About 11 years before this episode, I sat in my newspaper office in Campbell River, British Columbia, at 3:00 P.M., finishing off a 10-hour day that was wrapping up with the last page proofed and sent to the back room for final cutting. As one edition was being put to bed in the quiet confines of my office, the hustle and bustle in the outer offices was already preparing for the next edition. New deadlines, new problems, new news. Another day, another holler.

The phone rang and I muttered darkly while picking it up, wondering why the whole world had no idea I was on deadline. "They're jumpin' all over the place," an Irish accent growled, "right in front of the house. You better get down here." Even a silence of several seconds failed to clue me in. The voice continued, "Is this Neil?"

"Uh, yes it is," I said, unsure to whom I was talking.

"It's Bill. We talked in the Legion t'other day. You were asking . . ." His voice trailed off, then snapped back, "Oh, the lovely bastards are jumping all over! You asked me to call, so I did." Then he hung up.

It was as if the electricity had charged through the phone line. I banged the receiver down and bolted out of my office, right into the boss. "Hey, Neil, you got a minute?" he asked. "Just want to have a little meeting."

I figured I could be a steelhead and avoid the hook by charging right out the door. Or I could be a rainbow and suck the fly down slowly and wait for a chance of escape later. Instead, I became a wily old brown trout and impressed even my lying self. "Big accident," I said. "Reporters are all gone home. Gotta go!" Then I scooted quickly through the tailout and into the next run.

While driving south along the Island Highway toward Bill's home, I kept an eye on the Campbell River waterfront. I saw three fish move in the first half mile of that lovely, shallow stretch of ocean between the boat ramp and the Big Rock. Within half a minute I had covered the remaining half mile or so and saw a man standing up to his waist in the ocean. Fish could be seen moving around him, and I was sure he hooked one just before I dove into the trunk and started grabbing my gear.

I had fished near Bill before, so I positioned myself parallel to him, but slightly farther out, thereby receiving my first lesson in coho beach fishing. "If you step on their backs, they tend to not take so well," Bill said quietly, dropping his fly onto another swirl. I fished beside him, touching nothing, but intently watching his technique, picking up pointers. His quick, precise casts to moving fish, the pick-up of several feet of line from one direction to drop it in another. Both were important, I learned, but not as important as the strip-retrieve.

Bill's strip could best be described as jerk-and-pull. Imagine him holding a wool sock in one hand and plucking off bits of lint in quick, fluid pulls with the other. That's the first 6" (15 cm) of each strip. The last 6" or so is as if he casually throws that bit of lint off to the side. I mention this because I believe the strip is the most important thing in beach fishing, even ahead of the fly and its presentation.

Bill hit more than a few coho and a couple of cutthroat in that first hour, releasing them all. He had said little to me other than occasionally pointing out a fish to which I could cast. Which I did to no avail. The tide was changing, and even then I could sense that mysterious complacency nature uses to douse the most avid of feeding activities we call the bite.

Taking his cue, Bill reeled in his line. "Well, she's over. Would you care for a beer?" he asked and handed me a can of Lucky Lager. He had pulled it from the pouch inside the front of his waders, freely and easily because a fly vest didn't impede him. He wasn't wearing one, which was my second lesson in beach fishing.

Bill asked to see my fly, and I sheepishly showed him a fry pattern I had picked up in a local tackle shop. "Yes, that would work," he said, handing it back to me like it had lice. "Come and see my fish." The "would" part of his pronouncement was not lost on me as I followed him to shore. There, nestled in the shade and wrapped in grasses, was a 6-lb (2.7-kg) coho. That night it would find its way onto Bill's dinner table, but within a second of seeing its lovely flanks, dark and silver and regal, I knew an insatiable appetite had been whet for me as well.

We sat for a bit while Bill watched the last few fish of the tide show themselves. Then he handed me his rod and showed me the fly he was using. "It's a Michael Five or Micheil Coolig," he said. Then, winking at his Gaelic pronunciation, "Some people call it a Mickey Finn."

I had seen them before, of course, but had never seen one perform on the business end of a 9' (2.7-m) leader like I did that day. Bill explained that his friend, Jack, had tied the flies for him, and I felt honored when he handed me one. "So they really work, eh?" I asked.

"You betcha," Bill replied, smiling and patting the coho's side.

Near the end of the beer, I happened to ask, "What other flies do you use?"

Bill sort of cocked his head to one side, smiled that good-natured Irish smile of his and replied, "Oh, lots of them. Would you like to see?" With that he pulled a fly box from the hand-warmer pouch of his waders and handed it to me. I looked at the box, then at him questioningly. "Go ahead," he urged, "have a look at them—there's quite a few." I opened the box and when I looked up he was smiling even wider. There certainly were a lot of flies in his box, and they were all Mickey Finns.

SALT IN THE WOUND

I went directly to the tackle shop, bought a gazillion Mickey Finns, put them into a brand-new fly box and tucked it into one of my vest pockets. A habit I picked up early with beach fishing was to keep my rod, waders and so forth in the back of the Jeep at all times. This facilitated two things: First, from mid-June to mid-November, just about any beach or estuary bordering Queen Charlotte Strait, Johnstone Strait or the Strait of Georgia can come alive with pinks or coho at any time. My beat happens to be the east coast of Vancouver Island between Courtenay and Port Hardy. When I'm out and about it's simply a matter of stopping the vehicle and taking a quick stress leave. Secondly, it avoids having to tell the War Department that while I am loading waders and rods into my Jeep, it is only to take them in for "servicing," not for actual fishing.

After that day with Bill, work kept me from fishing for four or five days. When I finally got out, it was again south of Campbell River to the beach between Salmon Point and Oyster River. My friend and fishing partner, Dave Hadden, mentioned that Rory Glennie had been going there on a regular basis. That was good enough for me. I parked at the trail head right beside the Fishermen's Lodge pub, then hoofed it the quarter mile (402 m) or so down to the Oyster River mouth. I arrived to see a few fish moving but opted instead for Cutthroat Haven, an elusively nondescript spot on the beach about 1,500' (457 m) north of the mouth, where not only the cutthroat congregate at times, but also coho and pinks. I had seen Rory work that spot on several occasions, taking fish regularly while others on either side of him touched nary a thing. Of course, most of that was Rory's skill, but this spot also has a certain magic about it. And on that day, with no anglers within sight, it was so once again.

I could see fish moving in the distance while I hurried as best I could along the gravel beach. Sweating and panting, I strung up my rod, then tugged the zipper on the pocket with my boxful of Mickey Finns. It wouldn't budge. I yanked again and again while still looking out at the fish, before realizing something was amiss. Glancing down I saw the problem—the zipper was rusted shut. Closer inspection revealed that all of the zippers were rusted shut. A picture of Bill flashed through my mind. He was standing waist deep in the ocean, and he wasn't wearing a fly-fishing vest. I recalled how at the time I had thought it strange, even feeling a sort of smugness at how much better prepared I was than Bill for the day's outing. After all, my vest contained everything from an earthquake preparedness kit to three other fly reels, complete with line and backing—just in case. I also remembered that while fishing beside Bill that day, the fish rolling farther out had seduced me into deeper water while attempting to cover them. And how heavy my fly vest had become as the ocean water soaked into it.

None of the zippers would budge—and the fish were mocking me once again. There was nothing else for it. I took out my pocket knife and cut along the zipper, then withdrew the fly box and opened it. The Mickey Finns had all been arranged in neat rows, stuck into the ridges of white Styrofoam. I gasped at the orange halos encircling the shank of each hook. All. Every one. Oh, I salvaged some by scraping away the rust with my knife, and I even hit a few fish. However, confidence did not enhance my fishing, nor did thoughts of what havoc the orange death had wreaked on other gear inside my vest and, ultimately, onto an already spousally challenged fishing budget.

The lesson learned there should never be forgotten. Whenever fishing a beach you must always remember that you are in *salt water!* Yes, some very knowledgeable anglers recommend specially designed saltwater reels, and I suppose if you're going to do it on a regular basis that's fine. But not many local people fish the beach on a regular basis and, for sure, neither do visitors. So what are you supposed to do? Buy different gear just for beach fishing?

No. I believe you can use your regular freshwater tackle as long as you rinse it with fresh water when you are finished fishing. Not after a few beers and a couple of hours of trying to out-lie your partner, not the next day and certainly not any later than that. I won't bore you with the sordid details of how my three spare reels fared from their neglect in my fly vest. Suffice it to say they were not a pretty sight.

One of my favorite post-fishing haunts is the pub at Fishermen's Lodge, which is located right on the northern bank of the Oyster River, midway between Courtenay and Campbell River. If I decide to stop in after fishing and know I'll have a couple, I put my reel in my pocket and rinse it out in the washroom. If I'm going to have more than a couple, which isn't exactly eclipselike seldom, I'll walk the few feet from the pub parking lot and dunk my entire ensemble into the Oyster's fresh water. That keeps things reasonable until I can get a hose and really give it a good going over. With such frequent flushing, the reel gets re-oiled often throughout the season.

I have used two reels for beach fishing, and both are still in fine working order. My first and favorite is a British-made Leeda LC 80 I've had for eight years, the other a Hardy Ultralite No. 6 I've had for three. I think most readers will appreciate the prices involved. Although those who know me consider me totally magnanimous and generous to a fault, I simply will not take a chance on wasting that kind of money by not properly maintaining these pieces of expensive equipment. This is not to imply that the saltwater fly fishing tackle available now isn't any good, and it's no indication that I'm becoming frugal or parsimonious. It's just that, well, like I said, my fishing budget is spousally challenged.

THE FLY'S THE THING

When I arrived at the beach, a gentle southeast wind rolled lazily toward shore. Barking little waves popped up and tugged shoreward as if straining at an imaginary leash. A fine, mistlike rain joined the frolic, bringing the sea's hard freshness to nostrils and skin. It was the kind of day when most beach anglers stay home. Terrible, I thought, how many good fishing experiences bad weather has crushed in their infancy. However, this wasn't really bad, merely threatening. Every fall it's the same. Mild summer weather brings fish and anglers to the beaches. Then the first small blow hits. Most of the fish become dour and their numbers dwindle weekly, then daily as they sniff the fall freshets and slip into nearby streams to have sex and die. But any good beach angler knows fresh fish can, and usually do, show up throughout the autumn. As does Art Limber.

On that late October day, I had trudged about 1,500' (457 m) along the beach, pausing now and then to be fooled by this small, errant whitecap and that small, errant whitecap. I had even seen one or two coho but nothing worth spending time over because they were well out of casting range. While continuing on, I noticed in the distance the figure of the only other angler on the beach. As I got closer, I wondered if I was seeing things or not. Not only were fish showing near him, he was backing slowly toward shore with his rod bent double.

I cozied on up to him and recognized Art immediately. "Hi there," I called out as I started wading in. He glanced quickly at me, then continued fishing without saying a word. "How's the fishing?" I asked.

"Shitty!" he snapped.

"Looks like there's a few around," I played along.

"A few . . . not many." His abruptness started to bother me, but I pressed on. "Looks like a fresh little run."

"Naw, same old fish. Ain't takin' nothin'. I'm about ready to leave." Just then a fish jumped, obviously bright and obviously fresh. Normally, Art would be after it like a rattlesnake, picking up whatever line he had out from one direction and laying it on that fish's nose before it hit the water again. But he didn't—and I knew he had seen the fish.

"Mind if I cover that one, Art?" I asked.

His head whipped around and he peered at me. "Who the hell is that?" he demanded. "My glasses have rain on 'em and I can't see that well."

"It's Neil, Art," I said. "I was just—"

"Jesus Christ, Neil, get in here!" he was suddenly plowing toward me in a slow-motion gallop. "It's a fresh run and they're really taking." Art reached me just after his bow wave did. He pulled out a fly box and said, "Here, take these. They're Candy Flies. Just tied 'em up." With that he was gone again, heading back to his spot, casting at fish as he went.

I glanced at the Candies. They were small, almost jewel-like creations of pink and green, glittering from within what appeared to be a clear, glasslike coat. I tucked the Candies in my pocket and spent 15 minutes fishing with my Mickey Finn. Art played and released another two fish during that time and had a handful of follows. Not being the dullest hook in the fly box, I finally tied on a green Candy Fly and cast. Four, five, six strips and a fish hit. It was a good coho (although I've yet to see a bad one), and it took me on a trip. Within seconds, however, the line came back slack. I inspected the tippet and noticed the pigtailed end just as Art did, he having sidled up beside me. "Those flies take a long time to make," he said. "I ain't giving you any more if you don't learn to tie a proper knot."

Now Art has made his mark on the fishing scene with his line of beautifully crafted polar bear hair streamers that are used to troll for salmon. But being an avid beach angler, he had started dabbling with some mysterious synthetic materials and various types of epoxy, and eventually came up with the Candy Fly. I relate this to you because I learned two things that day: that Art's flies worked like hot damn and that it's important know how to tie a proper knot.

I really do forget the number of fish I hit that day, but one thing I did know was that I was hooked on Candy. The Candy Fly became my weapon of choice for several years, and it is still a major part of my arsenal. Like renowned fly tier, fisherman, friend and fishing historian Art Lingren once told me, if he had to fish with only one fly it would be the black General Practitioner. This is the way it is with me, the beach and my sweet tooth.

FIVE-FINGERED DISCOUNT

When I was the editor of *BC Outdoors* and *BC Sport Fishing* magazines, I worked in downtown Vancouver but maintained my home in Campbell River. I went to the city for three or four days, then came home for a week to do most of my editing. One of the biggest treats, of course, was heading home. Not because I wanted to get out of the city so badly, and not because I missed my girls so much, but simply because I usually stopped off in Courtenay at Bob and Vera Jones' house.

Bob was the fishing editor and columnist for *BC Outdoors,* and a veritable wealth of information on anything to do with fishing. He's also a very nice man who didn't seem to mind this young information sponge stopping off with a litany of questions. He had two other things that I greatly admired: a beer fridge to die for and scads and scads of flies scattered all over the workshop adjoining his basement office. But of all the times I stopped in, one in particular stands out.

I had just arrived and a beer appeared in my hand as if by magic. Then Bob said he was busy looking for something that had gone astray. As he puttered around his workshop, cussing and muttering under his breath, I sort of poked around his fly-tying bench. Suddenly, it was love at first sight! There, perched daintily in a small block of Styrofoam, were two dozen miniature Clouser Minnows tied on No. 8 hooks. I had certainly seen Clousers before but never dressed so scantily and looking so perky. They were dainty and really quite alluring, but what really caught my eye were the four strands of copper-colored Flashabou nestled atop the chartreuse and white negligee of polar bear hair that was their main dressing.

As I reached out to touch one, Bob growled, "They're counted Cameron!"

I whirled around, indignant that my motives could be misconstrued as anything but those of an ardent admirer. I told him that, too. Right there and without shame. I informed him that my pride, nay, my very heart, was mortally wounded. I questioned what type of friendship we really had if his level of trust was so . . . so shallow. Then, I thought, maybe I had been too harsh. Perhaps my words had wounded him as deeply as his had wounded me. He still hadn't spoken.

Bob gazed at me much as a father would his son, and I sincerely believed I had touched his soul. Then his eyes narrowed and he said in a flat, emotionless voice, "Listen, Magnet Fingers, there were 24 when you arrived, and there had better be 24 when you leave."

That could have ended our beautiful relationship, but I rose above it. I had always repented on past occasions, when other recently tied flies had disappeared simultaneously with my departure. So I placed my right hand over my heart and took a solemn oath of allegiance—to Bob, to his flies and to my respect for him. I humbled myself, subjecting the very honor of the Cameron name to horrid and insidious retrospection.

"Neil," he said paternally, "you're so full of it your eyes are brown." And with that he turned back to his search.

Now all of this time I had been watching the march of time on the clock, rushing forth as it does when an ideal tide is threatened by encroaching darkness. I weighed that against my friendship for the man. I weighed it against my somewhat studentlike hope that I could make him proud. That I would, for ever after, adhere to the very principles of rightness and goodness that he constantly and quietly lived by. So, when the crotchety old bastard turned away from me, I slipped 12 flies into my pocket, quickly said my goodbye and was fishing the beach within 30 minutes.

If those flies looked good on the shelf, they looked deadly in the water. While the Candy Fly and other patterns resemble tiny salmon fry, Bob's concoction looked very much like a sandlance, locally known as the needlefish, a slender baitfish whose importance to the salmon's diet has only been realized in recent years by fly fishers. They worked like a charm on coho and cutthroat alike, and I dare say a huge swirl and a broad head-and-tail turn off Willow Point during the fall of 2000 looked very much like I had just missed a chinook.

The trickiest part of this fly was how to get more. By now Bob would have realized those dozen had somehow walked off on their own. Fearing a fate worse than death, I picked up the phone. "Hi, Robert," I said jovially. "It's your beloved editor. Have I ever told you how much I like your writing?"

"So—what do you really want?"

"No, really—I've never really told you how much I appreciate your work and how much I consider you a dear, dear friend."

"Spit it out, Hoover Hands. What do you want?"

"Well, now that you mention it, I was wondering—" and here I held my breath, "if you might have any more of those Cameron's Copper Clousers."

If silence can be deafening, the roar at the end of the line was a sonic boom. Then came his reply: "'Cameron's Copper Clousers?' First you steal them, and now you're naming them after yourself?"

"Well, no . . . I mean, um . . . well, I didn't know what to call it."

"The 'stolen goods' might be a start."

"But Bob . . ."

"Never mind the crap. Did they work?"

"Hell, yes. The other day I—"

"That's good enough. Drop by and pick up some more, but don't forget to come bearing single malt."

INTO THE FRY PAN

Although it says somewhere that one should never a borrower or lender be, I can't help it. I'm a fly fisherman who doesn't tie flies. In that regard I am most fortunate to know Van Egan of Campbell River. Van is a traditionalist tier and his patterns are as effective as they are exquisite. Mostly, I arrive at Van's on bended knee, begging for General Practitioners, his Secret River Specials and, come to think of it, most of my other river and lake require-ments. It was only recently that I began using his Fry Fly imitation, which he tied for Art Lingren's book *Fly Patterns of British Columbia.*

Van varied the Fry Fly for my use, knowing that I was heading to the beach area and estuary of the Campbell River. He changed the pale blue at the throat to a light pink. This, he said, would imitate the alevin's yolk sac just before it is completely absorbed into the tiny salmonid's body. The effectiveness of this pattern was astonishing, even though I used it in the brackish water of the Campbell River's estuary, and even though I used it pre-dominantly for the annual late-winter cutthroat fishing there. But I think the key to all of this is that late-winter cutthroat fishing is very much like beach coho fishing in that you cast to a fish when it shows, then quickly strip/retrieve the fly.

Dave Osberg and I were on the Campbell's estuary one cold April morn-ing as the tide came in. Dave was killing time before starting work at the River Sportsman outdoor store in Campbell River, and before long he would be heading off for the summer to guide saltwater anglers in the Queen Charlottes. We were fishing cutthroat trout, but there was something strange about the way the fish were acting. Dave cast to a circle, and it disintegrated into white froth as a fair-sized fish thrashed about on the surface. When he finally worked it in, it proved to be a young coho about 16" (41 cm) long and in very good condition. What a coho that size was doing away the heck up in fresh water in April was a real puzzle. As we continued fishing, Van's Fry Fly took another coho almost the same size as the first, and another two or three got off, but we could tell they were coho by the way they fought. When Dave landed another about the same size, he proclaimed that he was winning on fish counts.

"No," I replied. "We're fishing for cutties—cohos don't count."

Later, still pondering why we had encountered those coho where we did, I posed the question via e-mail to Craig Wightman, the senior steelhead biol-ogist on Vancouver Island. Craig responded, "Good question. . . . They may be holdover smolts (i.e. two-year-olds or even three-year-olds that were trapped in headwater areas for some reason or another). They may also be hatchery fish (still holdovers, perhaps) that experienced accelerated growth before release (so-called super smolts). If you catch more, some scale samples would be very instructive."

OFF TO SEE THE WIZARD

Our accidental meeting in the tackle shop parking lot was hurried and short. Art Limber emerged from his truck at the same time I got out of my Jeep. Usually, we only see each other on the beach every late summer and fall, so this early summer meeting was unexpected. As we said our hellos, Art's eye's twinkled like he was bursting to tell me something. After quick pleasantries, he said, "Got a new fly for the beach. I call it the Wizard."

He handed me one. To be honest, it looked too thick for a beach fly. It had an epoxy head, but that was about the only thing beachy-looking about it. I wondered if Art called it the Wizard because the dressing flumed out from the head like Merlin's gown. Then I noticed its red throat. It was more a protuberance than part of the dressing. I wondered if it would simulate what a fish might see if a small baitfish flared its gill plates.

"Here," said Art, dropping more flies into my hand. "I only did two variations, so take a couple of purple and a couple of olive." We chatted for a few more minutes; then he was off. But before leaving he said, "They're darn good flies, Neil, but nothing's as good as a pink Candy as far as I'm concerned."

I didn't see Art again until early fall. There were a few other anglers on the beach that day, but Art had found a nice little school of coho to himself, so we fished and chatted for a half hour or so. I told him that I had been fishing almost exclusively with his Wizards, and one day, while beach fishing with Dale Brin, publisher of the *Kamloops Daily News,* and Bill Laurin from the *Victoria Times-Colonist,* I hooked into my largest coho of the season on an olive Wizard, a 12-pounder (5.4 kg).

Art waded over and pulled out the fly box. "This is the new Wizard," he said. "I've only got a few and I haven't fished one yet, but I think it'll work."

It was white but with the distinctive red throat like the original Wizards. He handed me one and we went back fishing. As he waded back to his spot, I thought about what he had said: "Haven't fished one yet. . . ." I tied on the new Wizard and started casting. I've never cared much about records in angling, but at that moment I desperately wanted to be the first to catch a fish on the new Wizard, especially since the guy beside me was the one who invented it. My fishing became even more fervent then, right in front of Art,

I had two huge follows. This was strange because the fish had seemed rather dour up until that point. Art asked what fly I was using and I answered, "Snow White."

"Snow White?" His brow furrowed in puzzlement. "What the hell kind of fly is that?"

"The new Wizard you gave me. I've just named it."

Art chuckled and we continued fishing. Then it happened: Almost as if a dream had come true, a fish swirled 30' (9 m) out and we both covered it. Even before I felt the tug, Art knew I had it. "That's a nice fish," he said, and in an instant my fly-line-to-backing connection rattled through my rod guides and streaked out toward the ocean like a miniature cable car without brakes. When the salmon's run stopped, its violent head shakes telegraphed up the taut line, jarring my arm. Then it rocketed toward me, and I cranked furiously on my reel while stumbling backward, trying to regain slack line. Suddenly, it turned sharply and headed out again. My line went sickeningly slack.

I was stunned. I was using an 8-lb (3.6-kg) test tippet, and even though it was a good fish, we had parted on rather queer terms. One second it was running with my line going out smoothly behind it, and the next, everything went dead. I reeled in quickly, holding my rod to the side, blocking Art's view of my leader. Sure enough, there was another pigtail. I couldn't bear to tell Art, so I tried an evasive tactic. "Well, I guess I go down in history as the first one to catch a coho on the white Wizard." Another fish swirled and Art cast to it. "There it is," said Art, and he was fast into a good coho. Then, as an afterthought, he said, "But you didn't land it, so it doesn't count. And besides," he paused to let his fish run, "you still can't tie knots worth a fiddler's fart."

BORNE BY AIR TO FAR-OFF PLACES

While the entire east coast of Vancouver Island is a great place for beach fishing, it is also a jumping-off point for many remote inlets cutting deeply into the mainland. Most have several rivers and creeks draining into them, and each estuary offers great potential for cutthroat and Dolly Varden that are, on average, bigger and more abundant than those found in more accessible areas. The key word here is *remote*—and reaching these angling Shangri-las requires long trips with seaworthy boats or, better yet, helicopters. Dolphins Resort in Campbell River offers some great helicopter trips from late February into April, then again in the fall. Early fall is my favorite peri-od because in addition to cutts and Dollies, the estuaries offer outstanding opportunities for coho, pink and chum salmon.

Several resorts now offer helicopter trips with guided fishing as an option. While it may be a bit too expensive for some people's bank accounts, the experience of fishing remote waters that seldom see other anglers is price-less.

GEAR, TACKLE & TECHNIQUE

Fly fishing the beaches of British Columbia is one of the most exciting and rewarding forms of angling there is. It can also be one of the most troubling and exasperating. To help you avoid some of the frustrations and pitfalls, fol-lowing are a few pieces of advice I have picked up over the years. Most have been gleaned from much better anglers,; others are based on trial and error.

Waders

Remember that the water is cold. While breathables might get you to and along the beach more comfortably, they'll also freeze your knees off. I prefer neoprene waders with the attached boot foot to keep me warm. They're also easy to slip into and out of—an added benefit if you're driving beside water and an opportunity to fish comes along. Besides, I'm not too sure how good salt water is for a pair of expensive wading boots.

Fly Vest

I don't wear one while beach fishing. If I have anything to carry, I use a back pack and leave it on the beach—above the tide line—while wading. About all you require for beach fishing are a couple of spools of tippet material, clip-pers, pliers and a box of flies. All can be accommodated in your wader pouch. If I plan to keep a fish, providing the regulations allow it, I carry with me a cooler with ice in it. I believe in care of the catch and can't believe the anglers who kill a fish, then leave it on the beach under some rocks while they con-tinue fishing for a couple of hours.

I clean my fish right away and get it on ice. If you don't have a cooler, clean your fish and wrap it in cloth dipped in ocean water. If you keep fishing for a while, repeat the process to keep the meat as cool and as firm as possible.

Fly Line

I don't know of many who use anything other than an intermediate-sink line. A floating line leaves a telltale wake on the surface as you retrieve, a fast-sink line will frequently hook you up on bottom and sink-tips are not much fun to cast. I use the Cortland 444 Clear Tip but have cut it back so there is only 12–15' (4–4.6 m) of the clear portion. This line's medium sinking action will get my fly below the surface but not too far. It will also accommodate those who like to let their fly sink before stripping, especially when fish aren't taking well at the surface.

Leader

The subject of leaders is open to interpretation. I know one guy who simply ties on 6–8' (1.8–2.4 m) of straight 8–10-lb (3.6–4.5-kg) test. Others stick with a basic 9' (2.7-m) tapered leader down to 6-, 8- or 10-lb (2.7-, 3.6- or 4.5-kg) test. All get good results. I usually prefer a tapered leader of up to 18' (5.5 m) long, which I tie myself with a tippet of 6–8-lb (2.7–3.6-kg) test. I'm not that great at casting, so this increased length allows for flubbed presentations that might otherwise put fish down with a shorter leader. The one drawback with building my own leaders is that when there's a lot of kelp and seaweed in the water, the knots will catch them no matter how closely they are trimmed.

Casting

One of the keys to successful beach fishing is casting to jumping fish. The quicker you get your fly over that ring, the better. With the longer leader I like to drop my fly either right in the ring or just beyond it. All the while, however, I'm conscious about not letting the thicker, butt portion of my leader land too close, because this often puts the fish down. I believe it is so important to get my fly to a moving fish that I'll pick up about 30–40' (9–12 m) of line from one direction, then cast it in another to cover a fish that has just jumped. There is no telling how many hundreds of fish from whose mouth I've pulled my fly while doing this, but such is the excitement of the moment.

CASTING FOR COHO

Beach fishing for coho is like hunting. You get there, you scout the shoreline, you find the fish, then you sneak up on them. For this, a good set of binoculars will help, especially those with polarized lenses that cut the surface glare and help you see fish jumping several hundred yards away. If there aren't any fish jumping in front of you, start walking along the beach. The schools usually move parallel to the shoreline, stopping here and there for whatever reason. Some anglers like to pick a spot and cast to coho as they swim by. I prefer the chase, and as a result I get lots of exercise during the course of a day. Believe me, I wouldn't be trudging up and down the beach in waders on a hot day if it didn't work.

Sometimes you'll find a school of pinks or coho that is just beyond casting range. You may try wading farther out, and occasionally you might even be able to cover them. In most instances, however, the fish are out that far because you and the other anglers are, too. Knowledgeable beach anglers will take charge and inform everyone to move back toward shore, so the fish will move back in. If someone refuses to retreat to shallower water, loudly threaten that several of you intend to bring out some spinning gear and make him the target of a few well-placed casts with large Buzz Bombs.

The Retrieve

Successful beach fly fishing depends on a retrieve that has a good pace to it. Leave your stripping basket at home. It won't allow you the "full pull" of a good retrieve. Just let your line fall in the water. With the exception of high and low slack periods, the tide is usually running one way or another, and it will straighten out in that direction while you retrieve. The line trailing in the water will create resistance for your next cast. But if you give the trailing line a yank between false casts, just like a dog that won't heel, you'll set the line on the water's surface just long enough so that your cast will go out unimpeded.

Sometimes, when fish are moving well on the surface but not taking, try letting let your fly sink. It's almost like chironomid fishing and can be exciting. However, remember that you are in shallow water, so don't let the fly sink for too long.

The Take

There is nothing more exciting in fishing than seeing a V-shaped wake behind your fly as you retrieve (with the possible exception of it being created by a killer whale). Your first instinct will be to stop retrieving. Don't do this. Believe me, I know. The second thing you might be tempted to do is speed up your retrieve, either consciously or because of the adrenaline rush. Don't do this, either. This is the voice of frustrated and disappointed experience speaking to you. The best thing to do is exactly what you were doing when the fish first appeared. And do it right up to your feet. That's right— some coho will follow that fly right to your feet. Simply move your rod to the side, even point it behind you if you have to, while continuing the strip. If you're lucky, you will not only see the fish, you will see that broad white flash of lighting that is a coho in shallow water taking your fly back to the depths. Do not, repeat, do not move your feet or legs. You will tend to turn sideways and move your feet while retrieving, but twist from the waist up only or kiss your fish good-bye.

A PASSION FOR PINKS

Before the coho show up on local beaches, chances are the pinks (also called humpback salmon) will be in. The fighting quality of these smallest members of the Pacific salmon family was overlooked in the past, mostly because they were caught on gear designed for larger fish like chinook and coho salmon. However, fly fishers have since discovered that with 5- or 6-weight fly tackle, pinks will give you all you can handle and more.

These small salmon are chrome bright when they first appear off the beaches, during which period they are excellent eating when properly cared for. If low water levels prevent them from entering the rivers, the males darken somewhat and start forming the noticeable hump for which the species is nicknamed, and the females develop irregular, olive green vertical markings on their sides. In this advanced stage of maturity, their eating qualities deteriorate, so it's best to release them.

The primary difference between fishing for pinks and fishing for other salmon and coho is that the strip/retrieve is much slower. The fly is usually fairly small and varies from pale to hot pink, but I've seen anglers do remarkably well with patterns incorporating pale green and blue. Generally, the most dependable fly is Rory Glennie's Pink 'n' Silver, which is tied on a No. 8 gold hook.

I still use a medium sink-tip but shorten my leader to 4–8' (1.2–2.4 m)— usually just a length of 6-lb (2.7-kg) nylon monofilament. I still sight cast but not as urgently, and I usually let my fly sink for a count of eight to ten, then start stripping in with slow, long pulls.

When schooling off the beaches, pinks and coho can be differentiated by the pink's almost sideways jump from the water. The coho will be more varied in size, from 3–10 lb (1.4–4.5 kg) and over. Pinks will invariably be 5–6 lb (2.3–2.7 kg).

FLOAT TUBES

I would be remiss if I didn't mention how float tubes and pontoon boats have affected (some would say interfered with) beach fishing. Sometimes, when fish are holding just out of reach, they do so for frustratingly long periods. I admit to having lusted after something that could give me even another 10' (3 m). I have seen float tubes and pontoon boats used effectively in these instances, but, unless the operator uses common sense and courtesy, they can interfere with the fish and other anglers. These flotation devices also can be life threatening. I saw one character of questionable intelligence tie off his float tube to a piece of kelp about 30' (9 m) from shore during low slack tide. Now tides along this stretch of beach near Campbell River reach speeds of 7–12 knots, and as the incoming tide started building it pushed against the float tube, which pulled against the kelp, which was solidly anchored. I was close enough to see the look of abject fear on the angler's ashen face as he struggled to loosen the knot, and had he not succeeded there was nothing I could have done but call the Coast Guard to recover his body.

If you decide to use a tube or pontoon boat, fine, but understand two things: the water and the fish. In very short order you can get caught in a tide that will sweep you away. Too, your presence on top of schooling fish near the beach will ruin the experience for everyone else. Consider that one of a salmon's greatest fears is being attacked by a seal. With your flippered feet and neoprene-covered legs thrashing around in the vicinity, how long do you think they will hang around?

So how can you tell if you're too close to a school of salmon and in danger of dispersing them? By the Buzz Bombs, of course, that other anglers start whizzing by your ears.

And now, dear reader, please excuse me while I go back to my knot-tying practice.

Noted conservationist Father Charles Brand enjoys fly fishing for pink salmon off the Oyster River estuary.

Ralph Shaw leads a pink salmon to hand at Royston, near Courtenay.

Rory Glennie has his hands full with a scrappy pink salmon.

Chapter 17

Inshore Fly Fishing from Boats

ROBERT H. JONES

THOSE UNFAMILIAR with open ocean fly fishing might think it is relatively new, but anglers have been out there casting flies for several decades. True, not many, but I recall seeing occasional fly fishers south of Campbell River in the late 1950s, offshore from the Black Creek and Oyster River estuaries. I didn't see these obviously demented anglers very often and never observed them catch anything, but they were out there trying.

For the most part, when beach fly fishers started venturing offshore in small boats, they concentrated their efforts around the same shallow estuaries where they had waded while casting to sea-run cutthroat and Dolly Varden, occasional steelhead, plus—depending on timing and location—coho, chinook, chum, pink and sockeye salmon. What probably prompted them to take to boats was the maddening habit these fish have of staying at precisely one's maximum, hernia-inducing casting range, plus 15' (4.6 m). Eventually, some of those pioneers started traveling farther offshore, which should have tipped off the rest of us that they were having some degree of success. Nevertheless, their numbers remained relatively low, and, for the most part, they stayed extremely close-mouthed about their activities. They had learned very quickly that despite having the entire Pacific Ocean at their disposal, locations suitable for inshore fly fishing were relatively scarce and often fairly small in area.

Those pioneer anglers also discovered that water depths of much beyond 30' (9 m) were difficult to fish efficiently with the type of fly-casting tackle available in those days, especially when strong tidal currents, brisk winds and wave action were factored into the equation. Over time they located shallow areas with islands, reefs, shoals, kelp beds, channels, bays and estuaries—combinations of submerged structure and water depths that attract schools of small baitfish and the larger species that feed on them.

As much of the British Columbia population base is clustered in the Lower Mainland, most beach and inshore fly-fishing action was originally concentrated around the Vancouver–Howe Sound area and northwest along the Sunshine Coast. Southern Vancouver Island has the next largest population density, and there fly fishers probed the waters from around the Sidney area, southwest past Victoria to Sooke and on the central eastern coast between Nanaimo and Campbell River. In all cases, fishing was restricted to fairly small, very specific locations, usually adjacent to estuaries.

There was some increased interest in saltwater fly fishing around Campbell River during the 1980s, when April Point Lodge on Quadra Island started promoting it. While their guests often did quite well, especially around Wilby Shoal at the southern end of Quadra Island, the interest remained fairly localized. The big boost came in 1995 with the publication of two books written by British Columbians: *Salmon to a Fly* by Jim Crawford (Frank Amato Publishing) and *Saltwater Fly Fishing* by Barry Thornton (Hancock House). During that same year, Dick Close and Holly Baker, owners of Weigh West Marine Resort in Tofino, were having a 17' (5.2-m) fiberglass boat designed and constructed specifically for fly fishing in Clayoquot Sound. After testing and finetuning the prototype, three "Flyfisher" models were added to their charter fleet in 1996, and more have been added since. I mention this because by 1997, thanks to a few magazine and newspaper articles and lots of word-of-mouth advertising (always the best kind) Tofino had become the uncontested center of attraction for saltwater fly fishing on the coast of British Columbia.

ON THE TOPIC OF BOATS

This is directed at you who plan on taking your own boat on a saltwater fly fishing vacation to British Columbia, and more specifically, to you who are experienced sailors but not on saltwater. It's not uncommon to see solo fly fishers operating from 12' (4-m) cartoppers or two of them casting from 14-footers (4.3 m). While both lengths are suitable when weather conditions are reasonable, the general consensus is that a boat of 16' (4.9 m) or longer is a far better and safer choice.

Get your boat, motor and trailer serviced before making your trip. Then make a shakedown trip in your home waters to ensure that everything is working properly.

FOUR MUST-HAVE ITEMS TO MAKE LIFE SAFER

Fog is a fact of life on the West Coast, especially during the summer months. Combine fog with clusters of islands and unmarked channels, and getting lost can become a reality for those who are unprepared. Ensuring your boat has the following equipment on board might save you the embarrassment of getting confused or turned around (guys never get lost) and could even save your life.

1. Marine charts: Study a current marine chart before going on the water to familiarize yourself with the area you intend to fish. In addition to orienting yourself with the overall area, it will help you locate the edges of shoals, pinnacles, pockets and drop-offs that are attractive to fish.

2. Compass: Even a small hand-held model is better than nothing. Used in conjunction with the marine chart, it will help you plot your course to and from the fishing grounds.

3. Global Positioning System (GPS): This can be programmed beforehand by using marine chart coordinates and then used on the water to locate—and relocate—potential or known hot spots. Of far more importance, if fog suddenly rolls in, you will have the one device that can lead you back to the dock or launch site with relative ease. In many ways a GPS is superior to a compass—but only if the batteries are good. A small, handheld GPS will provide all the information you need to move around.

4. Voice communication: Cell phones are now quite popular, but if you're depending on one, make sure you are in an area where it will work. While a CB radio might be fine elsewhere, it is not recommended for marine use, meaning a VHF radio is really your best all-round choice.

Also of importance, albeit more to improve your fishing prospects than as safety equipment, are the following items:

1. Depth sounder: This extremely important device will reveal what is beneath your boat: bottom contours, schools of baitfish, even individual fish (it won't make them bite, though).

2. Tide guide book: This must be a current issue and for the area you intend to fish. Use it well ahead of time to determine the peak high and low slack tides. Then plan to be out there and in position in time to take advantage of these prime periods.

You don't require a big, expensive depth sounder with all the bells and whistles. I have friends who get by quite nicely with ancient flasher units, but small, very basic sounders with a Liquid Crystal Display screen are economical and serve the purpose quite well. But, hey, if you can afford the big, fancy outfits, by all means get them. Just remember, having all of these items at your disposal is of no value unless you know how to use them. If you don't know how to read a marine chart, use a compass, decipher a tide guide or program a GPS, get someone who does to check you out. Preferably before you leave shore.

WHERE TO GO & WHY

Of the hundreds of sounds and inlets along coastal British Columbia, four on the west coast of Vancouver Island are easily accessible by road and the fifth, Kyuquot Sound, requires a boat trip of about 15 mi (24 km) from road's end at Fair Harbour via Zeballos. All offer excellent potential for inshore fly fishing. On the eastern coast of the Island, the lower Strait of Georgia is dotted with small islands and shallow estuary regions. The northern east coast of the Island is on a major salmon migration route, and plenty of the open and protected waters throughout Queen Charlotte Strait and Blackfish Sound are worth investigating.

Clayoquot Sound

Clayoquot Sound contains examples of virtually every situation fly fishers will encounter elsewhere along the coastline. Located on Vancouver Island's central west coast, it is road accessible and the outside waters have long been popular for salmon and halibut fishing. It is the protected waters inside the sound that now attract legions of fly fishers, but as it covers an area of approximately 480 sq mi (1,243 sq km) there is little danger of overcrowding. The fishing headquarters is Tofino, located at the end of Highway 4 on the tip of Esowista Peninsula. Although there are several resorts in the area, most of the fly-fishing action continues to occur out of Weigh West Marine Resort, which caters to anglers. Their charter office has a selection of proven fly patterns on hand, and the adjoining restaurant and marine pub are great places to swap yarns and gather information about where and when the action is occurring.

Clayoquot Sound contains three large islands—Flores, Vargas and Meares—plus hundreds of smaller islands, islets, exposed rocks and shoals. Much of the water throughout the sound averages less than 30' (9 m) deep, and the outer islands act as buffers against offshore winds and high swells rolling in from the open Pacific.

To these near ideal conditions add an abundance of fish, for this is a year-round feeding ground for juvenile chinook and coho salmon and a major feeding area for various stocks of mature salmon on their southward spawning migrations. In addition, several rivers and large creeks draining into Clayoquot Sound are spawning destinations for runs of chinook, coho, sockeye and chum salmon, and virtually all the estuaries have healthy, year-round populations of sea-run cutthroat trout.

Migratory chinook first appear on their southward odyssey around mid-April, but being 3–5 mi (5–8 km) offshore and up to 200' (61 m) deep, they are of no interest to fly fishers. When migratory coho arrive between late May and early June, the inshore fishery quickly heats up. They are a mix of immature local fish averaging 2–3 lb (.9–1.4 kg) and more mature migratory examples of 6–8 lb (2.7–3.6 kg). By feeding voraciously they quickly gain weight, and when the migratory coho continue southward in early July, some might weigh up to 12 lb (5.4 kg). The smaller coho remaining now average 3–6 lb (1.4–2.7 kg) and will continue to be joined by later runs of coho as the season progresses. By late September, it is possible to catch coho of 15–20 plus lb (6.8–9 kg).

Chinook to 50-plus lb (22.7 kg) are available until early September, then they either move into their home streams or continue on their southward migration. The best period for sockeye is throughout July and early August. Late-running coho and chum salmon are possible until well into November—assuming that heavy rains and foul weather don't keep you ashore. If there is, in fact, an overlooked fishery, it is this late run of chum salmon, not only in Clayoquot Sound but wherever they are available. Pound for pound, these are probably the toughest of the five salmon species, and their strong, bulldogging antics when hooked will test the fishing skills of any angler, plus the quality and strength of tackle.

Other Places

There are plenty of other areas to consider. Some already have established fly fisheries to some degree; others are waiting to be discovered. Generally speaking, most of the easily accessible places with fair to good fishing prospects are already well known and well used by anglers using standard saltwater fishing tactics. What the fly fisher must do is determine whether there are shallow areas the trollers and moochers might avoid but where salmon go to feed. True, we pay the same amount for our licenses and have all the same rights to fish these hot spots, but I suggest this approach for the simple reason that we can fish these shallow areas quite readily, thereby avoiding congestion, confrontation and tangled lines. Don't worry about being lonesome, though, because you will likely be joined by a few drift jiggers—but there is usually plenty of room.

To those with the time and money, consider visiting remote central and northern coastal areas where few anglers go to fish. Places that come to mind include Kyuquot Sound, the tangle of channels between Ocean Falls and Milbanke Sound on the Central Coast and various places around the Queen Charlotte Islands. I had the opportunity to accompany three very accomplished saltwater fly fishermen to Langara Island in July 2001. Martin Paish, Tim Tullis, Jim Brown and I made the 90-minute flight from Vancouver to Sandspit, on the southern end of Moresby Island, then the final 40-minute leg over Graham Island to the southern end of Langara Island in a Turbo Otter floatplane. Our destination was the MV *Marabell,* a Second World War minesweeper that has been converted into a comfortable floating resort.

We went to determine whether or not Martin, Northern Operations Manager for the Oak Bay Marine Group, should promote the saltwater fly-fishing potential of Langara Island and to offer our collective advice on setting up such an operation. The first part took all of an hour or so, surrounded as we were by large numbers of brawny coho and some of the heftiest pink salmon we had ever seen. There were also scads of chinook around, but they were scattered and too deep to be considered serious contenders as fly-fishing targets. Nevertheless, the opportunity is there.

What proved a real hoot were half-acre–sized schools of black rockfish that would suddenly begin flipping and cartwheeling on the surface. When that happened, which was often, we grabbed our 6- and 7-weight outfits and tossed out a high-floating popper. Rather than pop it, we simply twitched it occasionally until the fish saw it. Then all hell broke loose. The blacks would leap from the water, arch over and snap at the popper as they came back down—except there might be two, three or four in the air at the same time, colliding and bouncing off of each other. Rather than set the hook, we simply waited and watched the fun until one, somehow, finally hooked itself.

Although the fishing action was somewhat faster than anything I have ever experienced at Clayoquot Sound, there was obviously much more time, effort and money involved than simply jumping into my vehicle and driving there. That's usually the price you pay in order to fish remote destinations, but believe me, it's worth it.

Finding remote locations is mainly a matter of sitting down with a map of the coastal region and doing some serious daydreaming. Rivers Inlet, for example, contains some of the largest salmon in the world. As these behemoths migrate up the inlet to the Chuckwalla, Kilbella and Wannock rivers, they start favoring the layer of fresh water laying on top of the salt water, possibly acclimatizing themselves for their final journey into their home rivers. As this layer is only about 8–10' (2.4–3 m) deep, the trollers and moochers fish with fairly short lines—15–30' (4.6–9 m)—even though the water below that layer is nudging 900' (274 m) deep. From a fly-fishing perspective, this might seem ideal, but we have to factor in one very important point: Other people know about this place. Lots of them. Rivers Inlet Regulars. They arrive in big yachts, small boats and everything conceivable in between, or they fly in and stay at various lodges throughout the inlet. No, much as the thought of using your fly rod to catch one of those 70–80-lb (31.8–36.3-kg) chinook might seem like the ultimate challenge, I don't think you really want to be there amid that maze of heavy nylon line and downrigger cables.

BASIC TACKLE REQUIREMENTS

For my money, the single greatest boon to saltwater fly fishing has been the fairly recent introduction of fly lines designed specifically for our purposes.

Yes, graphite rods are marvelous casting tools, and anodizing processes have brought corrosion under control, but most of us could go back to fiberglass or cane rods if required and even program ourselves to conscientiously wash our equipment with fresh water after every use; however, having to give up our ultra-fast sinking lines, intermediates and sink-tips might cause severe bouts of melancholia, even a mass exodus back to trolling hardware or mooching with cut-plug herring.

While 8-weight tackle will handle most situations, having two or three outfits suited for specific tasks—rigged and ready for use—makes it easier to meet changing conditions. On a given day, your fishing locations might include rock-strewn shoals, shallow bays with sandy bottoms, fast-flowing tidal narrows, steep drop-offs into deeper water and river estuaries.

For early-run coho, cutthroat trout, rockfish and greenling (all usually caught in shallow water) many anglers favor 6-weight tackle with a sink-tip or slow- to intermediate-sink line. For larger coho, sockeye, chum salmon and rockfish, use an 8-weight with an intermediate or fast-sinking line. A 10-weight with a fast-sinking line gets the nod for chinook, late-running chum, or big lingcod and halibut. To reduce arm and wrist fatigue while tussling with fish, a fighting butt on the rod handle is recommended, even on 6-weight tackle.

Shooting heads are generally preferred to full-length lines, and the reels storing them must have enough capacity for a minimum of 450–600' (137–183 m) of backing. A smooth, easily adjustable drag is an absolute must, especially for large coho that can strip a reel in seconds and big, brawny chinook that pull like runaway trucks.

Neither salmon, trout nor bottom fish appear to be leader-shy, so a 7–9' (2.1–2.7 m) tapered leader with 12" (30 cm) or so of 8–10-lb (3.6–4.5-kg) test as a replaceable tippet will suffice. Tippets testing 12–20 lb (5.4–9 kg) are a better choice for chinook and lingcod.

WHAT SALMON EAT & HOW TO IMITATE IT

The fly box of an inshore angler tends to be large and, at first glance, filled with all manner of patterns. However, closer inspection usually reveals that most are similar in style and shape but tied in different sizes and color variations. When on a feeding binge, salmon will take virtually anything presented, but they can also be maddeningly selective and snub all but one size and color of a specific pattern, and then only if it's retrieved in a very precise manner.

At the basic level there are two main food groups on which salmon feed throughout their ocean years: crustaceans (euphausiids, amphipods, isopods, shrimp and prawns) and schooling baitfish (herring, anchovy, sandlance, pilchard, shiner seaperch, surf smelt and eulachon). The variations in sizes, colors and body patterns of these two types of creatures are mind-boggling, but the basic shape of each group remains similar. A tiny euphausiid and a large prawn may differ in size and color, but their silhouette is similar, and whereas sandlance are long and slender while shiners are short and deep-bodied, there is no mistaking that they are fish-shaped. To a lesser degree, but important nevertheless, chinook and coho also feed on squid, free-swimming sand worms and crab larvae or small crabs floating helplessly in the currents. Again, the colors and sizes may vary, but their basic shapes remain the same. Bearing this in mind, a well-stocked fly box for salmon should contain mostly patterns that imitate crustaceans and baitfish, plus a few representing squid, worms and crabs.

As juvenile pink, sockeye and chum salmon are pelagic, they are too far offshore during most of their saltwater phase to be of interest to anglers, but many juvenile chinook and coho salmon remain fairly close to inshore water throughout their rearing and growing periods, so let's take a look at their eating habits.

Coho

While still in fresh water, juvenile coho feed not only on various aquatic insects, larvae and pupae, but also target sockeye salmon fry quite heavily. Initially, after swimming downstream to the estuary, coho smolts remain in these littoral areas for a few months until they are acclimatized to the saltwater. Being voracious, opportunistic feeders, they eat pretty well anything that gets in front of them: small amphipods like kelp fleas and beach hoppers, tiny crustaceans, sticklebacks, bullheads and the fry of chum and pink salmon. As they move offshore, crustaceans become an important part of their diet until they reach a point in life where an increased piscivorous diet becomes necessary to provide the size and body fat reserves necessary to take them back to their natal streams. This transition from "pink feed" to baitfish happens in the final year of their life, usually starting in mid- to late spring. From this stage on, coho become insatiable eating machines, and, assuming there is an abundance of food, their growth rate is absolutely phenomenal.

Coho weighing 3–4 lb (1.4–1.8 kg) in May might tip the scales at 15 lb (6.8 kg) by September, and some late-running northern coho could be in the 30-lb (13.6-kg) range.

Chinook

The life cycle of chinook salmon is similar to that of coho, but they do not appear to feed on other salmon fry in either fresh or salt water. However, once they move offshore, chinook become very efficient predators. Most spend two or three years in the ocean, but some remain for up to seven years. Generally, the older fish are the largest, with the heaviest on record a 126-pounder (57.2 kg) caught at Rivers Inlet many years ago by a commercial fisherman. Just pause here for a moment and consider hooking something like that on a 10-weight outfit.

Shrimp in Their Many Guises

Most of us probably think of shrimp as pink, tightly curved, tasty little morsels because that's precisely what they are after cooking. However, the body of a live shrimp in the water has only a slight curve, and while they certainly come in varying shades of pinks and reds, others range from nearly transparent to pale white to drab colors like olive green and brown. Some local examples on the West Coast include broken-back shrimp, which are almost transparent with slight tinges of red, green, gray or brown; coon-stripe shrimp, which are pale red with blue stripes and white spots on the body and striped brown and white legs; crago shrimp, which are mottled brown, gray and black; opossum shrimp, which are transparent gray; and smooth skeleton shrimp, which are pale tan, greenish and rosy hued. I mention all of these simply to illustrate why the fly boxes of saltwater fly fishers have such a wide range of colors.

A typical shrimp imitation may be as simple as a tuft of appropriately colored hair, hackle or acrylic yarn affixed to a hook, or they can be amazingly realistic and made with long, trailing antennae of dyed bucktail hairs, beady black eyes fashioned from nylon monofilament melted at both ends, a segmented shell of translucent plastic and a body combining hackle fibers and combed-out dubbing to represent legs and a cluster of roe. In recent years, some very popular and durable patterns have been developed that involve covering the entire fly body with an evenly distributed layer of clear, fast-drying epoxy.

During May and June, early-run coho are feeding almost exclusively on euphausiids, so small, imitative patterns are used. No. 8 shrimp patterns in white or pale shades of pink, orange or green are stand-bys, but occasionally the fish turn on to attractor colors like chartreuse, hot pink and orange. Once coho switch to baitfish, much of this guesswork is eliminated. If a pattern looks and swims like a baitfish, it usually attracts attention.

Baitfish imitations can, for the most part, be reduced to variations of three basic patterns: the traditional bucktail or streamer with hair or synthetic material stacked in layers atop the hook shank; Lefty's Deceiver, a productive but somewhat fussier pattern utilizing hair, feathers and synthetics; and the Clouser Minnow (née Clouser Deep Minnow), one of the easiest yet most effective patterns around. These cover the three typical baitfish body shapes, which can be varied according to length, color and weight.

The remainder of the foodstuff—squid, worms and crabs—may also be imitated with patterns as simple or intricate as you wish to make them, as long as you remember to vary their sizes and colors.

Baitfish Patterns

Whenever saltwater fly fishers get together to swap yarns, the usual topics of conversation are fly patterns—types, sizes and colors—and the best methods and speeds of retrieves to use with them. Coho can be especially confusing as they often prefer extremes from dead slow to zipping through the water as fast as possible. The general consensus is that choosing a fly is more art than science, for there are periods when coho in particular will smash anything they see, yet other times when they become maddeningly selective about color, size, shape or combinations thereof. A productive fly may suddenly turn off, instantly and totally. The solution might simply mean switching to a smaller or larger version of the same pattern, but it could also involve having to work your way systematically through assorted sizes, shapes and colors of different patterns before discovering the right combination.

Bob Clouser's Amazing Minnow

In the late 1980s, Bob Clouser, a noted fly tier and fishing guide, developed this pattern to attract smallmouth bass in his home state of Pennsylvania. The first time his friend and mentor, Lefty Kreh, saw one, it appeared so

sparse that he thought Clouser hadn't finished tying it. The inventor explained that rather than fully dressing the fly to represent the outline of a baitfish,
he had used only enough material to create an almost transparent illusion of
the back and sides, but with emphasis on its large eyes. Without realizing it,
Clouser had developed what has since become one of the two most popular
streamer fly patterns in the world, the other being Kreh's equally famous
Lefty's Deceiver.

Clousers are among the easiest of flies to tie. The original used bucktail,
but polar bear, goat (or almost any type of long guard hair for that matter)
and a wide range of synthetic hair all work well. Depending on the material
used, Clousers can be 1–12" (2.54–30 cm) long. Friends and I have found 5–6"
(12.7–15 cm) a good length for coho, chinook and bottom fish, with a
fluorescent chartreuse back and white belly best for low-light conditions in
mornings and evenings, and a fluorescent pink back and white belly good for
bright, sunny days. Occasionally chinook have been hooked with both types,
but these have been accidental rather than intentional.

In the late 1990s, when Martin Paish was the Marina Manager at Weigh
West Marine Resort, I sent him a selection of flies to try for lingcod. Fashioned from twisted mohair yarn, the flies were designed to duplicate 8" (20-
cm) -long green plastic worms, which I had used successfully in the 1980s. I
tied two dozen in various colors, and because there was still a bit of space
left, I added a half dozen 6" (15-cm) -long Clousers made with synthetic
Ultra Hair, three each in chartreuse/white and pink/white. Imagine my surprise when Martin phoned to say he had received the flies, and while tact-
fully reserving judgment about my worm patterns, he was totally cranked
with the Clousers and was going to use them on coho. Two weeks later he
phoned to ask for, nay, demand, more Clousers as he was down to one fly,
which had been chewed down to about 3" (7.6 cm). I was driving to Tofino
the next morning to spend four days fishing with Martin, Jack Simpson and
Rory Glennie, so I thought it prudent to tie the flies. It was a good move
because when Jack, Rory and I drove to Tofino, I had two dozen Clousers
ready and waiting.

Over the next four days, Rory and Jack fished together, while Martin and
I teamed up. As a full-time freelance outdoor writer, I had taken along four
cameras in order to get photographs of anglers fly fishing. In such cases one
either fishes or shoots photographs, so Martin wasn't surprised when I con-

fined my fishing to early mornings and late evenings when light conditions were not suitable for photography. Despite these restrictions I managed to blunder into a 12-lb (5.4-kg) coho, the largest of our trip, on the second morning. Although I seldom mentioned this fact more than 10 or 20 times a day over our remaining time in Tofino, for some reason my companions grew testy and abusive.

Although Clouser recommends Tiemco 811s hooks in No. 6 to 2/0, I prefer No. 2 Tiemco 9394 hooks for saltwater as they have a slightly longer shank. I secure the eyes about ½" (13 mm) behind the hook eye using figure-8 wraps of thread and a drop of Krazy Glue.

A few words here on eyes. When trying to get a fly down to where fish are suspended, there is no such thing as eyes that are too heavy. That said, there are times when fish are just beneath the surface, so lightweight eyes are much preferred. I use either standard manufactured lead eyes in medium or large sizes (1/24 and 1/16 oz) or large-sized bead chain. For super-heavy eyes, I cut ¼" (6 mm) diameter lead sinker wire in lengths of ¼ and ⅜" (.63 and .95 mm), then carefully waist the center of each piece by squeezing it with round-nosed (not needle-nosed) pliers while rotating it. This produces eyes of up to ¼ oz (7 g), which calls for slow, careful casting strokes. Flak jackets and steel helmets are optional.

I tie lead eyes onto several hooks before painting them and setting them aside to dry. I usually opt for white, followed by a black pupil on each side. The original Clouser calls for tying about 20 strands of white bucktail ahead of the eyes by the butts. Don't stack the hair, and be sure to comb out the under-hair. Hold the hair in position against the shank and bring the thread back behind the eyes to make two wraps. Do this by angling the thread back under the eyes, making the wraps, then angling it forward—again under the eyes—and wrapping once in front of the eyes and tying a half hitch. Thus, when the hook is reversed in the vise, the two crossover wraps will be on top and covered when the remaining material is tied in.

Reverse the hook in the vise, which is the way it will ride in the water, then tie in about 20 strands of Krystal Flash that are about ⅛–¼" (3–6 mm) longer than the hair. Follow this with 20 more strands of bucktail the same length as the belly, then wrap a tapered head and tie off. That's it. Choose your own color combinations, but don't forget that Clouser recommends the Krystal Flash always extend slightly beyond the hair tips.

Clousers tied onto the leader with a loose loop knot have a much better up-down-up-down swimming action than those tied with conventional knots. I favor Lefty Kreh's Non-Slip Mono Knot, which is easily tied and tests at nearly 100 percent strength. If you're not into learning fancy knots, simply tie a small Sampo Duolock wire snap to your tippet with a Clinch or Palomar knot. The fish don't seem to mind.

Lefty Kreh's All-Purpose Deceiver

The Lefty's Deceiver is more of a tying style than a specific pattern. When Kreh started toying with the design around 1958, it was a simple white pattern with a feather wing and a collar of bucktail tied about 4" (10 cm) long to resemble an alewife. As time passed he experimented with color combinations and added some red at the throat to imitate gills. There are now Deceiver offshoots and variations galore tied in every color combination imaginable. Nevertheless, whether tied full-bodied or slender, the finished product should always have a distinct shoulder behind the head, then taper gracefully toward the tail. Those we use range from 2 ½–5" (1.5–12.7 cm).

THE STANDARD BUCKTAIL

My only advice here is to tie some examples sparse and some a tad overdressed. I much prefer polar bear hair to bucktail, but some synthetics also work well. Three patterns considered dependable are the Coronation, Catface Streamer and Glennie's Pearl Mickey.

Fill-In Patterns

We are left with squid, sand worm and small crab imitations for those rare occasions when salmon turn onto them. In 1996 I fiddled around with some pearlescent white braided Mylar piping and natural white polar bear hair, and fashioned a small squid pattern. While I was relegated to photographic duties, Ralph Shaw used one of my squid flies to hook an amazing number of coho, of which he led 14 to the boat and lost at least as many. When word got out, everyone wanted one of my flies. It became the must-have pattern for that season, probably for no other reason than almost everyone was using it. Pretty well everyone who used it thought it looked more like a sandlance than a squid, so further arguments were quelled by dubbing it the Weigh Wester. When saner heads prevailed and anglers started using other patterns, the Weigh Wester became just another fly that was nice to have on hand at times, which is as it should be. But I still consider it a squid pattern.

Sand worms are usually found in quiet bays or under pieces of debris floating on the surface. These very impressive beasties grow to lengths of 12" (30 cm) or more and are light tan with an iridescent sheen of pink, blue or green—quite something to see as they swim ever so slowly near the surface on bright, sunny days. Martin Paish told me of friends guiding at a resort in the Queen Charlottes who discovered that while casting from the dock on brightly moonlit nights, they could take salmon feeding on sand worms. Martin suggested that my twisted mohair worms would make reasonable imitations. I now make them by back-twisting mohair yarn, then adding a bit of Root's Dubbing Enhancer to the material before doubling it and letting it twist back up on itself. With the mohair fibers and enhancer teased out, it looks more suitable for largemouth bass, but Martin assures me that it works fine when fished just under the surface with a slow, hand-twist retrieve.

At times, salmon feed heavily on crab larvae, which are usually found floating within 6' (1.8 m) of the surface. These events, known locally as a "crab spawn," vary in time, location and intensity, but June appears to be a fairly reliable period. As crab larvae are free-swimming during this phase of their life, simply cast out a Chan's Crab and let it drift with the current or use a dead-slow retrieve.

WHERE, WHEN & HOW TO FLY FISH FOR SALMON

Despite what some usually self-appointed experts might have you believe, fly fishing does not rank up there with brain surgery and rocket science. Well, maybe freshwater fly fishing is getting close, what with all those tiny chironomids, backswimmers, gomphus nymphs, scuds, leeches and what-have-you, but saltwater is pretty basic.

After locating salmon feeding on the surface, you may see baitfish leaping and skittering across the water in panic. If, on the other hand, salmon are feeding on crustaceans, you won't actually see them, but the gulls and terns will be feeding on them like mad.

After figuring out what the salmon are feeding on, determine whether the school is moving or stationary. If it is moving, run slightly ahead and to one side, then cast toward it. Try matching your boat's drift speed to that of the fish, and avoid getting too close. If the school is feeding in one general area, position your boat "upstream" from it, then anchor so you can cast and retrieve.

If there is a truly wild feeding frenzy under way, casting for salmon is often just a matter of dropping your fly along the edge and hanging on. In most cases, however, you must determine the depth, speed and type of retrieve that will produce strikes through a process of elimination. Try short, jerky strips to imitate shrimp, slightly longer but erratic strips to resemble a crippled baitfish or long and fairly steady strokes to suggest baitfish fleeing from danger—or combinations thereof. Once it all comes together and the fish start taking, try to memorize as many conditions as possible. Then jot them down in a diary when time permits. A combination of conditions that turns on the fish one day might shorten the guesswork on another day with similar conditions.

As mentioned previously, avoid popular areas where anchoring conflicts with the movements of trollers, jiggers and moochers (they don't mind being called that). Besides which, should you happen to hook a fish on your cast fly, trying to handle an average-sized coho, let alone a large, unruly chinook, is nearly impossible among those curtains of downrigger cables.

Once salmon move into the shallows, they are fair game for fly fishers and the jiggers. When coho move in, it's not unusual to see them herding baitfish into shoreline waters that are scarcely knee deep. However, when chinook move into the shallows, their schools spread out and may even break up entirely. When this happens, your chances of hooking a chinook become limited to chance encounters rather than anything on which you can plan. As a result, most of us fish for coho and hope for an occasional shot at the larger beasts.

Just prior to Jim Crawford's book *Salmon to a Fly* being published, he asked me to accompany him to Clayoquot Sound to photograph him releasing a chinook—he hoped. On our first day, he and Dave Lornie left the dock at Weigh West Marine Resort in his 17' (5.2-m) Boston Whaler, with Holly Baker and I following behind in her identical boat. It was dull and cloudy when, barely two hours into the exercise, Jim hooked a chinook we guesstimated at nudging 25 lb (11.3 kg). After a fine tussle he coaxed it toward his boat, and Holly moved in close so I could record the event. The clouds parted and the sun spotlighted them for a full minute—long enough to shoot the dozen or so frames of slide film left on the roll in my camera.

We spent five more days on Clayoquot Sound, and while Jim and Dave lashed the water to a froth and caught plenty of coho and black rockfish, that was the only chinook they hooked. Talk about timing.

PLACES TO LOOK

The three most critical factors affecting saltwater fishing are wind, tide and water conditions. Worst case scenarios on exposed waters are tidal currents running one way, a stiff breeze blowing the other way, large swells rolling in off the open Pacific and a nasty cross-chop whipping from wave top to wave top. All you can do is stay well inshore and look for a large island or peninsula, and tuck in close on the lee side. It might not be perfect, but at least you can fish.

Best case scenarios are high or low slack tides with no wave action, current or wind. Such occurrences are so rare on the West Coast that when they do happen, you should take photographs or videos to mark the occasion, and then rush back to shore and buy a lottery ticket.

In open waters like Queen Charlotte Strait and the Strait of Georgia, knowledgeable salmon anglers often concentrate their fishing around the southern ends of islands. I am not suggesting that salmon are never at the northern ends or along the sides, but for some reason they favor those southern ends.

If you find good action on the downstream side of a bar, shoal or kelp bed while the tide is running in or out, try the opposite side after the high or low slack period when the tide starts running again.

At times salmon seem to disappear or develop lockjaw. Rather than chase around looking for them, tuck in beside a kelp bed and enjoy some bottom fishing, but keep your eyes peeled for birds flocking and diving or those sparkling, mirrorlike flashes of leaping baitfish.

If anchoring, try to position yourself so you are casting toward the sun or at right angles to it. The theory is simple: When close to the surface, salmon don't like looking into the sun any more than you or I do.

As a season progresses, early local stocks will move closer inland toward their home rivers. If a popular spot starts becoming crowded, it may a better move to travel inland rather than out when looking for fish.

IT'S NOT FLY-CASTING BUT . . .

A trolling method referred to as "skip fly fishing" is commonly employed

while searching for feeding salmon. The rod is hand-held with the tip pointing rearward at a low angle to the water, and the fly is trailed from 15–60'
(4.6–18 m) behind the boat, skipping along the surface, often right in the
boat's wake. When a salmon is seen approaching the fly, suddenly pulling it
forward or dropping it back frequently results in a take, which, in turn, may
cause severe heart palpitations, loss of coherent speech and possibly even
bladder control. What I'm trying to say is that the take and what follows
immediately can be violent to the extreme. It's also a good indication that
other salmon are around, so don't expect too much assistance from your companion, who may well be doing the same thing.

THOSE "OTHER" FISH

There is more to life than salmon, and for those willing to give it a try, various species of bottom fish provide challenge and excitement galore. The
name bottom fish covers everything that isn't a member of the salmonid family. Of over 260 species listed in *Fishes of the Pacific Coast of Canada* (Queen's
Printer), relatively few bottom fish are of interest to anglers, even less so to
fly fishers. Some are simply too large, like basking sharks, which reach lengths
of 30' (9 m) and weigh up to 8,600 lb (3,901 kg), or too small, like eel pout
that max out at 4 ¼" (10.8 cm).

Many popular species are simply too deep to consider reaching with fly-
casting gear. For example, yelloweye rockfish are usually found at depths
starting at 200' (61 m), and halibut are frequently sought around 300–500'
(91–152 m). Fortunately, several species inhabit shallow waters (including halibut), providing some good fly-fishing opportunities. That most also make
for fine eating is an added benefit.

Brawling Black Rockfish

Of about two dozen species of rockfish available to inshore anglers, one that
quickly wins the respect of fly fishers is black rockfish. Erroneously called
black bass, they look like they were stamped from the same mould as smallmouth bass. Although they average 2–6 lb (.9–2.7 kg), blacks have been
recorded to 10-plus lb (4.5 kg), making them ideal for light- to medium-
weight tackle. What makes them unique among the rockfish family is that
large schools often drive baitfish right to the surface, then go on a wild feeding spree. This is often much to the dismay of salmon anglers who race

quickly toward the melee thinking they have found a school of feeding coho or chinook. Those familiar with blacks simply start casting and enjoy the fun because blacks will strike at anything dropped onto the water. A high-floating popper or deer-hair bug will provide exciting memories of these stocky fish leaping into the air, then arching over to take the fly on the way back down. They are strong, determined fighters, and their firm, pure white flesh is considered excellent table fare. Black rockfish have salvaged many otherwise dud fishing trips for gear-slingers and fly fishers alike.

If you are fishing the bottom for species like lingcod or cabezon and the tide starts running too fast to continue, start cruising around to look for schools of black rockfish feeding on the surface. They favor the downstream side of kelp beds, especially those located around sheer bluffs, rock piles, small islets and points of rugged shoreline. As tidal currents speed up, baitfish move into the protective lee of these structures, making them attractive targets for the voracious blacks.

Although you can take blacks right on top while using a floating line, your best all-round choice is a sink-tip or intermediate-sinking line. As they herd baitfish from below, you can also find them deeper; nevertheless, locating a large school of blacks on top can provide some of the fastest-paced fishing you will ever encounter in saltwater—or anywhere else for that matter.

An Ethical Dilemma

Although many fly fishers practice catch-and-release without giving it much thought, when it comes to rockfish you are probably releasing fish that will die shortly afterward, even those that look fine and seem to dash off in great haste when unhooked. With the exception of black rockfish that are already close to the surface, those swimming deeper—even blacks—often suffer from decompression when drawn to the surface from water as shallow as 30' (9 m). For this reason, Fisheries and Oceans Canada urges anglers to keep any rockfish they catch (up to their legal bag limit, of course) or to move if they don't wish to catch any more. Unfortunately, this is often easier said than done because you never know what is down there.

Greenling, lingcod, cabezon, flounders, sole and halibut don't seem to be bothered by decompression, but mackerel will often bleed profusely from the gills, even though they are hooked only in the jaw.

Lurking Lunker Lingcod

Of the so-called heavyweights, lingcod are second only to halibut and they are usually a lot easier to locate, hook and land. Although lingcod have been recorded at weights exceeding 100 lb (45.4 kg), the average lingcod taken in inshore waters is about 8–20 lb (3.6–9 kg). This is excluding immature juveniles, which must always be released. Lingcod are strong and determined fighters that put up a good account for themselves. Although considered excellent eating, the smaller fish are your best choice for eating. Larger fish to 15 lb (6.8 kg) or more are usually spawning-age females, so many of us release them.

Lingcod seem virtually indestructible, making them a logical choice for release. I recall Ralph Shaw and I jigging at 300' (91 m) in Blackfish Sound. Ralph hooked a small rockfish right on the bottom and had just started reeling it in when a large lingcod grabbed it. This is a very common occurrence, and in most cases the lingcod will hang on tenaciously until it is dragged right to the surface, where, if its head doesn't break the surface, it can be netted or gaffed. In this case it was a lingcod of well over 40 lb (18 kg) with a 5-lb (2.3-kg) quillback rockfish gripped crossways in its mouth. As Ralph didn't wish to keep the big fish he drew its head through surface and it promptly opened its mouth, turned and started swimming around in circles, obviously looking for its lost prey. Unable to find it, the lingcod dove and swam swiftly from sight, none the worse for wear from its 300' (91-m) trip to the surface.

Racy Little Greenling

Greenling are smaller relatives of lingcod. There are four species common to British Columbia waters: kelp, painted, rock and whitespotted. Of these, you will probably encounter kelp greenling most often. Amazingly swift and strong for their size, they usually peak at 21" (53 cm)—about 3 lb (1.4 kg)—but during my Langara Island trip in 2001, I landed a nearly football-shaped female that was nudging 5 lb (2.3 kg). They are also quite streamlined and strikingly colored. The male kelp greenling is medium olive brown with beautiful, irregular-shaped turquoise markings around the head and shoulders. Females are a much lighter, almost reddish brown, covered with dark brown spots and have an orange hue to their fins. Rock greenling grow a tad larger—up to 24" (61 cm)—but are not as common. Their color ranges from brown to greenish, with irregular bright crimson stripes along the sides. All greenling are excellent table fare.

The Pug-Ugly Cabezon

Possibly the homeliest fish you might ever catch on a fly—or anything else for that matter—are cabezon (Spanish for "big head"), the largest members of the sculpin family. Although targeting "bullheads" might seem a bit odd, be warned that you will never forget your first encounter with one. Recorded to weights of 30 lb (13.6 kg), the average size found inshore will be about 8–20 lb (3.6–9 kg). They possess the size, strength and stamina to guarantee memorable encounters. Mottled brownish green, these critters have a large-diameter head and pectoral fins of equal size. When pulled toward the surface, their flared pectoral fins make them appear as wide as they are long. When they open their huge, rubber-lipped mouth, the skin inside may range from pale green to turquoise. Although the flesh is of good quality and taste, there appears to be so little of it compared to the overall size of these fish, I have never kept one. A word of warning if you do: The roe is extremely toxic.

Those Fighting, Flavorful Flounders

Although flounders and sole will never win any beauty contests, they have three positive things going for them: They bite eagerly, give you a surprisingly strong and active tussle and are one of the finest-tasting fish. Look for flat, sandy bottoms at depths of 20–60' (6–18 m) and simply drag a Clouser Minnow right on the bottom. Matched against a 6-weight outfit, a 12" (30-cm) flounder will outpull most freshwater fish of equal weight. If you luck into a bed with fish of 16–18" (41–46 cm), count your blessings and don't forget that lottery ticket when you get back to shore.

Don't Knock Dogfish

Most anglers consider spiny dogfish a nuisance, which they are if your target is salmon or more desirable bottom fish. However, if you set aside your prejudice and judge dogfish fairly, they are worthy opponents on fly tackle. These small sharks peak at about 4' (1.2 m) and 20 lb (9 kg), but one of half that weight will give you an extremely good workout on 8-weight tackle. Dogfish often school close to the surface in unbelievably large numbers, and when they go into a feeding frenzy, they bite at anything and everything. Once hooked, they will outfight and outpull freshwater game fish like largemouth bass and walleye and will certainly last longer than pike or muskie of equal size. Be warned, however, that once at the boat these fish can be dangerous to handle. The most important thing to remember is that they have two dorsal fins, and in front of each is a long, sharp spine of solid bone that can deliver painful gashes and punctures when the fish starts thrashing and writhing in a very eel-like performance. Although their teeth aren't large, there are hundreds of them in several rows, and all are razor sharp. For this very reason, a wire leader is recommended when intentionally fishing for dogfish. The flesh of a dogfish is pure white, firm and quite tasty, but it must be processed immediately. This involves killing the fish, promptly filleting and skinning it, then chilling the flesh.

Those Marvelous Little Mackerel

Whenever the El Niño current swings close to the West Coast, it usually brings with it hordes of Pacific mackerel. When this occurs, salmon anglers tend to set their hair on fire and run around in ever-increasing circles, while fly fishers dig out their 6-weight outfits and get ready for some truly fast-paced action. Pound for pound, mackerel will swim farther than salmon and do it a heck of a lot faster. These marvelous little gamesters, which peak at about 3 lb (1.4 kg), often school right on the surface and, like black rockfish, will take bass poppers and floating flies. They also are excellent table fare but should be bled and chilled immediately if being kept.

Are Halibut Worth the Hassle?

Halibut will take a fly. Heck, being high on the food chain, big ones take pretty well anything they want. From the fly fisher's perspective, the main problem is locating them. They are almost exclusively deep-water fish, but they do come into the shallows on occasion. A few years ago at Port Hardy, a young fellow fishing off the Seagate wharf landed a 127-lb (57.6-kg) halibut that he hooked on a drift jig in less than 20' (6 m) of water. I was present when Murray Gardham, owner of Double Bay Fishing Resort on Blackfish Sound, hauled out a 139-pounder (63.1 kg) he had hooked on a handline while fishing from his dock, which was floating in about 35' (11 m) of water.

Although they normally inhabit the bottom, halibut will follow schooling baitfish right to the surface. Jerry Donaldson of Sandy, Utah, told me that while fly fishing in Alaska for coho, he and a friend hooked several halibut of 15–35 lb (6.8–15.9 kg) on flies. Although they were in 90' (27 m) of water, all of their coho and halibut action was at 30' (9 m).

As mentioned previously, Martin Paish is an accomplished saltwater angler who has fished throughout coastal British Columbia, much of it with a fly rod. He recalls being off the Queen Charlotes and seeing halibut feeding on sandlance and herring that were scarcely a foot or so beneath the surface. Some of these halibut appeared to be 60–70 lb (27.2–31.8 kg).

The other problem with halibut is that you might hook into far more than you bargained for. Fish of 400 lb (181.4 kg) are still taken in the commercial catch, and a few sports-caught halibut exceeding 200 lb (90.7 kg) are typically caught each season. In some areas, 100-pounders (45.4 kg) will hardly rate a second glance at the dock. Most of these fish are caught on tackle designed for the task: stiff, pool-cue–like rods, big multiplier reels and lines of braided Spectra or Dacron testing 80 lb (36.3 kg) or more breaking strength. Many are still caught on handlines—200–300-lb (90.7–136.1-kg) test nylon monofilament—from which are suspended pipe jigs weighing up to 2 lb (.9 kg). We are not talking finesse fishing here, folks. And lest you think that halibut are logy, lethargic bottom-suckers, let me assure you that they are, pound for pound, as strong as any chinook salmon. They won't run as fast, but they are no slouches, and runs of 300–600' (91–183 m) or more are not unknown.

A third problem with fly fishing for halibut is a frustration similar that experienced when you hook coho while intentionally fly fishing for chinook salmon. Plan on catching a lot of nontarget species.

After considering these warnings, if try for halibut you must, give yourself a fighting chance by using suitable tackle and doing your homework prior to selecting an area to fish. This means a minimum of 10-weight tackle, with 12-weight an option. A reel loaded with at least 600' (183 m) of 30-lb (13.6-kg) test backing, 100' (30 m) of running line, 600 grain shooting head, 20-lb (9-kg) test leader and, as Martin Paish would say, a honkin' big Clouser.

Know how deep you can get with your fastest sinking line and heaviest Clouser Minnow, and use that as your maximum water depth. In some cases it is possible to get down 80' (24 m) or more, but conditions must be perfect, and they seldom last very long. Look for areas where the bottom is relatively flat and preferably covered with sand or gravel. Halibut also frequent rocky, uneven bottoms, thus increasing the probability of hanging up on obstructions.

At some remote fishing resorts, the guides have areas they refer to as "chicken coops"—places where customers can catch small halibut of 15–40 lb (6.8–18 kg). In some cases these halibut hot spots are relatively shallow, meaning less than 100' (30 m), so such places are certainly a consideration—if you can locate them. Clayoquot Sound and Kyuquot Sound have several places around the outer islands and shoals where halibut are taken in fairly shallow water—40–60' (12–18 m)—so it's simply a matter of studying your marine chart of the area or asking locals for advice. They will probably think you quite mad, but that's the price we pay for being saltwater fly fishers.

THE ONLY FLY YOU NEED

When it comes to fly fishing close to or right on the bottom you need only one pattern in your fly box: the Clouser Minnow. Period. Trust me on this. Other than casting for surface-feeding black rockfish and mackerel, you'll use it exclusively. It rides over and around obstructions, and the hook point rides up, which is important because your fly is usually down below you rather than out in front at a shallower angle.

You will likely be fishing with the fastest-sinking line you have, possibly even with a 3–6' (.9–1.8-m) length of lead core trolling line looped between your line and leader butt for that extra little bit of weight. A Clouser with the heaviest eyes you can handle on your rod also helps, and there are times when the tide is running that you definitely need all the help you can get.

Most salmon anglers agree that the prime fishing periods are high and low slack tides, plus a half hour or so on each side when tidal currents are fairly slow. It's the same for bottom fishing, so you must decide whether to target salmon or try for whatever might be down there lurking around on the bottom. Believe it or not, a few of us actually opt for the latter on occasion, simply to change the pace and satisfy our curiosity about what might take our fly on the next cast. Once in a while it's even a chinook or coho salmon, but I have never heard anyone complain about this.

The most effective way to cover the bottom is from a stationary boat. Anchor from the bow, and position anglers at the bow and the stern. Getting to depths of up to 20' (6 m) seldom poses a problem, but if you must get deeper, use the slack line drop method. Cast out as far as you can comfortably, then strip another 30–40' (9–12 m) of line from your reel and let it lay in loose coils on the deck or, better yet, in a plastic tub or box to prevent it from hanging up or getting stepped on. Strip in the line, then cast your fly "upstream" into the current and quickly shake the remainder of the slack line through the guides. This allows it to sink in a more level configuration rather than swing down like a pendulum. Make your casts in such a way that the anchor rope will be avoided and, if possible, so your line won't drift under the boat.

A good way to judge how deep you are getting is to compare the depth indicated on the depth sounder to the length of your cast. This only works, of course, if you know how far you can cast. Many people seem quite shocked and irate when, while practice casting on grass, their 80' (24-m) casts actually measure at 50–60' (15–18 m).

If the sounder reads 60' (18 m) and you are casting 60', your fly won't be anywhere close to reaching bottom because surface tension on the line will cause it to belly, lifting the fly back toward the surface. If you are reaching out 80' (24 m) or more, your fly might barely get down, but it still won't cover much of the bottom. However, shaking that loose line through the guides after each cast allows your fly to reach the bottom and remain close over a reasonable distance. You will know that your fly has reached bottom when you feel it dragging and bumping against obstructions. The length of time it remains down and the distance it covers will depend on such variables as your line's diameter and density, water depth, current speed and, of course, whether or not a fish grabs it.

Strip in line just fast enough to stay in touch with the fly, giving it occasional erratic twitches, until it hangs perpendicular from the rod tip. Once more, shake out a few feet of line, and wait until it starts to straighten before paying out more. This increases the time your fly is down there fishing. When the drift is finished, don't be in too great a hurry to strip it in for the next cast. The current will belly the line and lift your fly upward, and fish will often swim up off bottom to follow it for surprising distances—even flatfish like flounder and halibut.

While some might question the wisdom, perhaps even the sanity, of someone seeking bottom fish with a fly, it is simply another facet of this interesting, challenging and somewhat obsessive sport that is worthy of investigation.

Martin Paish with a chrome-bright coho taken on a cast fly at Langara Island in the Queen Charlottes.

Martin Paish with a hefty lingcod, a strong, stubborn fighter that more fly fishers are targeting.

Tim Tullis watches Jim Brown fighting a coho hooked on a cast fly at Langara Island in the Queen Charlottes.

As Jim Crawford mugs for the camera, Dave Lornie releases a prime coho taken on one of his Firecracker patterns.

Chapter 18

Favorite Fly Patterns

Note: Where known, the pattern's originator is provided in brackets.

DRY FLIES

Palmered Brown Bug
(Rory Glennie)

Generic dry fly for trout and summer-run steelhead.

HOOK	Mustad 94842, No. 12–8
THREAD	Uni-thread, black
TAIL	Mixed gray and red fox squirrel tail hairs
WINGS	Mixed gray and red fox squirrel tail hairs, divided in two upright portions, set facing forward
BODY	Tying thread, palmered heavily with brown/red saddle hackle feather, counter-wrapped with 2-lb (.9-kg) test monofilament line for durability, bottom portion clipped into an inverted V.

Pink Polly Wog
(Rory Glennie)

Surface-churner for coho, chum and summer steelhead. For higher contrast on dark days, substitute black for pink.

HOOK   Mustad 9049, No. 2–2/0

THREAD   Uni-thread or Kevlar, fluorescent pink

TAIL   Pink marabou with several strands of Krystal Flash

BODY   Deer body hair, dyed pink, spun around shank, roughly trimmed to a thumb-sized, potbelly shape

Snootli
(Rory Glennie)

Reverse-tied dry for trout and summer-run steelhead.

HOOK   Mustad 9671, No. 14–8

THREAD   Uni-thread, black

WING   Red fox or gray squirrel tail hair, tips extending beyond hook eye at least one full body length, butts aligned with hook barb. Bind hair down along shank.

HACKLE   Natural red neck hackle for red fox squirrel, grizzly for gray. Palmer closely over tied-down hair portion

---

Tom Thumb

HOOK	Mustad 9671, No. 16–8
THREAD	Uni-thread 6/0, black, waxed
TAIL	Deer body hair
BODY	Deer body hair
WING	Deer body hair

1. Wrap thread rearward until even with hook point, then back to center.
2. Position small clump on top of shank so tips extend one hook gap-length beyond bend. Trim butts slightly past center, tie in, wrap tightly back to hook point, then forward and cement.
3. Cut clump three times diameter of tail. Position so tips extend one to two shank-lengths beyond bend. Hold firmly in place, tie in butts ⅛" (3 mm) behind eye, make well-spaced wraps back to hook point, then forward.
4. Fold wing forward to form back, make two loose wraps and draw tight, then two tight wraps.
5. Lift wing and wrap thread under front base to hold it upright.
6. Form head, tie off, trim and cement.

WET FLIES & STREAMERS

Baggy Shrimp
(Richard Anderson)

HOOK	Tiemco 2457, No. 16–10
TAIL	Dubbing olive to dark green
BODY	Dubbing olive to dark green
SHELL	¼" (6 mm) wide strip from clear plastic bag
RIB	Gold wire, fine

Backswimmer
(Jack Shaw)

Note: Tools required include a small beading needle (available at hobby shops), a needle threader to pull rubber strand through needle eye and pliers to pull needle through body.

HOOK	Mustad 94840, No. 14–8
THREAD	Medium brown
BODY	4-ply tapestry wool, single strand, beige or light tan
1ST WRAP	Mylar tinsel, silver
2ND WRAP	Clear plastic freezer bag, ⅛" (3 mm) wide strip
WING	Turkey tail feather, dark brown, ½" (13 mm) wide section folded and tied in at tips
LEGS	6 cock pheasant saddle hackle fibers, reddish gray
PADDLES	Herl from peacock sword (stronger than from eyed tail feather)

1. Cover shank with even thread wraps to start of bend and cement.
2. Tie in wing, tinsel and plastic strip; wind thread forward.
3. Tie in wool and wind back evenly then forward again, overlapping in the center to create an oval-shaped body.
4. Wind Mylar forward, then plastic.

5. Bring wing forward, tie down, add legs, form head and trim.
6. Push beading needle crossways through center of body (above or below shank), and use it to draw rubber strand through. Fold rubber strand back and trim even with rear of hook.

Bead Head Cat Fur
(Jim Crawford)

A variation of Nick's Bead Head Leech. Crawford's wife's Norwegian Forest Cat had the perfect mix of browns, blacks and softness to match the long-strand, very soft wool used for the original.

HOOK	Mustad 94840, standard or 1XL, No. 8
THREAD	Black or brown. Use Kevlar or gelspun that wraps tightly.
BEAD	Black tungsten or brass
TAIL	Marabou tips, black and brown—not too dense—about ½ body length. Blend in a few strands of tiny black or red-black holographic Mylar. Tie in at hook bend.
BODY	Wrap shank evenly with thread, then cement. Wrap material evenly around tail binding so it trails halfway along tail. Wrap another section at midshank, another behind the bead. Tail should be wider than head. If necessary, trim body top and bottom to flatten.

Blood Leech
(Jack Shaw)

HOOK   Mustad 9672 3XL, No. 10–4
THREAD   Black
TAIL   Dark reddish-brown mohair
BODY   Dark reddish-brown mohair

1. Tie in mohair strand at top of bend and wrap forward to hook eye while stroking mohair rearward.
2. After tying off, brush hair to loosen, then stroke along sides forming a top and bottom wing.
3. Grip hook eye with pliers, dip fly in boiling water, then smooth wings rearward.
4. After wings dry, trim them so tips curve together ½" (13 mm) behind hook bend.

Cameron's Copper Clouser
(Bob Clouser)

HOOK   Tiemco 9394 4XL, No. 8
EYES   Bead chain, small. Paint white with black or red pupil
THREAD   8/0 chartreuse
BELLY   Polar bear hair or small diameter synthetic, white; blend in pearlescent Krystal Flash
WING   Polar bear hair or small diameter synthetic, chartreuse
TOPPING   Copper Flashabou, 4 strands

Candy Fly
(Art Limber)

HOOK	Tiemco 9394 4XL, No.
THREAD	Red
TAIL	Hackle fibers, hot pink
BODY	Tinsel, silver Mylar
BACK	Krystal Flash, pink
EYES	Adhesive, 1.5 mm, red
EPOXY	Clear, 5-minute

1. Apply eyes.
2. Grip hook eye with locking forceps, mix epoxy and apply to body with toothpick. Rotate fly, tilting as required so epoxy coats body evenly.

Copperhead Leech
(Rory Glennie)

For steelhead and big trout.

HOOK	Mustad 9049, No. 2–2/0
HEAD	Copper bead, medium
THREAD	Uni-thread, black
TAIL	Full marabou plume without stiff center quill, black, tied long
BODY	Rabbit fur crosscut strip, black, hide wound around shank

Crappie Basher
(George Will)

HOOK	Mustad 9672, No. 8–6
THREAD	Black
BODY	Medium, silver Mylar (weighted or unweighted)
WING	Sparse clump of white bucktail (or FisHair) sandwiched between two similar-sized clumps of yellow. All clumps about 1 ½ times body length.

Dale's LFB
(Rory Glennie)

For winter steelhead on dark, overcast days.

HOOK	Partridge Bartleet, No. 2
THREAD	Uni-thread, black
WEIGHT	Lead wire, medium, wrapped on full shank
TAIL	Marabou, mauve
BODY	Chenille, burgundy/purple
RIB	Tinsel, silver Mylar in open spirals
PALMER	Saddle hackle, mauve, sparse open turns
COLLAR	Saddle hackle, brown and black, two turns of each
HEAD	Black thread, lacquered

Fry Fly
(Van Egan)

HOOK	Partridge N (Low Water Salmon), No. 8–6
THREAD	Gray
TAIL	Golden pheasant crest feather
BODY	Tinsel, flat silver
RIB	Tinsel, fine oval silver
THROAT	Hackle fibers, pale blue dun or grizzly
WING	Narrow, married strips of green and blue goose wing veiled with light mallard flank and slender strips of dark mallard or teal overall

Gloria's Green/Pink Skirt

HOOK	Mustad 36890, No. 6–2
THREAD	To match
BODY	Fluorescent chenille, rear half red, front half chartreuse (or salmon/pink)
HACKLE	Chartreuse or hot pink, bisecting body colors

Harrison Minnow
(Harry Penner)

HOOK	Mustad 9672, No. 10–6
THREAD	Black
TAIL	Marabou, dark olive
BODY	Silver Mylar tubing. Use a dark, olive green permanent marker to darken top of Mylar. Coat Mylar with head cement, then squeeze from sides to form a minnow-shaped body.
THROAT	Marabou, red
HEAD	Build up with thread, paint black
EYES	Dab of white paint or adhesive eyes

Nick's Bead Head Leech
(Nick Soloman)

HOOK	Mustad 9672, No. 12–10
BEAD	Black or bronze
THREAD	Black
TAIL	Marabou, blended green and light brown, about length of hook shank
BODY	Weight with 10 turns of lead wire. Dubbing is a blend of soft wool to match color of leeches from various waters: maroon, black, olive and brown. Add a bit of sparkle with dubbing enhancer. Pick out dubbing and comb back over tail to streamline.

Pearl Mickey
(Rory Glennie)

Good for coho from tidewaters to headwaters.

HOOK	Eagle Claw 1197B, No. 6–2
THREAD	Uni-thread, red
BODY	Silver tinsel, embossed
WING	Polar bear hair, layered, ¼ red over ¾ yellow
TOPPING	Flashabou, pearlescent white

Pink Polliwog
(Rory Glennie)

An egg pattern for winter-run steelhead.

HOOK	Mustad 9174, No. 2
THREAD	Uni-thread or Kevlar, fluorescent pink
TAIL	Pink/white variegated chenille, twisted and doubled
BODY	Antron yarn, 4 pieces pink, 1 piece black or chartreuse for eye spot, spun and clipped spherically

Red, White & Silver
(Rory Glennie)

Traditional colors for salmon and steelhead. Use chartreuse to create the equally effective Green, White & Silver.

HOOK	Mustad 36890, No. 8–1/0
THREAD	Uni-thread, black
TAIL	Bucktail, bright blood red
BODY	Tinsel, flat silver
WING	Polar bear hair, natural white
COLLAR	Saddle hackle, bright blood red

Weigh Wester
(Bob Jones)

HOOK	Tiemco 9394, No. 6–2
THREAD	Danville's monocord 3/0, light gray
TAIL	Polar bear hair, bucktail or synthetic, white
BODY	Braided pearlescent Mylar tubing
EYES	Adhesive, 2 mm, red
CEMENT	Krazy Glue
EPOXY	Clear, 5-minute

1. Bind tail on top of shank, spiral thread forward to hook eye.
2. Slide end of tubing over hook eye and tie in behind, trim thread, stroke tubing rearward, turning it inside out over shank.
3. Use dubbing needle to tease out trailing strands, pull them rearward, bind body to shank at top of bend, glue thread collar and nose, allow to dry.

4. Apply eyes ⅛" (3 mm) ahead of collar, grip hook eye with locking forceps. Mix epoxy, apply to body with toothpick, rotate fly, tilting as required so epoxy coats body evenly. (For a slimmer fly, pluck off several strands of trailing Mylar.)

Wizard
(Art Limber)

HOOK	Mustad 34011, No. 8–6
THREAD	White Danville's Plus
HEAD	Clear monofilament thread
BODY	Diamond Braid, silver
TAIL	Hackle fibers, red
BELLY	Polar bear hair, white, and pearlescent Krystal Flash
BEARD	Fluoro Fiber, pink
WING	Blend of olive polar bear, rolled teal feather, lime Fluoro Fiber and a few strands of purple or olive Krystal Hair
EYES	Adhesive, 1.5 mm, silver or red (epoxy head after mounting eyes)

Wizard, Snow White
(Art Limber)

HOOK	Mustad 34011, No. 8–6
THREAD	White Danville's Plus
TAIL	Hackle fibers or synthetic, hot pink
BODY	Diamond Braid, silver
BELLY	Polar bear hair, white, blended with pearlescent Krystal Flash
BEARD	Fluoro Fiber, pink
WING	Blended white polar bear hair, rolled teal feather and white Krystal Flash
EYES	Adhesive, 1.5 mm, silver or red (epoxy head after mounting eyes)

CHIRONOMIDS & NYMPHS

Bead Head Chironomid

Tie in any color with contrasting ribbing. If using ceramic or plastic beads, weight shank with lead wire.

HOOK	Tiemco 2457 or 2487, No. 18–10
THREAD	Uni-thread, 6/0 or 8/0, to match body color
BEAD	Black brass
BODY	Black Midge Larva Lace or equivalent (original used floss or acrylic yarn). Taper tightly from halfway down hook bend, gradually enlarging toward bead. Keep it thin!
GILLS	Tiny tuft of CDC, white. Tie in before mounting bead
RIB	Extra small, black. (Rainbow Holographic flat tinsel gives three-dimensional look to larger No. 12–10 patterns.)
TAIL	(optional) Tiny tuft CDC or marabou, dark gray

Brown Pheasant Chironomid
(Jack Shaw)

HOOK	Mustad 9671, No. 14–12
THREAD	Black
BODY	Cock pheasant tail fiber
TAIL	Grouse, sparse
SHELL	Cock pheasant side feather, copper
THORAX	Peacock herl
BUBBLE	White wool

CDC Emerger
(Kelly Laatsch)

Fish wet in the surface film.

HOOK	Light wire, No. 18–14
THREAD	8/0 fine, color of body
TAIL	Tiny tuft of light gray or white CDC
BODY	Antron, light olive or cream, lightly tapered
THORAX	Build up slight shoulder about ⅔ up hook, and tie in another tuft of gray or white CDC. Add another pinch of dubbing in front so it sits upright, parachute style and not too high. Taper down to eye.

Marabou Damsel Nymph
(Dave Whitlock)

Tie in light colors, use permanent markers to match color of naturals. Keep fly length under 1" (2.54 cm).

HOOK	Mustad 94840, No. 10
THREAD	Small diameter to match body
TAIL	(actually the gills) Marabou to match body. Fairly dense, ¼ of body length, extending rearward.
BODY	Ultra Chenille, micro-size, white or tan
HEAD	Ultra chenille to match body or slightly darker. Build up to form distinct head.
HACKLE	To match body. Make two sparse turns around shoulder, trim top and bottom to form legs straight out from sides. Total width about same overall length as fly.
WING CASE	(optional) Hen pheasant tail fibers over shoulder hump

Mill Lake Chironomid
(George Will)

HOOK	Mustad 94840, No. 14–10
THREAD	Black
TAG	Mylar, silver (thin)
BODY	Floss, black
RIB	Antron, white (thin), five turns
SHELL	Pheasant tail section, dark
THORAX	Antron, black (slightly picked out)
GILLS	Small piece of white Antron tied just behind and above hook eye

Contributors' Biographies

NEIL CAMERON

When not busy publishing the *Campbell River Courier Islander* and *North Islander* newspapers, Neil haunts the nearby beaches and estuaries with his fly rod in hand and a small box of begged, borrowed and/or purloined flies in his shirt pocket. His house is right beside a beach south of town, so he need wander only 100 yards or so to be fishing for his beloved cutthroat trout or coho salmon. Neil edited and co-authored *The Ardent Angler,* and he contributes to various outdoor magazines. He is a member of the Outdoor Writers of Canada, the Haig-Brown Kingfisher Creek Society and the Tyee Club of British Columbia, and he is active in local conservation projects. He left newspaper publishing for two years in the late 1990s and became editor of *BC Outdoors* and *BC Sportfishing* magazines. When asked to return to the newspapers by his old friend Bob McKenzie, Neil considered two things: working in downtown Vancouver or working in downtown Campbell River. The choice, he said, was easy.

JIM CRAWFORD

Born and raised at north Lake Tahoe, Jim has a BA from Menlo College (1965) and an MBA from the University of Santa Clara and Stanford University. He moved to Canada in 1969 with Jostens Inc. and has lived in British Columbia, Alberta, Saskatchewan, Manitoba and Ontario. He retired from Jostens as Senior VP in 1993 and is now president and CFO of Campus Images, a division of Castle Operating Enterprises with over 500 photographers dedicated exclusively to digital electronic imaging. A co-author and photographer for *The Gilly*, Jim's first book, *Salmon to a Fly* was published in 1995 and more recently he co-contributed to *Fly Fishing Canada*. His second book, *Trout to a Fly*, is scheduled for publication in 2002. He is the Alaska and Western Canada Field Editor for Mike Fong's *The Inside Angler* newsletter, and he has written over 200 feature articles for North American magazines. A specialist in saltwater fly fishing, he has fished in nearly every state and province, and much of Mexico. Jim and his wife, Linda, presently have homes on Flathead Lake in Montana and in Courtenay, British Columbia.

RORY GLENNIE

Born in Southern Ontario, Rory is a self-taught fly-fishing specialist who began designing and tying bass flies in 1962 at age ten. Moving to British Columbia in 1970 introduced him to saltwater, and he has since been credited with developing and publicizing several popular fresh- and saltwater fly patterns. He has represented Canada at two World Fly Fishing Championships and is a professional fly-fishing guide and industry advisor covering coastal British Columbia. An impassioned conservationist, Rory sat two terms as president of the Steelhead Society of British Columbia and seven terms as chairman of its Comox Valley Branch, during which period it received a National Recreational Fisheries Award. He sat for an unprecedented eight consecutive terms as president of the Haig-Brown Kingfisher Creek Society. Rory is a member of the Atlantic Salmon Federation, International Game Fish Association and the Outdoor Writers of Canada. Since 1975, he has contributed articles and photographs to various magazines and newspapers, co-authored the prized *Ardent Angler* anthology and written a book about his experiences as a fishing guide. He is currently the West Coast Editor of *The Canadian Fly Fisher* magazine and Editor of *Casting About,* the monthly newsletter of the Comox Valley Fly Fishers.

ROBERT H. JONES

A writer since 1975, full-time since 1980, Bob contributes to several regional, national and international publications, and edits for Johnson Gorman Publishers. Born in Vancouver, British Columbia, in 1935, he left school at age 14 to become a logger—the same year he started fly fishing. A military career spanning 27 years allowed him to travel and fish throughout much of Canada and Central Europe. A past president and life member of the Outdoor Writers of Canada, he has received the Pete McGillen Award for service to that organization and the Jack Davis Mentor's Award for his assistance to other writers. Bob is also a member of the Outdoor Writers Association of America and The Writers' Union of Canada. He has written three books, co-authored ten, edited six and won seventeen writing awards. Bob and Vera, his wife and fishing partner, reside in Courtenay, British Columbia.

MARTIN LAMONT

As a child in Scotland, Martin's parents encouraged him to explore freely. He quickly discovered angling and recalls the assistance given by neighbors, friends and renowned professionals during his formative years. A dentist by profession, an avid outdoors man, conservationist and fly fisher by avocation, Martin began competition fly fishing in 1987. He was a Fly Fishing Canada team member when it entered its first World Championship in England, preceding eight wonderful years of overseas competition and learning that culminated in Kamloops, British Columbia, in 1993. He embraces the diversity and thoughtful, imaginative dimensions of interest and creativity, natural history, science, technology and artistry of fly fishing. As the pursuit of fish—one of mankind's oldest activities—has been documented throughout the history of literature, Martin is proud of his associations with the Outdoor Writers of Canada and Fly Fishing Canada. He has contributed to several books, most recently *Fly Fishing Canada,* to which he was a major contributor and an associate editor. He and his wife, Helen, live in Comox, British Columbia.

RALPH SHAW

Born at Cold Lake, Alberta, in 1926, Ralph started fishing six years later—catching shiners with a piece of string and a bent pin. This progressed to catching trout when he and his brother began dangling flies from willow poles. Since that early beginning, Ralph has specialized in fishing trout with artificial flies and more recently to taking salmon and bottom fish in saltwater. A lifelong crusader for sane fish and wildlife conservation practices, he retired as a school principal in 1983 after 35 years in education but continues his conservation activities. He received the Order of Canada in 1984 for his work in these endeavors and the Canada 125 Medal. His popular weekly outdoors column in the *Comox Valley Record* has won several writing awards, and he contributes regularly to *The Outdoor Edge, BC Outdoors, Outdoor Canada, Island Fisherman* and *Island Angler.* He has contributed to several books over the years, including *The Gilly* and *Fly Fishing Canada.* His first book, *Ralph Shaw's Vancouver Island Adventures,* was published in 2000. Ralph and Elaine, his wife and partner for over 50 years, live in Courtenay, British Columbia.

GEORGE WILL

After George took up fly fishing in the 1960s as a teenager, he came to know and appreciate the undiscovered trout fishing opportunities available on the Flatlands. When he moved from Manitoba to British Columbia in the 1970s to pursue a post-graduate degree in archaeology, he found the year-round angling much to his liking, often fishing up to 200 days a year. After teaching anthropology and archaeology at Simon Fraser University and the University of British Columbia, he did an eight-year stint as editor of *BC Outdoors* magazine and was the founding editor of *Action Outdoors* magazine. During the 25 years George lived in North Vancouver, he gained an intimate knowledge of the fishing opportunities available right at his doorstep, going so far as to obtain a Guiding License for the region. Over the past several years, he has been involved in the development of digital photography programs in Alaska and then the Lower 48. He has recently resurfaced in Kamloops, British Columbia, where he freelances to various magazines and was a major contributor to *Fly Fishing Canada.* He may frequently be seen lobbing flies from his pontoon boat at favorite lakes such as Pass, Hyas or Duffy.

Index